AMERICAN HERALDS
OF THE SPIRIT

Emerson, Whitman, and Melville

AMERICAN HERALDS of the SPIRIT

Emerson, Whitman, and Melville

John F. Gardner

© Lindisfame Books, 1992, 2020

Published by Lindisfame Books
an imprint of SteinerBooks/ Anthroposophic Press, Inc.
402 Union Street, No. 58
Hudson, New York 12534
www.steinerbooks.org

Earlier versions of Chapters Two and Three appeared as publications of the Myrin Institute for Adult Education: Chapter Two as Proceedings of the Myrin Institute Number 28 and Chapter Three as Proceedings of the Myrin Institute Number 32 (© 1974 and 1977 respectively by the Myrin Institute, Inc. for Adult Education) Used with permission.

ISBN 978-1-58420-907-2

All rights reserved. No part of this book may be reproduced in any form without the written permission of the publisher except for brief quotations embodied in critical reviews and articles.

Printed in the United States of America

CONTENTS

Preface : 9

1 American Heralds of the Spirit : 13

2 The Idea of Man in America : 29

3 Melville's Vision of America : 66

4 Walt Whitman: The Poet of Death and Life : 112

5 Walt Whitman: The New Columbus : 148

6 Emerson's Christianity : 181

7 Emerson's Goal: A Science of the Spirit : 204

8 Radical Individualism and Social Reform : 239

Epilogue : 273

Appendix A : 289
Appendix B : 292
Appendix C : 298

I think that the reasons for the crisis in which the world now finds itself are lodged in something deeper than a particular way of organizing the economy or a particular political system. The West and the East, though different in so many ways, are going through a single, common crisis. Reflecting on that crisis should be the starting point for every attempt to think through a better alternative. Where does the cause of this crisis lie? . . .

I . . . feel that somewhere here there is a basic tension out of which the present global crisis has grown. At the same time, I'm persuaded that this conflict . . . is directly related to the spiritual condition of modern civilization. This condition is characterized by loss: the loss of metaphysical certainties, of an experience of the transcendental . . . and of any kind of higher horizon. It is strange but ultimately quite logical: as soon as man began considering himself the source of the highest meaning in the world and the measure of everything, the world began to lose its human dimension, and man began to lose control of it.

We are going through a great departure from God which has no parallel in history. As far as I know, we are living in the middle of the first atheistic civilization. . . . It seems to me that if the world is to change for the better it must start with a change in human consciousness, in the very humanness of modern man.

Vaclav Havel, *Disturbing the Peace*

PREFACE

Throughout my adult life, I have taken special interest in Emerson, Whitman, and Melville as spokesmen for the spirit—for the Universal Spirit, of course, but also for what is best in the American approach to this spirit. My interest has not been academic, nor constant, nor equally apportioned, but to these authors I have returned again and again, and always with wonder and delight.

The motive that kindled my enthusiasm in the first place, and kept alive the hope that some day I might feel able to write this book, had to do primarily with future readers who might be glad to share with me how beautiful the writing of these men is and how challenging their bold ideas are. It is to satisfy this aim that I have quoted so extensively throughout. The commentary introducing or following such quotations has been meant only to set off jewels that deserve, I think, to be viewed with wonder as well as pleasure.

My second motive has been a personal one: to see where I myself might be led if I attempted to work through some of the riddles the passages to be quoted represent. I wanted to convert the sometimes difficult thought-language of an earlier time in our history into that of the present day in order to test it against my own experience while considering its relationship to problems that face us presently.

Having been always somewhat of a teacher, I am reluctant to be accused also of preaching, but only my third motive for writing this book might be open to this charge: I do, of course, want and hope that the ideas set forth by these geniuses will make a difference. For I am convinced that Western civilization, especially what passes for civilization and culture here and now in our own United States, is trying to solve ever-multiplying, ever more crucial problems with the same simplistic thoughts, the same materialism indeed, that are themselves the original *cause* of these problems. I share the opinion of these three men that such an approach is doomed. I believe that not only some, but most, of the major difficulties our present civilization will be encountering from now on will prove unsolvable by approaches that take so little account of the spiritual.

What we need are new thoughts and a different way of developing thoughts that correspond with *reality*—in which Spirit is always basic. For the sake of sheer practicality, the time has come for intellectual arrogance to confess bankruptcy and to open itself to a more heartfelt approach to wisdom. In the greatest variety of ways, the modern soul and the modern world are both plagued by problems that take the form of seemingly irreconcilable conflicts. To none of these conflicting interests has materialistic, technological science as presently conceived, an answer. Its one-sidedness will always give rise to, and show itself helpless to deal with, the perverse outbreaks of its opposite one-sidedness, which appears in the form of anti-intellectualism and irrationalisms of every kind. When spiritually ignorant human beings are led to think of themselves as complex machines, their instinctive response is to repudiate the coldness of this conception by turning to crude demonstrations of animalistic vitality.

The way to genuinely reconciling and humanizing thoughts can be found, I believe, if for once we take seriously the words in which our native inspirers offered their counsel. These men are still, at times, fulsomely honored, but their real message and intent are all the more inexcusably ignored. No doubt the reason for this neglect is that their path-breaking efforts belong, indeed, more to the future than to the past. Yet that is also why they deserve to be freshly considered as heralds of the New Age we are still hesitating to conceive and create.

Time moves on. Certainly we cannot find everything we need today in the geniuses of yesterday, who after all were bound in certain respects by the limitations of their own time. But many of their intuitions are timeless, and can serve as I believe they were meant, to rouse and awaken us. They will do so, if once we muster that combination of humility and courage which is able to free us from stale thought-habits. Freshly harbored and pondered in open minds, the impulse of these pioneers will surely bear fruit in ways that accord with the demands as well as with the still unrealized possibilities of the epoch upon which we are entering.

Perhaps I should alert the reader before he or she begins, to the fact that although an attempt has been made to link the following chapters to one another with a semblance of logical continuity, the truth is that while most have been recently composed, several others were written some years ago as separate essays, with no thought as yet of serving as chapters in an orderly book. I offer this explanation of what will no doubt appear as unexpected, but one hopes not too disconcerting, shifts in tone and style.

1

AMERICAN HERALDS OF THE SPIRIT

When Nature has work to be done, she creates a genius to do it. Follow the great man, and you shall see what the world has at heart in these ages. There is no omen like that.
—Emerson, "The Method of Nature"

GREAT men and women, in an important epoch, are usually supported by a whole constellation of kindred souls. That is how it was in the eighteenth century with the Founding Fathers of our country, whose task was primarily political and economic. It was equally so in the following century with Emerson, Whitman, and Melville; their task, in the next generation of Founders, was cultural and spiritual. These three heralds were joined in the prophetic role by Henry Thoreau and Margaret Fuller and by many others of marked spirituality such as Amos Bronson Alcott of whom Emerson said, "The ideal world I might have treated as cloud-land, had I not known Alcott, who is a native of that country and makes it as solid as Massachusetts for me."[1] And though his outer role was a political one, Abraham Lincoln can be recognized as belonging also to those who contributed so notably to the deepening of the inward life.

In singling out Emerson, Whitman, and Melville for special attention, I have no wish at all to be exclusive, but only emphatic. These were great Americans, deeply joined with the destiny of their nation, and inspired for its sake. Their contributions were distinctively different, as though their inspiration came from, or through, quite different parts of the human soul: and as though it were meant to speak most intimately to differently constituted readers. But in what they had to say, they bore each other out. They all spoke for the spirit, as this could and should live in America.

In our first approach to these men, I should like to call particular attention to their distinctive styles of writing and being, because these have so much to reveal about the content of what each man had to say. [See also Appendix A]

EMERSON

Emerson's first major writing, the little book *Nature*, was published in 1836 when he was thirty-three. His first sentences after the Introduction place before us a definite style, of life as well as of writing.

> To go into solitude, a man needs to retire as much from his chamber as from society.[2]

Here, in the first sentence of the first page of a book that shall teach us about Nature, we are told how we may best find ourselves alone—how we may break off contact with the world. We should have expected, rather, a lesson on how to *make* this contact!

"But if a man would be alone," Emerson continues, "let him look at the stars. The rays that come from those heavenly worlds will separate him and what he touches." To achieve not union but separation is the first advice we receive. This book is surely meant to bring us close to

Nature; yet, to begin with, it sounds the note of withdrawal and separation.

Emerson's path into Nature thus begins with the stars. It is strict; it is chaste; it is lucid. It is purely spiritual. For him, the remote comes nearest, the abstract is felt concretely, and the universal is home territory. In "The Poet," he alludes to a "centrifugal tendency" that is present in all people but was particularly strong in himself. This tendency strives ever for "passage out into free space," that a man may "escape the custody of that body in which he is pent up...." ("The Poet," 333)

The opening pages of *Nature* reveal the author's outlook and the quality of his experience:

> In good health, the air is a cordial of incredible virtue. Crossing a bare common, in snow puddles, at twilight, under a clouded sky, without having in my thoughts any occurrence of special good fortune, I have enjoyed a perfect exhilaration. I am glad to the brink of fear.
>
> Standing on the bare ground—my head bathed by the blithe air and uplifted into infinite space—all mean egotism vanishes. I become a transparent eyeball: I am nothing; I see all; the currents of the Universal Being circulate through me; I am part or parcel of God.

In such pictures as these we see before us a lean, aquiline, economical, ascetic man in whom starlight, the still air, and snow on the ground, kindle a holy enthusiasm. Especially is the bare ground congenial to this lover of granite. "As water to our thirst, so is the rock, the ground, to our eyes and hands and feet. It is firm water; it is cold flame; what health, what affinity!" he wrote in a later essay, also entitled "Nature." (407) Especially snow, the heavenly moisture that falls in chill star forms, warms this man's heart.

Emerson seeks the highest point from which to view events. He will see the earth from above. In mentioning the stars, he is not so much looking up to them as down from them. From such a lofty vantage, we can understand why, for him, "the name of the nearest friend sounds then foreign and accidental." Climbing the hill behind his house of an early morning, he lets his soul wing forth into the empyrean, where it feels most at home.

> I see the spectacle of morning from the hilltop over against my house, from daybreak to sunrise, with emotions which an angel might share. The long slender bars of cloud float like fishes in the sea of crimson light. From the earth, as a shore, I look out into that silent sea. I seem to partake its rapid transformations; the active enchantment reaches my dust, and I dilate and conspire with the morning wind. (*Nature*, 10)

It comes to us as no surprise that one who could dilate and conspire with the morning wind was often likened even in appearance to an eagle. The eagle views earth's events from far and on high but with piercing vision. He sees the whole, but when the occasion warrants, he can descend to seize upon the specific with abrupt and iron grasp. He is universal in scope, sudden in attack, terse in grip. We remember the eagle as one of the three archetypal animals of whose conjoined forms, according to myth, our human form is made.

WHITMAN

As we pass from Emerson to Whitman, we find a polaric difference between them in their styles of both living and writing. In many ways, Whitman is to Emerson as bull is to eagle.

Emerson is a son of rocky New England. Whitman grew up on sandy Long Island—Paumanok, the fish-form nosing into New York harbor, yet still belonging to the sea. Whitman's hair and beard are flowing, his skin is exceptionally rosy, his countenance even scarlet, his eye contemplative. Robust but relaxed, seemingly indolent, he strolls with loose and rolling gait. He wears a soft hat, easy clothes, his shirt always open at the neck.

As Emerson's style of writing—notably in his poetry—is abbreviated and condensed to the highest degree, Whitman's is expanded, inclusive, and repetitive—also to the highest degree. As Emerson's thought is trenchant, Whitman's is, in the original sense of the word, ruminative. He sets the picture of himself before us in the first stanza of his first great poem, "Song of Myself":

> I celebrate myself;
> And what I assume you shall assume;
> For every atom belonging to me, as good
>   belongs to you.[3]

"I would be alone," said Emerson; "the name of my nearest friend sounds foreign and accidental." "I celebrate myself," is Whitman's reply, "but in doing so, I include you. I approach you and draw you near, even though we've never met." Both men are searching for the fundamental reality of the human self. Emerson seeks this in what purges him of physicality. Whitman finds it in what immerses him most deeply in the physical. Emerson rises coolly into the universal-impersonal. Whitman penetrates warmly down into flesh and blood. Emerson points to the inaccessible stars; Whitman, to "every atom" of his own immediate, miraculous body.

Emerson observed that in many hours "Nature satisfies by its loveliness, and without any mixture of corporeal benefit" ("Nature"), for then one rises into the ether, body-free. While many passages in "Song of Myself" show that Whitman, too, fully appreciated and wrote from this same freedom, the final lines of the first canto bespeak a contrasting orientation.

> The atmosphere is not a perfume—it has no taste
>   of the distillation—it is odorless;
> It is for my mouth forever—I am in love with it;
> I will go to the bank by the wood, and become
>   undisguised and naked;
> I am mad for it to be in contact with me.
>
> ("Song of Myself," 61-2)

Emerson is happy when there is no mixture of corporeal benefit, when he experiences the morning light and air as a purely ethereal being. His head is then bathed by this elixir of spiritual life; through eye and breath he passes over into it. Whitman, on the other hand, experiences primarily through the skin of his torso and limbs, through the most bodily sense, that of touch. He is "mad" for the touch of the air to caress him; he drinks it in through his mouth and through all the pores of his skin as mouths. While Emerson is glorified in transcending himself through the experience of the morning air, Whitman is glorified by bringing the transcendental air to transfuse and unite with him in his concreteness.

> I loafe and invite my soul;
> I lean and loafe at my ease, observing a spear of
>   summer grass.
>
> ("Song of Myself," 66)

Whitman experiences the earth through his entire body, especially his abdomen and limbs. He lays himself upon the earth at full length. His body feels expansively at ease, because the All has come to embrace it. This relaxed torso and these limbs are very different from the chiselled, compact head that Emerson lifts up, birdlike, when his soul is rapt by the All. If Emerson, as many of his contemporaries saw him, is an eagle, Whitman fully qualifies to represent the opposite archetype. He leans and loafs, and he has his eye on a spear of summer grass. It, like the air, is for his mouth forever. Clearly, it is no accident that the collected edition of all his books of poetry holds to the one title, *Leaves of Grass*. As Whitman said, "I guess it must be the flag of my disposition, out of hopeful green stuff woven."[4]

We have mentioned the terse control, the compactness, the axiomatic concentration, of Emerson's elegant style of thought and writing. All this can hardly be better typified than by reference to the king of birds. Yet the cruder and looser structure, the warmer and more liquid breath, and the earth-loving heaviness to be found in Whitman's style are equally distinctive. We are compelled to observe in the latter's way of comporting himself something thoroughly bovine, for Whitman grazes with appetite upon all facts, scenes, kinds of people. All are as grass for him. Grass is the color of hope, and he has hope for them all. His intake is immense; when he is full, he lies down and ruminates. He chews his cud over and over again, he salivates, he digests. And out of it all he patiently, lovingly distills the very milk of human kindness. Emerson wrote of Whitman, "He is a man of titanic abdomen," "a Minotaur of a man," a man "of buffalo strength." ("Nature," 406)

MELVILLE

Herman Melville proves to be as truly lion as Emerson was eagle and Whitman bull. In *Mardi*, the book that preceded *Moby Dick*, Melville clearly characterizes himself under the guise of describing a certain fictitious author of the past named Lombardo. When Media, the demigod, asks Babbalanja, the philosopher, what originally impelled Lombardo to write his *Kostanza* (that is, this extravagant, myth-making book itself), Babbalanja's answer is "Primus and forever, a full heart—brimful, bubbling, sparkling, and running over like the flagon in your hand, my lord." And shortly thereafter, to the image of the heart Melville adds that of the lion: "Hast ever seen a yellow lion, all day basking in the yellow sun, in reveries rending droves of elephants, but his vast loins supine and eyelids winking? Such, Lombardo...."

Lombardo was a dreaming giant, for "great fullness weds great indolence." Of all people, he was "by nature ... the most inert"—until "Want, the hunter, came and roused his roar. In hairy billows, his great mane tossed like the sea; his eyeballs flamed two hells; his paw had stopped a rolling world."[5]

Neither Whitman nor Emerson would have been disposed to conjure up such a picture of might, of sheer power—and of fatal torment—in order to portray himself thus in fictional guise. But the powerful lion image persists in *Moby Dick*, where the story's great protagonist, Captain Ahab, presided over meals at his cabin table "like a mute, maned sea-lion," whose "unsurrenderable willfulness" belonged to a man said to be "daft with strength." Moby Dick himself, the formidable white whale, confronts predatory Ahab as his opposite in power. Implacable force faces equal counterforce. A "wild vindictiveness" in the captain pits itself against "an infernal ... aforethought of ferocity" in the whale.[6]

Nearing the battle's climax, Ahab soliloquizes: "Here's food for thought, had Ahab time to think; but Ahab never thinks; he only feels, feels, feels; *that*'s tingling enough for mortal man!" (*Moby Dick*, 554)

While the lion as such is mentioned fairly seldom in Melville's writings, its human counterpart, the rhythmic heart and lungs of the chest, appears with astonishing frequency and vividness. In the passage on Lombardo, for example, we find sentences such as these:

> To scale great heights, we must come out of lowermost depths. The way to heaven is through hell. We need fiery baptisms in the fiercest flames of our bosoms. We must feel our hearts hot, hissing in us. (*Mardi*, 491)

And one remembers Ahab's pursuit of Moby Dick:

> He piled upon the whale's white hump the sum of all the general rage and hate felt by his whole race from Adam down; and then, as if his chest had been a mortar, he burst his hot heart's shell upon it.
> The White Whale swam before him as the monomaniac incarnation of all those malicious agencies which some men feel eating in them, until they are left living on with half a heart and half a lung. (*Moby Dick*, 183)

Perhaps a certain morbidity of torment and passion predominates in Melville, but by no means exclusively. There is also the robust joy and ringing cheer of a great-hearted man, a man who perhaps does not wing forth into the morning air of the hills so blithely as Emerson, nor drink the ocean's salt air through his bodily pores with Whitman's self-satisfaction, but who nevertheless uses the full capacity of his lungs. "Our brains should be round as globes, and planted on capacious chests, inhaling mighty morning inspirations." (*Mardi*, 490)

Both Emerson and Whitman, to say nothing of Alcott and Thoreau, speak often of the inspiring quality of air, especially morning air, as the very breath of Aurora, but in none of them do we sense, as in Melville, that it is the chest itself that is speaking. The mighty inhalations of a capacious chest, whether in grief or joy, may always be heard behind Melville's word—as in this passage near the tumultuous, tragic climax of *Moby Dick*:

> It was a clear steel-blue day. The fundaments of air and sea were hardly separable in that all-pervading azure; only the pensive air was transparently pure and soft, with a woman's look, and the robust and man-like sea heaved with long, strong, lingering swells, as Samson's chest in his sleep.

> Hither, and thither, on high, glided the snow-white wings of small, unspeckled birds; these were the gentle thoughts of the feminine air; but to and fro in the deeps, far down in the bottomless blue, rushed mighty Leviathans, swordfish and sharks; and these were the strong, troubled, murderous thinkings of the masculine sea.
>
> (Moby Dick, 531-2)

As seen here on nature's scale, this interplay of what comes from above with what comes from below—this exchange, in its beautiful mutuality and dire conflict—is the very signature of Melville's life and writing. In him as in no other American author, life is not only symbolic but also profoundly paradoxical. In all events, be they great or small, heaven meets hell, joy meets pain, light meets dark. Even as, for the human organism, the centrally placed heart and lungs must ever mediate between the upper and the lower body, between cerebration and visceral impulse, so all of Melville's work, from *Typee* to *Billy Budd*, is engaged in wrestling with the dualities of life. And this very wrestling is what is impressed into his way of composition as its distinctive tension, cadence, and rhythm. We encounter it not only in the themes of his novels taken as a whole, but also in the formation of sentences, parts of sentences, and parts of parts. Consider, for example:

> Strange wild work, and awfully symmetrical and reciprocal, was that now going on within the self-apparently chaotic breast of Pierre.
> ...by some ineffable correlativeness, they reciprocally identified with each other, and, as it were, melted into each other, and thus interpenetratingly uniting.... [7]

We observe in Melville's style what we encounter in his thought: the confrontation and interchange of opposites, "blurringly conjoining," as he would say. As ideas, these contrasts, contradictions, and oppositions lay in the realm of values, but underneath we can hear, as it were, the polaric streams of blood, the life-depleted and the life-renewing, passing each other in the heart, the alternate streams of breath passing in and out of the lungs, and the never-ceasing, rhythmical interchange between breath and blood in the lion-chest of the author.

THINKING, WILL, AND FEELING

Psychologically speaking, we find in the head the instrument of clear *thinking*, for it is there that we are fully conscious. In the metabolic and sexual center of the lower body, by contrast, instinctive life and the fire of *volition* have their seat. Between the two, lies the realm of *feeling*, which has always been associated with the heart and lungs. The quality of consciousness here is not so awake as in the head, nor so asleep as in the lower body. Rather, the one mixes with the other. In our feelings, as in our fantasy, we appear to be dreaming: half awake, half asleep.

Philosophically speaking, because *thinking* primarily seeks truth, we may say that its orientation is essentially scientific. By contrast, the most positive deeds of the *will* aim to further and establish what is right and good and better—as through moral and religious commitment. In the middle station between thought and will, the life of *feeling* finds expression in creative fantasy and the many forms of art.

In the trio here considered, Emerson stands out as the thinker. As Whitman, his friend of long-standing, said of him, "His quality, his meaning, has the quality of the light of day ... intellectuality dominates him.... He does not see or take one side ... only or mainly—he sees all sides."[8] His cool passion is to characterize and conceptualize the spiritual laws governing basic aspects of human experience. Thus he inquires into the distinctive dynamics of self-reliance, heroism, character, friendship, love, art, poetic genius, politics, social reform, and so on. Wherein lies the secret, and what are the further possibilities, of the power of thinking itself? What is right and what is wrong with the method of natural science? If we can speak of a "method" of nature, what is that method? And what is the relationship of the human being to the rest of the natural creation? Emerson never tires of tracing out the operations of human intelligence as it is and as it could be; and he finds the whole universe to be but the manifestation of divine mind.

> The world is mind precipitated, and the volatile essence is forever escaping again into the state of free thought. ("Nature," 421)

> In the divine order, intellect is primary; nature, secondary; it is the memory of mind. That which once existed in intellect as pure law, has now taken body as Nature. It existed already in the mind in solution; now, it has been precipitated, and the bright sediment is the world.... We may ... study the mind in nature, because we cannot steadily gaze on it in mind; as we explore the face of the sun in a pool, when our eyes cannot brook his direct splendor.[9]

> There is one mind common to all individual men. Every man is an inlet to the same and to all of the same.... Of the universal mind each individual man is one more incarnation. ("History," 123-4)

Whitman is the man of warmth, of life-force, and of sympathy. He is the lover, and his comprehensive acceptance encompasses all that exists. For him, what is most precious in things is not the specific law, the creative Idea, in which they find their beginning, but the germinal, future-looking possibility they share in common, which is that of becoming more than they have been or presently are. It is the spiritual *will* projecting them toward perfection that excites Whitman's imagination. He is slow to analyze but quick to encourage. He would be not critic but healer and savior; his mood in this sense is avowedly religious. Whitman's vision is directed toward a future for himself, for America, for humanity, for all natural beings, that reaches even beyond death, and justly so, because potentiality inheres in all, and potentiality is of the spirit, which knows not death.

> Urge and urge and urge,
> Always the procreant urge of the world.
>
> What is known I strip away,
> I launch all men and women forward with me into
>   the unknown.
>
> Births have brought us richness and variety,
> And other births will bring us richness and variety.
>
> I know I have the best of time and space, and was
>   never measured and never will be measured.
> I tramp a perpetual journey.
>   ("Song of Myself," 63, 123, 127)

RELATIONSHIPS TO TIME

It can be said that in many ways Emerson's gaze as thinker was essentially retrospective. It was as though he would remember a cosmic spiritual life before the soul's descent through physical birth. He sought the truth of things in their origin, being ever drawn toward the condensingly creative *involution* of divine wisdom into matter.

In comparison, Whitman's inspiration, which took the form of love, was prospective. His love is awakened less by the thought of how spirit, as primal Idea, has in the past entered into all things, making them what they now are, and more by the certainty that spirit is still lifting all things up and out of matter, through its *evolutionary* will, to an unlimited future.

Melville's orientation, characteristically, is toward the drama of life as it is being played out so enigmatically in the present, between the receding spiritual past, remembered as Light, and the approaching earthly future, envisioned darkly. He experiences existence as mortal warfare between the ideal and the real. His tone is apocalyptic, and with all his heart he could have agreed with St. Paul: "For we wrestle not against flesh and blood, but against principalities, against powers, against the rulers of the darkness of this world, against spiritual wickedness in high places" (Ephesians 6:12). He feels profoundly aware of noble aspects of his own past, reaching back through many lives; yet he is so caught in the toils of his painful experience of the present earth-life that the future tends to augur only more of the same: ever the heart-rending battle between good and evil.

* * *

In the lifework of these much honored yet too little assimilated authors, there are depths that should rescue them from mere enshrinement as heroes of the literary past, for they were truly pathbreakers and prophets of the future. The impulse toward spiritualization that came at a critical stage to a materialistically inclined America, for both correction and encouragement, no doubt required three such distinctly different kinds of men to typify it. Beyond their singular styles of speaking, however, which doubtless have the advantage of appealing specially to different kinds of readers, there is an inspired unity in the message they conveyed.

Precisely the "archetypal" difference in their ways of experiencing life is what enables these prophetic figures to offer us such a balanced picture of how life in America is turning toward, and away from, the spirit. In the following chapters we shall consider the three men in sequence: first Melville, because his parable plunges most dramatically into the storm and stress of the modern soul's experience; next Whitman, because his compassion shows one way of healing the fatal tendencies portrayed by Melville; and last Emerson, because his clarity of mind demonstrates the basic change that must occur in our ways of thinking, if humanity is to check the gathering momentum of its presently downward trends.

To class Melville and Whitman, or even Emerson for that matter, as "Transcendentalists" does violence to the radical independence of all three. Yet this name does point to certain truths that were fundamental for them. They were all intuitive thinkers, and as Emerson said, "Whatever belongs to the class of intuitive thought is popularly called at the present day Transcendental." ("The Transcendentalist," 93) We turn now to sketch the intuitive concept of what it means to be a human being, and how that human being is related to the rest of earthly and cosmic nature. (See also Appendix A)

NOTES

1. Ralph Waldo Emerson, in *Nature, Addresses, Lectures* (Boston: Houghton Mifflin, 1903), xxxiv.
2. Ralph Waldo Emerson, *Nature*, in *The Complete Essays and Other Writings of Ralph Waldo Emerson*, Brooks Atkinson, ed. (New York: Random House, 1950), 5. Page numbers for further references to this book will be given by essay title in the text.
3. Walt Whitman, "Song of Myself," in *The Portable Walt Whitman*, Mark Van Doren, ed. (New York: Viking Press, 1945), 61. Page numbers of further references to this book will be given by poem title in the text.
4. Ralph Waldo Emerson, quoted in *The Shock of Recognition*, Edmund Wilson, ed. (New York: Grosset & Dunlop, 1955), vol. 1, 266, 248, 252.
5. Herman Melville, *Mardi: And a Voyage Thither* (New York: New American Library of World Literature, 1964), 490-1. Page numbers for further references to this book will be given in the text.

6. Herman Melville, *Moby Dick* (New York: Random House, 1950), 147, 122, 514, 183, 182. Page numbers for further references to this book will be given in the text.

7. Herman Melville, *Pierre, or, The Ambiguities* (New York: Grove Press, 1947), 148, 118-9.

8. Walt Whitman, quoted in *Shock of Recognition*, op. cit., vol. 1, 272, 286-7.

9. Ralph Waldo Emerson, "The Method of Nature," in *The Complete Writings of Ralph Waldo Emerson* (New York: Wise, 1929), 60-1.

2

THE IDEA OF MAN IN AMERICA

What is man that thou art mindful of him?
and the son of man, that thou visitest him?
For thou hast made him a little lower than the angels,
and hast crowned him with glory and honour.
Thou madest him to have dominion over the works of thy hands;
thou hast put all things under his feet.
—Psalm 8*

IDEAS HAVE CONSEQUENCES

THE feeling that prevails in society at a given moment is hard to characterize in a way that will seem true also of a slightly earlier or later time. The apparent national mood changes at remarkably short intervals. But beneath the surface ripples are larger, slower-moving waves; and below these, still more deliberate currents and tides. The periodicity of such underlying, long-lasting movements may span centuries, even millennia.

Many today look back upon earlier epochs of American history as having been comparatively robust and happy, because people then were presumably closer to nature,

---

* The meaning of "man" in traditional usage, as in the Psalms and among the New England Transcendentalists, had no sexual connotations. It obviously included women as well as men. And it had equal room for the feminine aspect (*anima*) of a man's soul and the masculine aspect (*animus*) of a woman's.

more leisurely, and more godly in their orientation than we are. But if these things were true of the last century, as imagined, how shall we account for what the severe but discerning eye of Thoreau observed among his fellow citizens in New England nearly a century and a half ago—six years before the Civil War?

> The mass of men lead lives of quiet desperation. What is called resignation is confirmed desperation. From the desperate city you go into the desperate country.... A stereotyped but unconscious despair is concealed even under what are called the games and amusements of mankind.[1]

And what was Walt Whitman sensing in the wake of the War between the States, when he reported in *Democratic Vistas* his own prophetic observations?

> Shift and turn the combinations of the statement as we may, the problem of the future of America is in certain respects as dark as it is vast.... Unwieldy and immense, who shall hold in behemoth, who bridle leviathan? Flaunt it as we choose, athwart and over the roads of our progress loom huge uncertainty and dreadful threatening gloom. It is useless to deny it.[2]

In comparing the prevailing feeling of contemporary American society with that experienced by Thoreau and Whitman a century and a half ago, perhaps most people today would not agree that ours, like theirs, is a mood of "despair" or of "huge uncertainty and dreadful threatening gloom." But undoubtedly most New Englanders of that earlier time would not have agreed either with what was being said about them by our authors. In both cases, it is a matter of superficiality or depth of perception. It is in the deeper sense that one can hazard today an appraisal of the contemporary scene—even as presidents come and go—that corresponds very closely to the diagnosis of despair and gloom for earlier times.

There is a difference, of course, in the accepted ideas prevalent then and now, but the difference is slight and the similarity considerable. Perhaps today both thought and mood are lighter than then, but at the same time they are darker. Many things are better, but many are much worse. In some respects Whitman's vision of the future certainly remains relevant today. Despite a surface complacency that is encouraged by many of their leaders, Americans today are actually more apprehensive and more lacking in conviction and motivation than they perhaps realize. Many are losing confidence both in themselves and in their country. The question must be asked now as it was asked by our earlier heralds of the spirit, whether such underlying malaise in the midst of an abundance of creature comforts and services must not be traced primarily to dispiriting thoughts, as these play so great a role in shaping our lives. What else could result from an outlook on life, and centrally on humanity and its place in the scheme of things, that lacks grounding in the spirit?

The testimony of both Thoreau and Whitman helps us realize that what now ails America underneath all its complacency has been long in coming. If in the old days there was something at work on the scene that loomed darkly "athwart and over the roads of our progress," that something has not ceased to influence us. It is a spirit that expresses itself in certain ideas—ideas whose inhumanity, unless thoroughly exposed and dealt with, will continue to subvert the peace, health, and happiness of humankind not only in America, but worldwide.

We manage our lives according to the ideas we hold about who we are and how we are related to the rest of humanity, to the cosmos, and to fate. These ideas develop in us through our education—an education that has increasingly tended to inform our heads with concepts that prove useful in controlling some aspects of external life while at the same time undermining our confidence in ourselves and others, robbing life of much beauty and joy, and in the end paralyzing truly *human* initiative.

Even the best schools today feel no compunction in insisting upon such ideas with their students. They take for granted that the planet upon which we live in cosmic loneliness had its beginning in consequence of a Big Bang (mechanically conceived and morally meaningless), and that it will find its end at long last in an equally insignificant, equally meaningless heat death—unless human perversity precipitates that end before its time. The sciences being absorbed by the young have nothing to tell of any higher Intelligence, or Love, or Meaning within, above, or behind this physical sequence of events. If there is any such higher awareness and caring, it cannot be discovered by the methods we currently rely on in building our lives. For science, the human being is an animal, albeit a clever one. He is engaged in a struggle for survival of the fittest. For the solution of his problems, he is advised to trust technological ingenuity, which represents the maximum of human cleverness.

Such ideas were well on the way to acceptance by many intellectuals of the last century in New England, but for intuitive thinkers they were the enemy. Transcendentalists knew that if education is to prepare human beings who will be fully human—which is to say, men and women who are strong enough to take control of their personal and national destinies—it must return by new ways to an older, nobler conception of human nature.

In what follows I shall attempt to suggest in my own way some presuppositions of the earlier, intuitive view of our true nature and destiny. Admittedly, my formulations of these understandings were never set forth in so many words by any of the last century's idealists, but perhaps they will serve to prepare some present-day readers for their first encounter with Transcendentalism. My picture, I believe, will find ample confirmation in the direct quotations that follow.

THE TRANSCENDENTAL IDEA OF THE HUMAN BEING

The old high idea of the human being is voiced in the first book of the Bible: "Let us make man in our own image!" With these words, divine powers expressed their will for humanity. Its origin is high; its destiny shall be equally high. As appointed, humanity shall have dominion on the earth. So spoke the ancient revelation.

But we live in a much later time. Does there still exist a native teaching in the West that is capable of renewing in modern terms the Eastern, Biblical conception of humankind's divine origin and destiny?

Let us consider what the cultural and spiritual builders of our own nation thought, felt, and believed in the last century. These men were not traditionalists. They were not merely repeating churchly doctrines. Indeed, as Emerson testified before Harvard's Divinity School in 1838, the decline of religion was already far advanced in the last century.

> I think no man can go with his thoughts about him into one of our churches, without feeling that what hold the public worship had on men is gone, or going. It has lost its grasp on the affection of the good and the fear of the bad.... And what greater calamity can fall upon a nation than the loss of worship? Then all things go to decay. Genius leaves the temple to haunt the senate or the market. Literature becomes frivolous. The eye of youth is not lighted by the hope of other worlds, and age is without honor. Society lives to trifles, and when men die we do not mention them.[3]

The Transcendentalists felt that the work to be done in their time was to halt or slow the downward momentum of humanity resulting from scientific materialism. This limited and limiting way of looking at things, however justified in some areas, proves incapable of accounting for beings that have life, soul, and spirit. It has no way to recognize the higher nature of humanity, or its central position here on earth. In his first book, published in 1836, Emerson held that the human being

> is placed in the center of beings, and a ray of relation passes from every other being to him. And neither can man be understood without these objects, nor these objects without man. (*Nature*, 25-6)

This is the outlook that has always given dignity to human beings by viewing them as the epitome of the world process. It enables each of us to feel at home in the universe—to experience ourselves as a microcosm that is intimately and centrally related to the macrocosm. We can say with Whitman: "I am the acme of things accomplished, and I am an encloser of things to be." ("Song of Myself," 124)

"He who would understand nature," said Thoreau, "must practice more humanity than others." These words are hard to understand, but Emerson's similar affirmation helps to clarify their meaning.

> Nor has science sufficient humanity, so long as the naturalist overlooks that wonderful congruity which subsists between man and the world; of which he is lord, not because he is the most subtle inhabitant, but because he is its head and heart, and finds something of himself in every great and small thing. (*Nature*, 37)

Chapter Seven will attempt to shed light on these difficult statements as they relate to a more spiritualized method of scientific investigation. My purpose here is simply to call attention to the conviction held by Thoreau and Emerson that, if the human soul is to know truly the world in which in all respects it occupies a unique position, a full response, not merely an intellectual one, is indispensable.

First, I should like to trace some of the "rays of relation," in Emerson's words, that demonstrate this human uniqueness, a uniqueness that becomes evident when we think through the respective implications of our ability to know, our virtually unlimited practical abilities, and our creative originality. The central position of the human being among all of earth's kingdoms will stand out most dramatically when we make the effort to imagine the magnificent course of evolution as Emerson, Alcott, Thoreau, or Whitman visualized it, despite Darwin's new theory of lowly rather than exalted origins.

To build the short ramp of thoughts needed to raise us to the level at which we shall be further quoting these idealists, let us do a little preliminary reasoning of our own.

THE HUMAN BEING AS KNOWER

Children in almost every school today are taught that human greatness, such as it is, consists in our being extraordinarily clever animals. We are said to be the cleverest of all earth's inhabitants: we are the animals that can think.

This teaching is accepted without question; yet it is based on an assumption the Transcendentalists would never have agreed with, namely, that human beings differ from the animal in degree but not in kind. Do we not, indeed? The "thinking" of animals is instinctive, dreamlike, and concerned strictly with their own necessities. Is there any animal that devotes its life of "thought," as we do, to the study of other animals? Which animal goes beyond the habits of its own kingdom to ponder the wonders of plant formation and rock strata?

We are unique in that our interest in *other* beings of all kinds is essentially limitless. Such interest goes far beyond organic instincts and species behavior. Ultimately, our interest as human beings is, as we say, disinterested. Our quest for objective, universal truths demands that the preferences of our own self-centered organism be completely stilled. Our thoughts may start from desires for personal benefit, but they soon pass to the general law; their goal will sooner or later be self-transcending. Indeed, the human being is free to focus attention upon all of earth's creatures, on each for its own sake—and, wonderfully, as the nature of the *other* being lights up for us, we always feel *ourselves* fulfilled.

The cognitive possibilities of an individual who could live long enough would be unlimited; for in any reflective moment, any one of us can say: Behold, my body is a tiny point in the universe, but my consciousness can be as large as the universe itself. Potentially, I am privy to all secrets of whatever kind; I can share the life of every creature to which I choose to give my attention. While each creature's perception of the world is limited by its particular point of view, the human being alone can go beyond immediate perceptions and instinctive reactions to them. Any human being can choose to remember and *think* about perceptual experiences; and when we do so, we rise above any single point of view. Thus, in *thinking* the multitude of possible views, we are either not a "creature" at all, or we are the one and only Universal Creature.

THE HUMAN BEING AS DOER

A comparison of our practical abilities with those of any other created being on earth tells the same story. Where is the limit to what we can master and make? The rabbit thumps, the frog croaks, the bird sings; but the human individual will accurately imitate all these sounds, and with unlimited variations to boot. The spider spins its threads; the wasp conjures with paper; the swallow builds a nest of mud and sticks; the groundhog digs a burrow. We will make any and all of these kinds of habitats in imitation of these animals, or we can build in altogether new ways. Whitman, especially, loved to suggest the innumerable applications of human inventiveness and industry.

There is no predicting whether people will live in this kind of house or that, or how they will be clothed, or what they will manufacture, or when, or for how long. Human abilities command all possible materials, all possible methods, all possible goals. We go beyond ourselves to understand earth, water, air, and fire; we draw these elements to ourselves and bend them to our use.

If we were an animal, we would be the animal that collects, houses, studies, domesticates, and selectively breeds other animals; the animal that uses one creature for this purpose and another for that—tomorrow differently than today or yesterday—and the one that has the power to succor or to ruin every other animal species.

But there is no such animal! The human being, who can do these things and far more, is essentially either not an animal at all, or is the one and only Universal Animal.

THE HUMAN BEING AS CREATOR

Potentially, it is within our power to *understand* all creatures and to *control* them. And yet we go beyond both of these possible functions. Were we to regard ourselves only as mirror and master of all that is, we would still not have taken our measure. Characteristically, we go beyond everything that already exists, to fashion what has never existed before. For example, into the midst of nature we introduce a synthetic kingdom of energies, processes, and machines that has been called the wholly new realm of "subnature." And again, out of natural substances, we build also the superkingdom we call art.

The beings of nature, of course, also bring forth artifacts in abundance, each after its kind. But human beings bring forth according to all kinds, to no kind, and to new kinds. The beings of nature create, but their creations in every case are necessitated organically; they are essentially the same for all the members of a given species; that is, they are not independent, free creations at all, but the necessary further expressions of an already created being, by necessity arising out of its given physique. Our creations have no such general character and no such necessity behind them. Whether they happen at all, and what they will be, depends upon the unpredictable will of the individual.

Thus at our best we are more creator than creature. We are creative precisely because we are, in the essential part of our being, still "uncreated." The original, undetermined, self-determining, all-creative *Ground of Being* comes to expression in the human soul. As creatures, we belong to the existing world order, but as creators we transcend it. In us the given world continually dies, and new worlds begin.

"Who," asked Emerson, "can set bounds to the possibilities of man?" We know, he says, that "man has access to the entire mind of the Creator, is himself the creator in the finite" (*Nature*, 35-36). God determined the world in creating it, by giving to each being its nature. But in creating humanity, God did not fashion such a fixed or determinate nature: He gave directly of Himself. It is therefore not an overstatement to say with Emerson that the human being alone of all earth's beings is himself, in his highest aspect, "the creator in the finite." For this reason and in this sense, we are not limited to being simply a part of nature—one of many—but we are the open channel on earth for the unlimited creativeness of Universal Nature itself.

These are commonsense ways in which we may approach the "Idea of Man" proclaimed by America's last-century heralds of the spirit. Their view acknowledges our triviality in our personal nature, and is keenly aware of the disturbing effects our ignorant self-will introduces into the world process; yet, their limitless expectations rest upon the certainty that in each individual there lives something capable of self-judgment, self-change, and of changing all else in accord with universal standards. This higher something is the clue to our greatness. It makes us not eccentric but concentric with the world process: productively central, first and last, even in the evolution of all the natural kingdoms that surround us on earth.

HUMAN BEINGS AND ANIMALS

Before we turn to the evolutionary past, however, we may profit by trying to gain a still clearer idea of where we stand at present in the hierarchy of earth's beings, particularly in our relationship to our animal "brothers." Since nothing so trivializes the concept of human nature as a facile Darwinism, let us go over this ground once again, to see if we can put right what has so often been put wrong.

As we have mentioned, students today learn, from teachers and textbooks alike, beginning in the earliest grades, that the human being is an animal—not just that we obviously have animal aspects and that a portion of us shares in animal experience, even as other parts of our nature are plantlike and mineral-like—but that in essential truth we *are* animals. We are the animal, it is said, whose brain is developed beyond that of the other animals. Supposedly it is this larger brain that gives us the ability to think: to reason abstractly, to remember and foresee, to develop the many forms of communication our society and culture are built on. And supposedly because we also have our forelimbs free, our clever brain can show us how to make things, to fashion the tools that permit us to satisfy our ever-expanding desires.

This information is true enough. Certainly, all the higher animals do have complex nervous systems. All do accomplish their work by combining elements of consciousness with distinctive physical abilities. All communicate to some extent, too, and live within some kind of social order. But the conclusion the student of biology is encouraged, and even compelled, to draw is untrue—namely, that in our highest achievements we are doing the same things as the "other" animals, only in a more complicated way.

This line of reasoning makes a powerful impression upon children, especially since youth loves animals and quite rightly wants to think of them in the most admiring terms. On the other hand, the thrust of the argument holds long past childhood—into the age when childhood's warm affinities have cooled. Then, when grown men and women no longer idealize animals quite as children do, but may even look down upon many of them, they are still asked to consider themselves as basically animals. And this opinion not only numbs but can eventually destroy what is uniquely human in them. People who imagine they are born only to serve their instincts, and who believe themselves to be competing with all other instinctive forms of life for survival, will progressively degrade themselves. Because they are actually not the animal they think they are, their liability to error, fear, and degeneracy will not be limited like the animals'. In their alienation from themselves, they will come to develop traits more tawdry and more terrible than any animal's.

The argument that classifies human beings as animals is more than merely faulty; it has consequences sure to prove disastrous.

What distinguishes the human individual from any animal is a difference in kind, not merely one of degree. It is pseudo-logic to say that because deer wag their tails and human beings use semaphores, because crows caw and human beings proclaim, both are of one kind: all are animals, and they differ only in the degree of their ability to communicate. In addition to the ability of every person to imitate the whole range of animal calls, cries, and gestures, we must take into account further capacities that enable us to pray and preach, to establish schools and parliaments. We do more than merely perform "signalling acts"; we are also such masters of communication as Aeschylus, Shakespeare, and Dante; Mozart, Bach, and Beethoven; Plato, Swedenborg, and Hegel; Tesla, Edison, and Marconi.

We may say that with human beings the power of expression has *arrived*. In animals, it is only a doomed potentiality. The difference may be seen in a comparison of human with animal "faces." The bird with its frozen beak, the horse or goat or monkey with its gross muzzle, wear masks. Compared to us, they are limited, at best, to positive or negative hints of expression. The human countenance is alive to the finest detail of forehead, eyebrow, eye, nose, mouth, cheek, and jaw. The features are balanced, the skin is soft, the musculature is infinitely subtle; the blood plays through to the very surface of the delicate skin. Every possible feeling and meaning can be expressed by and reflected on this countenance. And the same is true of our limbs, down to the tips of fingers and toes. Compare the improvisation of a great singer, violinist, or dancer with the highest expression apes can give to their dim, organic stirrings!

What holds true of function is equally true of form. If we were actually animals, we would be the kind that has a forehead, a chin, a fully opposable thumb, a broad rather than deep chest, a bowl-shaped pelvis, a straight knee, a true heel, and so on: in brief, the one that stands erect. But no animal stands erect, nor does any animal have any of these features of fully erect posture. Only we do; and the fact that by standing fully upright we project our whole physical organization into a vertical rather than horizontal flow of forces must delicately but decisively transform every bone, muscle, gland, and organ system in our body.

The *logic* of our relation to the animals may now be summarized. If it is reasonable to say that among rocks there are some that live, reproduce, and develop a green color—these being called vegetative rocks, or "plants"—and that among plants there are some that slink about with black-striped skins, snarl, and leap upon their prey—these being called tiger-type plants, or "animals"—and that among animals there are some that can do the innumerable things we know human beings do—these being called people-animals, or humans—then it is also reasonable to speak of a square in geometry as a special, advanced kind of "triangle" that has four sides.

Finally, it is not *our* achievements, however impressive, that set us apart. It is the unlimited creativeness of the Universal Spirit that expresses itself through us.

THE TRANSCENDENTAL THEORY OF EVOLUTION

Any outlook recognizing how the whole of creation comes to self-consciousness in humankind will accord humanity the central position in nature. Greek and Renaissance Humanism, German and English Romanticism, and American Transcendentalism all agree that humanity deserves this honor and bears this responsibility. "Nature," said Emerson, "is so pervaded with human life that there is something of humanity in all and in every particular" (*Nature*, 35).

> Nature is the immense shadow of man.... The world is thoroughly anthropomorphosized, as if it had passed through the body and mind of man, and taken his mould and form.[4]

If we think through the implications of these assessments with respect to our capacity to know, we see that our cognitive nature is essentially boundless, encompassing all that lies before and around us. This means that the secrets of all possible beings can come to consciousness in us—and, among earthly inhabitants, only in us. The whole world awakens in and through the human effort of thought. In us, the hidden life, the soul, of each and all gradually comes to tell its story.

In the course of its creative striving, the World-spirit has brought forth the kingdoms of nature; in some sense all have been but offshoots or by-products of its central purpose, that of realizing itself in and through humanity. The universal power that has been at work unconsciously in nature is the same that lives consciously in the human soul. Hence, we may consider ourselves—rather, the Universal Self within each of us—as the original source, the summary archetype, of all other creatures.

> The world proceeds from the same spirit as the body of man. It is a remoter and inferior incarnation of God, a projection of God in the unconscious. (*Nature*, 36)

Here we have the beginning of Emerson's humanist theory of evolution, which we can sketch in a general form, implied but never elaborated by Emerson himself.

Evolution is the path creation takes. The first act of every true creation begins not with a caused cause, but with an absolute or first cause: with what is self-existent, self-maintaining, and self-active. Such an absolute prime mover, said Emerson, can be found only in the spirit. "Spirit hath life in itself" (*Nature*, 15). "A Fact," he said, "is but the end or last issue of spirit" (*Nature*, 19).

Evolution must have begun when the divine spirit set before itself the highest possible ideal of creation, that is, when it undertook to *create the creative*. Divine love must have sought to express itself in and through a form that was to be capable of receiving and continuing divine life so immediately, so centrally—and yet so independently—that it would itself become absolutely and forever creative. This new being itself was to become a first cause, a prime mover, able to make radically new beginnings—and eventually "a new heaven and a new earth."

The vessel that was to house the universal spirit must, of course, not be limited by any bias or distortion. It must be of subtlest refinement and perfectly balanced; and to build up this material form from simplest beginnings would require a long development, passing through many stages. These stages would all be emanations of the divine power: sacrificial gifts of its own spiritual substance made by what was "in the beginning." As time would thus come into being out of eternity and as, in the course of time, more perfect bodily forms would develop, these forms would prove themselves to be ever more receptive and representative of the divine influx. The creative First Cause, which had sought Self-realization *in and through matter*, could of course actually appear upon earth only in the last form of all.

Walt Whitman paints this evolutionary picture:

> Afar down I see the huge first Nothing,
>   I know I was even there,
> I waited unseen and always, and slept through
>   the lethargic mist,
> and took my time, and took no hurt from
>   the fetid carbon.
> Long I was hugg'd close—long and long.
> Immense have been the preparations for me,
> Faithful and friendly the arms that have help'd me.
> Cycles ferried my cradle, rowing and rowing
>   like cheerful boatmen,
> For room to me stars kept aside in their own rings,
> They sent influences to look after what was to hold me.

....
My embryo has never been torpid, nothing could
 overlay it. ("Song of Myself," 124-5)

Whitman saw that evolution always follows from involution. As the generative spirit gives more and more of itself, involving itself ever more deeply in matter, progressively higher orders of being develop in the material world, and higher functions become possible. From the beginning, the divine gives of itself to all, but it cannot give the *essential* of its own being to any form until it has transformed that form again and again through creative inworking—up to the very last impulse that allows the vessel to *begin* to be a true image of the divine. The climax of evolution, therefore, will be reached by the being that has remained malleable the longest in the hands of the creative archetype that gave all things their start. "In the beginning was the Word" that created all things; in the end are human beings, who alone can release the Word out of themselves. Our word is presently weak, but has it not before it the possibility of being filled at last with the primordial power?

Those who are skeptical of the human being's centrality in nature here on earth think of human beings as merely a species added to the many other more or less evolved creatures. We have fought our way to the top, they suppose; but they cannot say whether we will last. That we arrived on the physical scene very late* is believed to prove that the evolution of the earth went on well enough by itself before we came and that it may continue to advance just as well, perhaps better, after we are gone.

The humanist, romantic, transcendental, anthroposophic view is that though humanity as a physical embodiment came last in the earth's history, the creative power, the

---

*"It is a mischievous notion," wrote Emerson, "that we are come late into nature; that the world was finished a long time ago." "The American Scholar," in *Essays*, 57-8.

source and goal of all earth evolution—the Human Being—was there from the beginning. The Human Being with a capital H and B is as central to all the other beings of nature as the germ and sap of a tree are to its sprouting branches and leaves. The "human form divine" is the energy behind all other forms. When Amos Bronson Alcott was asked by Theodore Parker "what he would do with the Mosaic account that gives the priority of creation to the elements," he replied that this

> was the historical, not genetic, account of the matter. It was the story told in the order of the senses.... The senses begin in the concrete, and analyze from the surface to the center. But this is not the order of generation. The *Soul* is prior to the elements of nature. It was the Soul which said, "Let there be light, and there was light." *Light* is generated by *the Soul*, and is the base of matter.[5]

In Alcott's view, the essential human being

> is older than nature. The synthesis of his being is broader. Nature is included within it. Matter, both organic and inorganic, is consequent and a sequel of his birth. He is older, and survives all its changes. Nature is the Soul's cast-off wardrobe.[6]

Or, as he said on another occasion:

> Say this, loosely: Nature is the waste man. The soul instinctively frees herself from all superfluous matter generated in building forth her own body....[7]

Obviously, Alcott's divine Soul is the same as Emerson's Over-soul. It is the eternal creativeness that chose to *involve* itself ever more deeply in the material process until, in the balanced, harmonious human body, it had *evolved* the temple it could call its own and in it stand upright.

When he speaks of "the human form, of which all other organizations appear to be degradations" (*Nature*, 25), Emerson is of one opinion with Alcott. Only the human form can be said to have been fashioned through and through by the ideal, or to be an individualized precipitate of the universal creative mind. It was the descending divine spirit that at all times led the way through and past the evolutionary stages at which other beings stopped. They, too, were once potentially human, for they expressed the same spirit we manifest, and they moved together toward the same end. But their complete development was sooner or later blocked, so that the Presence itself could never as fully enter them as it can now begin to enter us. While the creative power continues to stir them in varying degrees, it cannot raise them to full consciousness. It still hovers, as it were, at different levels outside of and above them. The divine, creative Selfhood of rocks lies far on high; while here below, the inert bodies sleep in the deepest trance. Bending closer to the sleeping plant than to the rock, the divine Selfhood awakens life processes. Finding its way still more deeply into the animal body, it brings about a dreaming, inward consciousness; it conjures sensation, feeling, and the power of movement. This same descending, causative, prime mover is the Spirit that now at last has begun to enter human beings—that has its foot actually inside the door of our house, so speak, and henceforth will enter it the more, the more we consciously, freely take our own development in hand. As we perfect ourselves morally, as we develop reverence and love toward all that surrounds us, and as we devote ourselves to the earth with compassion and initiative, the universal Mind can open up, and the creative Presence can make itself known ever more fully in and through us. The reality of the other forms of the world around us can begin to speak their secrets within our own consciousness.

Once the human soul begins to awaken, the study of nature awakens it ever further. "Man imprisoned, man crystallized, man vegetative, speaks to man impersonated," said Emerson (*Nature*, 21). We are able to know the beings of nature because a light can shine forth in us, which must remain dark in other beings because of their incompletion. When we look at animals, rocks, or plants, mysteries confront us to all of which we ourselves contain and will yet give the answer.

Novalis, the German Romanticist who considered himself a "transcendental physician," expressed the humanistic concept of our relationship to nature when he said:

> I do not know why people always talk of humanity as something separate. Are not animals, plants, and stones, stars and breezes also portions of humanity? [8]

Henry Sutton, the English poet, alluded similarly to the mystery of the tie between ourselves and nature:

> Man doth usurp all space;
> Stares thee, in rock, bush, river, in the face.[9]

When Whitman spoke of himself as "infinite and *omnigenous*," he must have been visualizing the self-existent, self-active source of creativeness that moves physical evolution forward while remaining hidden until it has developed the human form. In *this* form at last it comes to light as the conscious "I am!"

> I find I incorporate gneiss, coal, long-threaded moss,
>   fruits, grains, esculent roots,
> And am stucco'd with quadrupeds and birds all over,
> And have distanced what is behind me for good reasons,
> But call anything back again when I desire it....
>
> So they show their relations to me and I accept them
> They bring me tokens of myself—they evince them

>   plainly in their possession.
> I wonder where they got those tokens,
> Did I pass that way huge times ago and negligently
>   drop them?
> Myself moving forward then and now and forever,
> Gathering and showing more always and with velocity,
> Infinite and omnigenous, . . . ("Song of Myself," 99)

But is it not presumptuous to speak of human beings as infinite and omnigenous? Is humanity really so grand; is it not rather something far less? Emerson suggests that while we are undoubtedly small in what we have thus far made of ourselves, we are yet great in our origin and in our potentiality.

> Man is the dwarf of himself. Once he was permeated and dissolved by spirit. He filled nature with his over-flowing currents. (*Nature*, 39)

Once humanity was integral with the First Cause. In the beginning, our evolving form was not a condensed, limited physical body, earth-born and earth-bound. Instead, it was peripheral to the earth, ethereal, fluidic, but slowly condensing and descending from still higher, purely spiritual spheres. For the most part, we were still in and of the All-creative Spirit that translated itself gradually into the manifest forms of nature, until eventually it could cross the *t* and dot the *i* in the earthly human being.

> But, having made for himself this huge shell, his waters retired; he no longer fills the veins and veinlets; he is shrunk to a drop. He sees that the structure still fits him, but fits him colossally. Say, rather, once it fitted him, now it corresponds to him from far and on high.
>
> He adores timidly his own work. . . . Yet sometimes he starts in his slumber, and wonders at himself and his

house, and muses strangely at the resemblance betwixt him and it. (*Nature*, 39)

When the spirit of humanity was still integral with God, it participated causatively in the evocation and infusion of the whole of the natural environment it later entered—even, as Alcott said, of matter itself. The steps of the evolutionary ascent of earth's material forms were therefore at the same time, *for our essential being*, the stages of a descent into matter. When the eternal "I Am" could finally utter itself, as stillest, smallest voice, as tiniest spark, within an adequately evolved being on earth, that being was the humble but balanced human being. Of course, we can achieve at first only the echo of the great "I Am," but even this echo is an absolute. Potentially, it can speak the Word of God.

THE EVOLUTIONARY FUTURE

Thus, we are both infinite and limited. We are great, and we are small. We were from the beginning, yet of all creatures we appeared last. What of our future, since evolution is of the future as well as of the past? Will nature in time produce other creatures superior to us?

For the view we have presented, it is clearly impossible that the creative spirit could now go on to build up higher forms of physical beings. When the primordial creativeness began at last to enter consciously into human beings, it began at the same time to withdraw from the rest of nature, just as all parents eventually begin to withdraw when they have passed on to their offspring the power of renewal. We carry within ourselves the seed of the earth's further development. In us alone lies the quickening power for the future of all earth's kingdoms. Creativeness on earth has passed into our hands. Further evolution on the earth will be the consequence of our initiative and love, based on our gratitude. Advances, if there are to be any, will take place henceforth only by our choice. It is not the created being, of course, but only the eternal "I Am" working in and through it, that can further this work of creative evolution.

The battle for the future evolution of all the earth's creatures will be fought between the "higher self" and the "lower self" of human individuals. Should the battle be lost to the lower self, the whole of the natural creation, which, in Emerson's words, issued originally from "Man" and which is but the leaves and branches of his tree, will deteriorate. To the extent that the battle is won by the higher or universal Spirit—the authentic Self in human beings—not only human clay but all clay on earth will be uplifted.

As Alcott suggested, the human spirit, in the rhythms of its slow involution into matter, necessarily had to thrust out and set aside the material forms that resisted further evolution through their premature condensation, thus "precipitating" or depositing themselves at various levels as the several lower kingdoms of nature. Thus, it is only fitting that in our freely chosen evolution we should feel gratitude to the brothers who stayed behind so that we might go ahead. The top of the mountain, though still distant, is within our reach; but our brothers are the faithful servants who have pitched the base camps upon which our ascent has depended. Their sacrifice has served a great purpose. "Nature is thoroughly mediate" said Emerson. "It is made to serve. It receives the dominion of man as meekly as the ass on which the Saviour rode" (*Nature*, 22).

A leader must develop grateful interest in all those who have made and still make his or her success possible. The human being is not, as so many believe today, really in competition with nature. We are raised above nature by divine decree. Our task is simply to rule our kingdom as a good king would do: for the best interest of our subjects, remembering that insofar as our unique creativity adds new content to the world, it should be worthy of and a blessing upon what already exists. Since nature seeks fulfillment *in* and *through* us, we should live in such a way that all forms of the earth may indeed be fulfilled. Emerson observed that "In proportion to the energy of his thought and will, he [every rational creature] takes up the world into himself" (*Nature*, 11). Once humanity has come to itself, it has no other or higher task than to unite again in sympathy and service with the beings it has had to distance itself from for a time. If we are to be lifted up, we can and should draw nature with us. As St. Paul said:

> The whole creation is on tiptoe to see the wonderful sight of the sons of God coming into their own. The world of creation cannot as yet see reality, not because it chooses to be blind, but because in God's purpose it has been so limited—yet it has been given hope. And the hope is that in the end the whole of created life will be rescued from the tyranny of change and decay, and have its share in that magnificent liberty which can only belong to the sons of God! (Rom. 8:19-21, Phillips translation)

PRESENT AND FUTURE

The Human Being As Artist

Priests and poets, sages and seers have always seen the creative work of human beings as world fulfillment. In art, we are most ourselves and yet are, or should be, wholly "about our Father's business." While nature is God's work of art from which we start, art of the human kind is the new "nature" we go on to create out of ourselves. When an individual creates out of what is deepest in him or her, the work is thoroughly original, yet it continues nature. "A true announcement of the law of creation, if a man were found worthy to declare it, would carry art up into the kingdom of nature, and destroy its separate and contrasted existence." ("Art," 313)

Art begins when the divine in nature has awakened the divine in us. "Thus in art does Nature work through the will of a man filled with the beauty of her first works" (*Nature*, 14). To reach this beauty requires a deeper perception, one that passes beyond the already formed to the formative. The formative life, *natura naturans*, makes itself known not to the outward but only to the inward senses. "The lover of nature is he whose inward and outward senses are still truly adjusted to each other" (*Nature*, 6). To speak truly, Emerson said, the adults who can really see nature are few. "Too feeble fall the impressions of nature on us to make us artists. Every touch should thrill.... The rays have sufficient force to arrive at the senses, but not enough to reach the quick." ("The Poet," 14, 6, 321)

If every material fact is the end result of spiritual creativity—as we have affirmed—it is also true that *in* this material fact creativeness, which is of the spirit, comes to an end. It comes, indeed, to a "dead end." This is why any mode of knowledge that limits itself to physical facts will never produce art. It cannot do so because these facts are themselves the *last* issue of creative becoming. They can be intellectually known, but in this knowledge there is no force to go further. Inevitably, a fact-bound science will first ascertain what is, and then may try to preserve and mummify it; but in the end, it will disintegrate what is. Material fact is the last issue of spirit, and materialistic science is but the crumbling of that fact. Applied material science may seem to produce an "abundant" society, but it is actually an exploitative and disintegrative force and will eventually lay that society waste.

The importance of this insight cannot be sufficiently emphasized; for creative art is not simply the talent or the product of some especially gifted individuals. It is the destiny and health of all human beings. Business is art; politics and marriage and education are art. Are not farming and medicine and the dispensing of justice also arts? Above, beneath, and running through everything, human morality itself is the highest creative art. When free human beings choose moral goals, arts of all kinds, and life itself, prosper. When moral human beings express themselves creatively in any way, the evolution of the earth takes a step forward.

Emerson wrote more about poetry and art than about anything else, perhaps, except for Nature, God's art. He admitted that the American Transcendentalists gave highest value to Beauty, the goal of art. In his essay entitled "Beauty," he quotes Goethe's observation that "the beautiful is a manifestation of the secret laws of nature which but for this appearance had been forever concealed from us."[10] So it is important to realize that genuine art enables us to reach higher forms of insight: "The more poetic, the truer," said Novalis. "Poetry, if perfected, is the only verity," was Emerson's way of saying the same thing.

> Poetry is the perpetual endeavor to express the spirit of the thing, to pass the brute body and search the life and reason which causes it to exist;—to see that the object is always flowing away, whilst the spirit or necessity which causes it subsists.[11]

Through art we achieve insight, but at the same time we also do the deed the world of appearance needs to have done for it: we raise the transient to permanence. This was a major theme of Whitman's poetry, for example, of his "Crossing Brooklyn Ferry" (see Chapter Seven). And this function of art need not be considered abstruse. The world passes through human hands; inevitably, we will either *dis*figure it, or we will *trans*figure it. "Man is never weary of working it up . . . until the world will become at last only a realized will—the double of the man." (*Nature*, 22) Will the transformed world be made in the image of humanity as the materialist fancies it, or as the idealist-transcendentalist-humanist-anthroposophist knows it is and must yet further become?

Morality as Work of Art

Pervading all private and public life, all works theoretical and practical, is human morality. *Morality is the value we incorporate into our actions as a matter of choice.* Here, too, it is art that gives the clue to a wholesome, evolutionary creativeness.

As Schiller stressed in his *Letters on the Aesthetic Education of Man*, in the realm of logic human freedom of thought is bound; and in the realm of practical fact, our freedom of action is bound.[12] In neither world can we fulfill our very own creative impulse. Human striving for freedom seeks to bring forth a new reality that arises from the mingling of the worlds of thought and fact according to each heart's creative desire. This is the function of art, and of morality as the human art of living. In the fantasy with which the moral artist brings about this intermingling, he or she moves in freedom. Through moral imagination and technique, the human heart brings together intuitive thought and practical will to produce new, self-chosen values. *These values find their reason for existence in the moral artist's objective love for them.*

It is only the love we have for our deeds that makes them entirely ours. In doing "good" deeds, we may appear to act like moral beings; but we shall remain submoral until our heart is saying an emphatic "Yes!" to what we are doing. We can say that we love our deeds when we have conceived, imagined, and executed them as free expressions of what makes us truly, enduringly happiest. This is Schiller's view. It is also the teaching of Rudolf Steiner's *Philosophy of Spiritual Activity*,[13] and it is the belief of that self-reliant American, Emerson, who held that "the absolutely trustworthy" is seated in the heart and that "in self-trust all the virtues are comprehended." ("The American Scholar," 57)

Emerson's essay "Experience" explains the art of life as always attempting to hold the proportion between "power and form." ("Experience," 353, 352, 354) Will is power; thought is form. "Each of these elements in excess makes a mischief as hurtful as its defect." Therefore "the mid-world is best," because it lies between the anemic estrangement from the world of abstract thought and the hectic immersion into the world of practical life. "We may climb into the thin and cold realm of pure geometry and lifeless science, or sink into that of sensation. Between these extremes is the equator of life, of thought, of spirit, of poetry—a narrow belt." Morality issues from this narrow belt, where, because we have neutralized the habitual or customary or merely logical thoughts that would compel us, we are left free to choose from the center of our own being. It is hard to keep one's way along so narrow a path; indeed, "a man is a golden impossibility. The line he must walk is a hair's breadth." ("Experience," 354) But we human beings glory in doing the impossible. Precisely at the intermediate zero point within ourselves, where existing "forms" and "powers" come to rest, we discover, we invent, we will our own reason for existence. From this nothing we will bring forth our own something, namely, our uncoerced love for what we esteem good. Imbuing all that flows out from our lives with the values we love, we will begin to build the new world for which the evolution of the whole existing world was only preparation.

Human Life Eternal

There is an old saying that "art is long, but time is fleeting." We cannot conclude this sketch of the humanism envisaged by our American heralds of the spirit without taking the measure of this particular truth. If the fulfillment of human beings lies in the creative expression of their love, as artists in life, how scarcely will anyone *be* fulfilled within the brief span allotted in a single life-span on earth! And if the redemption of nature is our great task, how unlikely it is that any one of us will in one brief lifetime gain sufficient wisdom, love, and moral force to contribute adequately. Human life ends but shortly after we have begun to learn—and long before we have made good on the harm done while learning.

There is no doubt that art is long, but is life really so short? Emerson, Whitman, Melville, and Thoreau dug deep for their answers to this question. At one time or another, they all stated their conviction that the essential being of man, which did not begin with birth and will not die with death, must have an unlimited scope for its development. A few quotations will suffice to confirm their belief that human beings live many earth-lives and that learning and doing grow toward perfection through a continuing experience that, while often punctuated, is never ended.

As we do the day's work, then seek sleep for renewal, and, when we are ready, return to carry new inspiration into a new day, so it is with our course through one life on earth and into the next. Good deeds therefore have the fullness of time to bear their fruit, and time will wait forever for bad deeds to be made good. The prospects for positive development are equally unlimited. "I show that size is only development," said Whitman.

> Have you outstript the rest? Are you the President?
> It is a trifle, they will more than arrive there every
>   one, and still pass on. ("Song of Myself," 84-85)

Emerson believed that

> We must infer our destiny from the preparation. We are driven by instinct to hive innumerable experiences which

are of no visible value, and we may revolve through many lives before we shall assimilate or exhaust them.[14]

The idea of reincarnation appealed to Emerson. It came recommended by Plato, Eastern philosophy, the German idealists, his friend Alcott, and many other Transcendentalists of his time. The idea seemed reasonable and lifelike to him, but he could not quite assert it on the basis of his own intuitive memory.

> I cannot tell if these wonderful qualities which house today in this mortal frame shall ever re-assemble in equal activity in a similar frame, or whether they have before had a natural history like that of this body you see before you; but this one thing I know, that these qualities did not now begin to exist, cannot be sick with my sickness, nor buried in any grave; but that they circulate through the Universe: before the world was, they were.... I draw from this faith, courage and hope.[15]

Emerson perceived that "The love of life is out of all proportion to the value set on a single day," and "it is the nature of intelligent beings to be forever new to life." He quoted with approval Goethe's saying:

> To me the eternal existence of my soul is proved by my idea of activity. If I work incessantly till my death, Nature is bound to give me another form of existence, when the present can no longer sustain my spirit.[16]

Of course, the conviction of immortality is not yet the certainty of repeated earth-lives; yet, we know that Goethe and many of his friends believed strongly in reincarnation:

> The soul of man
> Is like to water;

From heaven it cometh,
To heaven it riseth,
And then again
To earth returneth,
Forever alternating....[17]

And when Emerson's beloved child Waldo died, in the poem "Threnody" he solaced his grief with the expectation of a later reappearance of the boy's soul. Perhaps, he thought, this child who seemed to augur much for the future had needed only so brief a life to make the connections he came for; perhaps his withdrawal from earth was only to make ready for rebirth in a time that will better help him to develop what he has already taken into himself.

Whitman and Melville discuss this subject again and again. "Do you believe," asks Melville, "that you lived three thousand years ago?" Probably not, he says, for "in some universe-old truths all mankind are disbelievers." But "The greatest marvels are first truths; and first truths the last unto which we attain.... It is because we ourselves are in ourselves, that we know ourselves not...."[18]

In a letter to Hawthorne, Melville tried to explain how he had already in his twenties, as a callow, half-educated American youth of narrow experience, come upon the deepest metaphysical problems and grappled them with strangely mature powers of soul. He felt that both the problems and the powers had awakened suddenly within him—full-grown, as it were. He thought he must now be dealing with the resumé of struggles and achievements belonging to times long past. He must be approaching the condensed essence of life-riddles posed by forgotten deeds and misdeeds of his own. "I am like one of those seeds taken out of the Egyptian Pyramids," he wrote as he tackled *Moby Dick* at the age of thirty-one, "which, after being three thousand years a seed ... being planted in English soil, it developed itself.... I feel that I am now come to the inmost leaf of the bulb."[19]

Melville's sense of the relationship between his past and his present comes to light repeatedly in *Mardi*. "My memory is a life beyond birth," he says; "Zoroaster whispered me before I was born."[20]

> Thus deeper and deeper into Time's endless tunnel, does the winged soul, like a night-hawk, wend her wild way; and finds eternities before and behind; and her last limit is her everlasting beginning.[21]

In *Moby Dick*, Melville used the chapter "Stowing Down and Clearing Up" to characterize the sequence from life through death and purgation, and on to a new existence.

> Yet this is life. For hardly have we mortals by long toilings extracted from this world's vast bulk its small but valuable sperm; and then with weary patience, cleansed ourselves from its defilements, and learned to live here in clean tabernacles of the soul; hardly is this done, when— There she blows!—the ghost is spouted up, and away we sail to fight some other world, and go through young life's old routine again.
> Oh! the metempsychosis! Oh! Pythagoras, that in bright Greece, two thousand years ago, did die, so good, so wise, so mild; I sailed with thee along the Peruvian coast last voyage—and, foolish as I am, taught thee, a green simple boy, how to splice a rope.[22]

Thoreau's belief that reincarnation gives us time to perfect ourselves, to learn, and to live out our inner being comes to light in many places. His journal entry of July 16, 1851, has this note:

> Methinks my present experience is nothing: my past experience is all in all. I think that no experience which I have today comes up, or is comparable with, the experiences of my boyhood. And not only this is true, but as far back as I

can remember I have unconsciously referred to the experiences of a previous state of existence.[23]

Another entry also leaves no doubt of his meaning:

I lived in Judea eighteen hundred years ago, but I never knew that there was such a one as Christ among my contemporaries. . . .
And Hawthorne, too, I remember as one with whom I sauntered in old heroic times along the banks of the Scamander amid the ruins of chariots and heroes. As the stars looked to me when I was a shepherd in Assyria, they look to me now a New Englander.[24]

While to most of the Transcendentalists, repeated earth-lives could be only a reasonable supposition, Thoreau seems to have spoken from personal memory and experience. Less specific perhaps than Thoreau's memory but nonetheless a matter of immediate consciousness that carried conviction in itself, was the illumination recorded by Alcott in his journal entry of February 1, 1850:

It was during these months that there came a period of surprising introversion . . . too remarkable, indeed, to be easily forgotten, yet not easily described. The state is faintly indicated in the following notes from my diary of that time:
"And this seems to be our apotheosis—shall we name fitlier by any other name what we see and feel as ourselves? . . . It is no longer Many but One with us, and we live recluse yet sweetly and sagely, as having made acquaintance suddenly of some mighty and majestic friend, omniscient and benign, who keeps aloof as if it were beneath some intervening umbrage, and yet draws me toward him as by some secret force, some cerebral magnetism, while he enjoins the writing of things he extends to me from behind the mystic leaves."[25]

We may think of Alcott in this experience as approaching his own immortal entelechy, the Self who in eternity stands as the One behind the many selves developed in successive earth-lives.

> I am drawn on by enchantment, and seem taking the leaves of the trees of lives then plucked for me, and to sojourn I know not whither through regions of spirit.... And now come the old memories into me, and I fear, almost, this blaze of being. This survival of the foregone periods in me shall blot from the memory forever the spots and forms and names I so lately knew.... Far too slender is the thread that holds me to this Now....[26]

A contemporary, Frederic Hedge, stated in philosophical terms what had come to Alcott as a direct intuition:

> What is the root? We call it soul. *Our* soul, we call it; properly speaking, it is not ours, but we are its. It is not one article in an inventory of articles which together make up our individuality, but the root of that individuality. It is larger than we are, and other than we are—that is, than our conscious self. The conscious self does not begin until some time after the birth of the individual. It is not aboriginal, but a produce—as it were, the blossoming of an individuality.... And the soul which does so blossom exists before that blossom unfolds.... Whatever had a beginning in time, it should seem must end in time. The eternal destination which faith ascribes to the soul presupposes an eternal origin.... This was the theory of the most learned and acute of the Christian Fathers (Origen).... Of all the theories respecting the origin of the soul it seems to me the most plausible, and therefore the one most likely to throw light on the question of a life to come.... A new bodily organism I hold to be an essential part of the soul's destination.[27]

It may be helpful to close this brief sampling of nineteenth-century American thought on the subject of reincarnation with the following quotation from a close friend of Emerson. James Freeman Clarke placed the concept into the context that has occupied us in this chapter, that of involution and evolution.

> That man has come up to his present state of development by passing through lower forms is the popular doctrine of science today. What is called evolution teaches that we have reached our present state by a very long and gradual ascent from the lowest animal organizations. It is true that the Darwinian theory takes no notice of the evolution of the soul, but only of the body. But it appears to me that a combination of the two views would remove many difficulties which still attach to the theory of natural selection and the survival of the fittest.... If we are to believe in evolution, let us have the assistance of the soul itself in this development of new species.
> For of the soul the body form doth take:
> *For soul is form, and doth the body make.*
> . . . .
> The modern doctrine of the evolution of bodily organisms is not complete, unless we unite with it the idea of a corresponding evolution of the spiritual monad.... *Evolution has a satisfactory meaning only when we admit that the soul is developed and educated by passing through many bodies.* (Emphasis added)[28]

* * *

The purpose in this review of Transcendental themes has been to place our three heralds, Emerson, Whitman, and Melville, in the context of an implicit world conception. They breathed an air and responded to an impulse of abounding new life that was prophetic of what is possible, and indeed necessary, for the healing of our own time. Theirs was a spiritual vision of human nature, and they based their wish and their hope for their country's future upon this vision.

We now turn more specifically to these three heralds, beginning with Herman Melville; but as we shall see in the following chapter, his impassioned soul's experience of life in his own time and place added up to warning rather than assurance.

NOTES

1. Brooks Atkinson, ed., *Walden and Other Writings of Henry David Thoreau* (New York: Random House, 1950), 7.
2. Walt Whitman, "Democratic Vistas," *The Portable Walt Whitman*, Mark Van Doren, ed. (New York: Viking Press, 1945), 464. Page numbers of further references to this book will be given by poem title in the text.
3. Ralph Waldo Emerson, "Divinity School Address," in *The Complete Essays and Other Writings of Ralph Waldo Emerson*, Brooks Atkinson, ed. (New York: Random House, 1950), 79. Page numbers of further references to this book will be given by essay title in the text.
4. Ralph Waldo Emerson, "Poetry and Imagination," *The Complete Writings of Ralph Waldo Emerson* (New York: Wise, 1929), 733.
5. Amos Bronson Alcott, *The Journals of Amos Bronson Alcott*, Odell Shepard, ed. (Boston: Little, Brown 1938), 125.
6. Ibid., 121.
7. Ibid., 379.
8. Novalis (1772-1801), quoted in Robert Lee Wolff, *The Golden Key* (New Haven: Yale University Press, 1961), 38.
9. Henry Septimus Sutton (1825-1901).
10. Goethe, as quoted in Emerson, "Beauty," in *The Complete Writings*, 608.
11. Emerson, "Poetry and Imagination," in *The Complete Writings*, 732, 731.
12. Friedrich Schiller, *Essays Aesthetical and Philosophical* (London: George Bell, 1884).
13. Rudolf Steiner, "The Idea of Freedom," *The Philosophy of Freedom* (London: Rudolf Steiner Press, 1970), 135-8.
14. Emerson, "Immortality," in *The Complete Writings*, 829.
15. Emerson, "The Method of Nature," in *The Complete Writings*, 69.
16. Goethe as quoted in Emerson, "Immortality," *The Complete Writings*, 831.
17. "Song of the Spirits over the Waters," quoted in *Reincarnation*, Head and Cranston, eds. (New York: Julian Press, 1961), 178.

18. Herman Melville, *Mardi: And a Voyage Thither* (New York: *The New American Library of World Literature*, 1964), 251.

19. Melville as quoted in Eleanor Melville Metcalf, *Herman Melville: Cycle and Epicycle* (Cambridge: Harvard University Press, 1953), 110.

20. Melville, *Mardi*, 305.

21. Ibid., 199.

22. Herman Melville, *Moby Dick* (New York: Random House, 1950), 426.

23. Thoreau, quoted in *Reincarnation*, op. cit., 242.

24. Ibid.

25. Alcott, *Journals*, 222.

26. Frederic Hedge as quoted in *Reincarnation*, 239.

27. James Freeman Clarke, as quoted in *Reincarnation*, 240.

3

MELVILLE'S VISION OF AMERICA

*As every one knows, meditation and water
are wedded for ever.*
—Melville, *Moby Dick*

MOBY DICK is said to be the most intensively studied book in American literature. Though it sold few copies and was scornfully treated by many of the critics who bothered to take notice of it when it first appeared in 1851, it began to come into its own in the 1920s. Since then, it has received numerous scholarly interpretations, been assigned to countless English classes in high school and college, and become generally recognized as a major work that has something of great importance to say about the condition of the modern soul. Many readers, indeed, have had the feeling that the tragedy of the *Pequod* under Captain Ahab is in some way prophetic for American society and the American ship of state.

My own acquaintance with *Moby Dick* came at the age of about nineteen. I was captivated equally by its strength and by its beauty. It was for me full of portents and presentiments expressed in language of extraordinary power. I did not get far in trying to lift the mystical truths I sensed on every page out of the language in which they were embedded, so I left them in it, simply reading and rereading many passages as they stood, until I had virtually memorized them. I delighted in the alliterative music of Melville's words and in the surging flow of his sentences. His was indeed "a bold and nervous lofty language." And its strange hints about the wonders and vicissitudes of human life were of fascinating interest to an inarticulate youth who was trying to fathom riddles in himself and cope with forebodings of the world about him. High daring, deep melancholy, ambition, anger, and wild defiance speak to the soul of youth—especially when they are "judgmatically" salted and peppered throughout with a robust, skeptical workingman's humor.

Youth longs to find life fair and good, yet inevitably it will encounter sordid impulses in itself and in others. Youth would like to believe that all is possible, but it cannot avoid observing how helplessly adults face their more serious problems. Youth has the wish to penetrate life's mysteries, but it finds itself being taught by learned people who are, as regards just these mysteries, know-nothings and believe-nothings. Above and beneath all, there are in most young persons a self-esteem and self-concern that are bruised by the indifference of the rest of humanity, all of whom have, of course, their own concerns. These conflicts between subjective idealism and objective reality are the very signature of young life trying, and failing, to find itself at home in the world. They can explain why *Moby Dick* tallies with the experience of many an adolescent, and who would want to say that in this meaning of the word he has entirely outgrown adolescence?

Throughout his writing career, Melville was preoccupied with the fact that the ideals the ardent self brings forth out of itself are apparently not to be reconciled with the harsh realities encountered in the external world. This discrepancy forms the substance of most of his books before and after *Moby Dick*, but in this particular tragedy it comes to expression in a way that far transcends mere youthful or private distress.

WATER AND LIVING THOUGHT

Possibly the most important fact to remember about the story of *Moby Dick* is that it takes place on the water. The first chapter, "Loomings," opens with an attempt to remind us of the obscure but deeply rooted feelings that bodies of water awaken at times in the human heart and mind. Somehow water contains mysteries we landbound human beings feel ourselves drawn to. In it, we sense possibilities of enlargement, even enlightenment. Water opens perspectives of an inward kind. It helps one to a broader, deeper capacity of realization. "As every one knows," says Melville, "meditation and water are wedded for ever."[1]

Meditative and imaginative forms of knowing bear the same relation to water that everyday logic bears to solid ground. Water is the symbol of the living, creative power of thought that sometimes fills us like a tide, lifting us out of everyday preoccupations, and opens our vision to more spiritual forces, presences, and events. To make an extended journey on the face of the greatest of all waters is therefore to venture at great risk into the unknown wonders of the soul, of nature, and of destiny.

Historically, the self-conscious, reasoning mind has arisen, as an island may rise from the sea, out of mere dreaming instinct and impulse. In this sense, the primitive water-consciousness is a thing we have done well to leave behind and below us. On the other hand, there is reason to believe that a higher kind of water-consciousness will be required in the future. The mentality with which our present world is unsuccessfully attempting to manage its affairs has grown stiff and hard. It is drying out. Only the moisture of new life will restore to it the powers of insight and creativeness it needs. One has the impression, from this perspective, that Melville's state of mind while writing *Moby Dick* was partly of the past, partly of the future. It was in part a subnormal dreaming consciousness, yet also a supernormal kind of prophesying.

Melville speaks of the whale as "this Leviathan" who "comes floundering down upon us from the headwaters of the Eternities." (*Moby Dick*, 455) Of what kind were those waters? In Genesis, when we read of darkness upon the waters, our habits of thinking probably bring to mind an image of darkest night surrounding the earth and its oceans. But there was no planet earth then, and there were no oceans, neither substance nor form of any kind. Nor, for that matter, was there a sun to be hidden, causing darkness. Earth and ocean, sun and stars, according to the first book of Moses, were all fashioned later. In the primal beginning, there were only the mysterious "waters"—and the "firmament" called heaven that "divided the waters from the waters." And the waters under heaven were gathered to become our planet earth and its oceans. But what of the other waters, those that remained "above" the firmament of heaven? Moses must have visualized these as being of a spiritual nature, some kind of purely ideal yet living source out of which all the heavenly bodies could be formed and by which they could continue to be nourished.

Primordial, living, ensouled *world-thought* must be pictured when we think of the waters through which swims the power of the White Whale Melville has in view. And as there are waters and waters, so there must be whales and whales. "Who can show a pedigree like Leviathan? . . . I am horror-struck at this antemosaic, unsourced existence of the unspeakable terrors of the whale, which, having been before all time, must needs exist after all humane ages are over" (*Moby Dick*, 454).

But more of Leviathan later.

The rhythms and imagery of Melville's writing, as well as his concepts, ask of readers that they loosen the hold of solid matter upon their mind and entrust themselves to a more buoyant, more far-ranging and deeper-diving consciousness. A simple consideration will suggest what is required if we are to feel at home in Melville's water-world.

We know that the modern individual, lifted out high and dry, as it were, from the flowing life of nature, is a self-conscious, self-directing, indeed, self-centered person. Each of us tends to be a law unto himself or herself. In this sense, each person may be compared to a stone whose force of coherence holds it together as a thing in itself, apart from other things. We know that our attention moves outward into the world from the centerpoint in ourselves we call the self or ego. Our consciousness is sharp and clear; its goal, as we say, is to be crystalline. Clear consciousness is seated in the head, and even as the head is the compact, still part of the body, so the consciousness with which we conduct usual affairs is not content until it has brought the ceaseless flux of events to a similar standstill and has defined every separate object and pinned it by its law. We moderns impose our static conceptions upon the flow of life.

But abstract concepts are not the only way we show our preference for fixity. We are also accustomed to seek confirmation of reality through that most material of the senses, the sense of touch. Our "understanding" always wants to plant its feet on the bedrock of physically tangible evidence. Because I sense, for example, that my writing paper rests on the blotter, the blotter on the desk, the desk on the floor, the floor on the foundations of my house, the foundations on subsoil, and the subsoil at last on granite, I feel that I understand the facts of my situation, and that all are well based.

But when we begin to inquire in this way about any kind of physical reality, there always remains a further step to be taken. Once we have grounded a preliminary fact in more basic facts, have dug down to the earthly root-fact on which all others appear to rest—in the case of the paper on my desk, down to the undoubted granite—must we not ask further: "On what does this alleged root-fact, the solid earth-mass itself, rest?" And now we come face to face with a non-fact, for all the inconceivably ponderous earth is not resting on anything at all. This enormous rock appears to be floating like a feather in the world ether.

Suddenly, we are disoriented. The ever-solider basis from which we had been accustomed to draw our sense of assurance has evaporated. To discover what continues to hold things in place, we can no longer think in the manner of stones that always settle towards the ultimate bottom. Cosmically, there is no such bottom. There is only empty "context." Not substance but relationships are what count now. These relationships no longer point inward toward the earth-center, but outward to all parts of the world-periphery. The unspeakably heavy earth-ball floats serenely in a sea of mere relationships. "O, vast Rondure, swimming in space!" exclaimed Whitman. "How like a whale!" might have been Melville's rejoinder.

When we leave earthbound experience and venture imaginatively into cosmic space, we must accustom ourselves to a new way of looking at things. This new way derives its assurance from the feeling of flowing buoyancy, even as the old way rested upon the feeling of solidity and weight. With this buoyant new consciousness we can appreciate what it means for the earth to swim in the world ether—and we can begin to reconsider events on the earth that we had hitherto studied only in the old way.

Regardless of what the launchers of physical space flight will say to our treatment of how the earth swims in the cosmos, this way of speaking may serve to conjure up a certain feeling that is, in fact, related to the psychological experience of water as Melville intends for us to sense it. Thoreau had this feeling when he said that in floating on Walden Pond he became a citizen of the cosmos. He could believe himself set free from gravity and placed in orbit as a small world in space—the neighboring worlds being felt no longer as remote and easy to forget but as intimately near, living, and related.

By becoming individuals, by learning to walk each his or her own way, we modern human beings have torn ourselves partly out of the universal continuum and have thereby lost our buoyancy. "Men of little faith," said Thoreau, "stand only by their feet." Yet he knew that it is possible to be modern, retain individuality, and yet learn to regain buoyant rapport with the All. His experience at Walden Pond is a good preparation for Melville's great adventure. "When most at one with nature," Thoreau said, "I feel supported and propped on all sides."[2]

Nature grows, evolves, transforms itself, and begets new life within the all-sustaining buoyancy of the universal context. This it can do only because it is liquid; fluency is life; fixity, death. And though the death process (witness the rigid skull, which crystallizes whatever it captures for cognition) may bring a human being to ordinary self-consciousness, it obviously cannot grasp the essence of life. For life is to be apprehended only by a consciousness that has reestablished its buoyant cosmic rapport. As Emerson put it:

> It is a secret which every intellectual man ... learns, that beyond the energy of his possessed and conscious intellect he is capable of a new energy (as of an intellect doubled on itself), by abandonment to the nature of things; that beside his privacy of power as an individual man, there is a great public power on which he can draw, by unlocking, at all risks, his human doors, and suffering the ethereal tides to roll and circulate through him....[3]

The ethereal tides are those of living thought. Through this kind of thought, said Emerson, we are caught up into the creative spiritual life of the cosmos. We come, said Melville, to "the headwaters of the Eternities."

LOOKING INTO LIFE'S MIRROR

If we may assume, then, that this whaling story means to launch us on the seas of inward experience, what is the goal of the voyage we are to embark on? On the third page, Melville offers the clue. In venturing upon the great ocean, he says, when the last bit of land has dropped wholly out of sight, a person is likely to feel overtaken by a "mystical vibration." Somehow one stands before, or in the very midst of, the mystery of existence, existence in general but also one's own in particular. Melville is reminded of the Greek myth of the fair youth Narcissus.

> Who because he could not grasp the tormenting, mild image he saw in the fountain, plunged into it and was drowned. But that same image, we ourselves see in all rivers and oceans. It is the image of the un-graspable phantom of life; and this is the key to it all. (*Moby Dick*, 3)

This is the key! In what sense is the story of self-enamored Narcissus also the story of Ahab and his fatal fascination with Moby Dick?

To answer this question, we must understand one peculiarity of imaginative experience. The imagination is fluid and makes fluid. It turns all things to self-transforming water. But water is a mirror, and like a mirror it reverses whatever it reflects. In genuine imagination as in many dreams, this strange reversal takes place. We discern that what seems to us as dreamers to be approaching from outside is actually welling up within ourselves. And even as the imagination holds up a mirror to life, there is a sense in which life itself is a great imagination, and thus a mirror for the fate of every human soul that passes through it. If we walk toward life with habitual gratitude, do we not encounter an uncommon number of people and events to be grateful for? Does not the suspicious or stingy individual pass through an uncommon number of events that seem to want to rob or gyp him? Does not the stubborn bruiser strike his head against one solid wall after another that rises before him as before no one else?

We must suppose that what Narcissus saw in the mirror pool of his imagination was the mystery of his own being, and that this revelation overwhelmed him through the self-love it awakened. He could not hold himself back from the fatal wish to plunge into the wellsprings of his own nature. We may well believe that the resulting self-immersion left him as one dead to the rest of the world. Certainly Melville was like Narcissus in being profoundly concerned with himself. He was irresistibly drawn to dive to ever deeper levels in his own soul. As Hawthorne testified in dismay on the basis of his personal friendship with Melville, the latter was what we may call a metaphysical plunger.

Melville's early years of seafaring gave him ample chance to indulge his overmastering propensity to brood. Through words he puts into the mouth of Ishmael, the narrator of *Moby Dick*, we get an idea of what no doubt had often transpired when he took his turn in standing watch aloft at the masthead. Though his assigned task was to look outward for physical whales in the physical ocean, he appears more often to have used these occasions to look inward for imaginations swimming through the bottomless waters of pure thought. "With the problem of the universe revolving in me," Ishmael says, "how could I—being left completely to myself at such a thought-engendering altitude—how could I but lightly hold my obligations" (*Moby Dick*, 156).

Conjuring nautical music as ever, Melville conveys this experience of the young man, both romantic and melancholy, who is sent aloft to look sharp:

> ... lulled into such an opium-like listlessness of vacant, unconscious reverie is this absent-minded youth by the blending cadence of waves with thoughts, that at last he loses his identity; takes the mystic ocean at his feet for the

visible image of that deep, blue, bottomless soul, pervading mankind and nature; and every strange, half-seen, gliding, beautiful thing that eludes him; every dimly-discovered, uprising fin of some undiscernible form, seems to him the embodiment of those elusive thoughts that only people the soul by continually flitting through it. (*Moby Dick*, 157)

There is no life in the mainmast sentinel now, "except that rocking life imparted by a gently rolling ship; by her, borrowed from the sea; by the sea, from the inscrutable tides of God." In this mood, Melville says, the conscious spirit "ebbs away to whence it came; becomes diffused through time and space; like Cranmer's sprinkled Pantheistic ashes, forming at last a part of every shore the round globe over."

We should not pass by this description too quickly, because it shows us something about Melville's constitution that accounted for the quality of his life-experience, which in turn provided the substance for his writing. The ability to dwell, as Melville-Ishmael did, in living thought, is not a brain-based but a body-free experience; it is a purely self-sustaining spiritual activity. Emerson speaks of the need an abstract thinker has for "periods of isolation and rapt concentration"—"almost a going out of the body in order to think!" ("Wealth," 711) At such moments "the intellect goes out of the individual, floats over its own personality, and regards it as a fact, and not as *I* or *mine*." ("Intellect," 192-3) This higher level of thinking "rends the thin rinds of the visible and finite, and comes out into eternity, and inspires and expires its air." ("The Oversoul," 266)

Whitman testified to the same experience: "I loosen myself," he said, and "pass freely."[4] "I fly the flight of the fluid and swallowing soul... I help myself to material and immaterial...." ("Song of Myself," 105) "My ties and ballasts leave me—I travel—I sail—my elbows rest in the sea-gaps; I skirt the sierras—my palms cover continents...." ("Song of Myself," 100)

As we have noted, Melville was much inclined toward this *expansion* of consciousness, and the monotonous life at sea further developed the tendency. Later in *Moby Dick* he continues his characterization of how the susceptible consciousness of young Ishmael, as he stood watch on high, was conjured out of itself by the unlimited sea at his feet.

> No resolution could withstand it; in that dreamy mood losing all consciousness, at last my soul went out of my body; though my body still continued to sway as a pendulum will, long after the power which first moved it is withdrawn. (*Moby Dick*, 283)

But Ishmael had the security of his perch on the mast to hold him. He was aloft in the air yet still aboard ship; otherwise his experience might have been the one Melville ascribed to poor, lost Pip, the castaway black cabin boy who during a chase jumped from his whale boat and was soon left a mile behind, completely alone on the shoreless ocean. Pip's soul was swallowed up by the boundless waters.

Melville had a basis in himself for knowing what Pip's experience was like: "The intense concentration of self in the middle of such a heartless immensity, my God! Who can tell it?" The castaway, alone on the surface of the deep, found that his "ringed horizon began to expand around him miserably." (*Moby Dick*, 412-3) His self was sucked out of itself. Though his finite body survived, "the infinite of his soul" was drowned; it could not recover itself from its overexpansion. It could not resume its self-possession or regain a proper footing on earth after having been transported into the cosmic world of living thought. The passage is worth quoting because it is so typically Melvillean both in its power of language and in its incalculable overtones. Pip's soul, says Melville, was

> carried down alive to wondrous depths, where strange shapes of the unwarped primal world glided to and fro

before his passive eyes; and the miser-merman, Wisdom, revealed his hoarded heaps; and among the joyous, heartless, ever-juvenile eternities, Pip saw the multitudinous, God-omnipresent, coral insects, that out of the firmament of waters heaved the colossal orbs. He saw God's foot upon the treadle of the loom, and spoke it; and therefore his shipmates called him mad. So man's insanity is heaven's sense; and wandering from all mortal reason, man comes at last to that celestial thought, which to reason, is absurd and frantic; and weal or woe, feels then uncompromised, indifferent as his God. (*Moby Dick*, 413)

THE WHALE EXPERIENCE

We now have a basis, not a solid but a watery one, for suggesting some of the meanings of *Moby Dick* as a projection of tendencies in the soul of its author—and perhaps also as a prophecy concerning tendencies in his native land. Having seen how Melville could portray a Pip's relationship to the world, we turn our attention to Ahab—Ahab who said that Pip bore the same relationship to him "as the circumference to its center" (*Moby Dick*, 524).

If Pip represents the extreme of the centrifugal tendency that Melville felt in his own soul, Ahab represents the extreme development of its opposite, the centripetal pull. Because both were extreme, both came to madness: "One daft with strength, the other daft with weakness," as the old Manxman said (*Moby Dick*, 514). Their madnesses were similar and symmetrical, in that they had to do with a disordered relation of the ego to its experience of spiritual reality. Yet they were polar opposites in that in Pip's case the self was too emptied of itself, and in Ahab's case it was too filled with itself.

All of Melville's writing is based upon polarities of this kind. Just as, in the characters of Pip and Ahab, Melville described the modern ego in opposite ways, so the particular experience confronted by the ego, namely Moby Dick, the great white whale, cannot be fathomed by a single interpretation; it too must be studied in dual form. Moby Dick was a qualitative experience of the soul of Ahab, seen in the mirror of imaginative reality. But I should like to suggest that Ahab's soul, at different stages of its development, as he changed in his own nature from youth to age and from one kind of ego experience to its opposite, saw two radically different whales.

The legendary White Whale is the projection of two contrasting kinds of experience in the soul of the mad captain. What precisely were those experiences? Can they be translated from the language of water to the language of land—that is, from images to concepts?

Narcissus looked into the pool, saw himself, and was fatally attracted. Ahab looked into his much larger pool and was equally obsessed by what he saw. He saw the essential in himself as a great white whale; but, since, as we shall try to make clear, the essential in him was *the conflict between polaric tendencies*, the whale he pursued, the whale that came against him, thus also partook alternately of two natures, the one developing alongside or out of the other. This unsuspected duality has introduced confusion into all simplistic attempts to interpret what is going on between Ahab and Moby Dick. We may begin to appreciate what is involved here if we visualize a certain sequence of experiences known to many a young man of modern times. Let us observe an "Ishmael" before he turns into an "Ahab."

Our hypothetical young man starts life as an idealist. He is ardent, ambitious, proud. He feels in himself giant possibilities. If he has the stature of a Melville-Ishmael, the young man may, indeed, be quite overwhelmed with intimations of beauty and grandeur, of moral elevation and spiritual power. Yet this young romantic is not rightly at home either in himself or in the world, for he is given also to doubt and despair. We see him brooding morbidly, self-absorbed, ready to be hurt. In this first phase he is innocent, impulsive, moved by passionately good intentions; yet he is by turns dejected, melancholy, and overtaken by he knows not what shadow. Sometimes his eyes search the stars; at other times, they are downcast upon the earth.

Now let us imagine the efforts of this highly endowed but somewhat morbid young man to make a place for himself in the conventional world. He may, of course, ignore the outside challenge and launch ever further into his private dreams of the ideal. On this tack, he will find himself increasingly alone with his own overheated fantasy, which may lead him to unbreathable heights or to unsoundable depths. He will become a Pip, too disoriented to judge and too weak to do anything about the mysteries—or are they illusions?—in which his spirit dwells. If, however, the young man takes his way at least partly into the "real" world, he will be shocked by what he encounters there: pettiness of spirit, violence, and vileness. He will feel opposed by persons and circumstances, appalled to find that what he thinks best in himself often seems to provoke the greatest antagonism in others. Eventually, he may come to feel that the world of people, the customs of society, the prevailing culture, above all the economic order, are worse than merely ignorant and unlovely: they may seem willfully deceitful and cruel. He cannot get on in such a world. He does not understand it but feels called upon to oppose it in outrage and as a matter of principle.

The young man so violently compressed may explode. If he is the kind of Ishmael that has the makings of an Ahab in him, his early pride will turn to burning resentment; his early ambition will become the desire for revenge; his once benevolent intelligence may be transformed into manic plotting.

If we walk another step with this young man who cannot help getting older even though he despises his elders, who must fight for a foothold in the very world he holds in contempt, and who cannot win except by the rules of a game that outrages him, we shall observe a remarkable change taking place in him. His initial egoism will persist, it will be deepened, but it will take on a different character: one that bears a close resemblance—whether he realizes it or not—to the very traits in the established world that caused him such distress in the first place. It is now his own heart that has hardened. It is he himself who has become skeptical, shrewd, and aggressive in the vengeful belief that the world deserves nothing so much as a double dose of its own bitter medicine. He undertakes this cure with a vengeance. He does not notice that he has been absorbed by the evil he thinks he is opposing. Ishmael has turned into Ahab.

Phase one tallies a good deal of what we know or can guess about the early character of Ahab before he lost his leg and became so grim; and we may take the young Ahab to represent a basic and original aspect of Melville's own nature. In this aspect we see him starting out with a purely spiritual idealism and ambition. He is, as it were, born of light and he aspires to the light. This part of his nature continues as he grows older, but through the encounter with life's adversities it also changes. His light darkens into fire. He feels himself capable of storming heaven, a Prometheus who would steal fire from the gods. The original light and the eventual fire mingle confusingly.

It was the older Ahab who exclaimed, "Oh, thou clear spirit of clear fire, of thy fire thou madest me, and like a true child of fire, I breathe it back to thee" (*Moby Dick*, 499); and in another context he soliloquizes, "Clear truth is a thing for salamander giants only" (*Moby Dick*, 337). Salamanders are fire beings, and Ahab considers himself such a one. He sees himself as Lucifer, the angel who started out as the high bearer of light, but fell and became the fiery dark spirit of pride.

> There's something ever egotistical in mountain-tops and towers, and all other grand and lofty things; look here—three peaks as proud as Lucifer. The firm tower, that is Ahab; the volcano, that is Ahab; the courageous, the undaunted, and victorious fowl, that, too, is Ahab; all are Ahab.... (*Moby Dick*, 428)

There is a proud eagle in some souls, he says,

> that can alike dive down into the blackest gorges, and soar out of them again and become invisible in the sunny spaces. And even if he forever flies within the gorge, that gorge is in the mountains; so that even in his lowest swoop the mountain eagle is still higher than other birds upon the plain, even though they soar. (*Moby Dick*, 423)

In the boundless ocean of spiritual pride and ambition, an ego such as Ahab's would naturally pursue only the greatest of fish, the whale, and the greatest of whales, the legendary, ubiquitous, immortal White Whale, for he is on the hunt for ultimate truth, the truth that is also highest power. "Unless you own the whale," Melville says, "you are but a provincial and sentimentalist in Truth" (*Moby Dick,* 337). "Speak," mutters Ahab to the severed Sphinx head hoisted alongside his ship. "Speak, thou vast and venerable head...speak, mighty head, and tell us the secret thing that is in thee. Of all divers thou hast dived the deepest" (*Moby Dick*, 310).

We find the Luciferic phase of Ahab's soul pictured in this description of the White Whale's glory:

> A gentle joyousness—a mighty mildness of repose in swiftness, invested the gliding whale. Not the white bull Jupiter swimming away with ravished Europa clinging to his graceful horns; with smooth bewitching fleetness, rippling straight for the nuptial bower in Crete; not Jove, not that great majesty Supreme! did surpass the glorified White Whale as he so divinely swam. (*Moby Dick*, 538)

Such a whale mirrors the part of Ahab's aspiring idealism that sought to approach the primordial powers of beauty and truth that made the world—yet that in doing so was also indulging in ambitious pride and self-conceit.

But we know that what we imagine as the Lucifer-phase of Ahab's young development was already past when the quest for Moby Dick, as told in this story, begins. The whale that now swam before the battered captain, in the seas that mirrored the radically changed condition of his soul, was a fundamentally different creature from the one described above. This new creature's essence had more to do with icy coldness than with seductive light and warmth, with calculating power than with spiritual illumination. He was, indeed, the very epitome of "intelligent malignity."

> The White Whale swam before him as the monomaniac incarnation of all those malicious agencies which some deep men feel eating in them, till they are left living on with half a heart and half a lung.... All that most maddens and torments; all that stirs up the lees of things; all truth with malice in it; all that cracks the sinews and cakes the brain; all the subtle demonisms of life and thought; all evil, to crazy Ahab, were visibly personified, and made practically assailable in Moby Dick. He piled upon the whale's white hump the sum of all the general rage and hate felt by his whole race from Adam down; and then, as if his chest had been a mortar, he burst his hot heart's shell upon it. (*Moby Dick*, 183)

A "Khan of the plank, and a king of the sea and a great lord of Leviathans" such as Ahab cannot cease to play the Titan. But his battle with life has taken something away from him and introduced something new into him. His crippled willfulness now takes a vindictive, hateful turn and its reflection is to be seen in the maimed aspect of Moby Dick:

the "vast, involved wrinkles" of his forehead, the "terrors of his submerged trunk," and "the wrenched hideousness of his jaw" (*Moby Dick*, 539). These betray an "inscrutable malice," an "infernal aforethought of ferocity" (*Moby Dick*, 162 and 182).

We must try to be more precise about this ambivalence, this shifting duality that makes Ahab and his mirror-image, Moby Dick, so hard to interpret. This same dualism, as we have said, pervades all of Melville's writing. *Moby Dick* was written between two other books: the earlier *Mardi* and the later *Pierre, or the Ambiguities*. In *Mardi*, a romantic quest by representatives of the philosophic, poetic, historical, and heroic aspects of the human soul—of Melville's own soul—is underway. Its goal: to find again and bring back the maiden of light, Yillah, who seems to have vanished. But the fellowship that goes wandering in search of Yillah is itself being pursued by the queen of darkness, Hautia. And in *Pierre*, the hero has promised his hand to Lucy, also a maiden of light; but the marriage does not take place, for Isabel, a raven-haired girl of tragic fate, intervenes. In both books, the conflict between light and darkness is the central theme.

In *Moby Dick*, the agents and their motives are equally ambiguous. Two basic tendencies in human nature, and perhaps in cosmic nature as well, are at war with each other for mastery over the captain's soul. Melville characterizes both in the chapter "The Whiteness of the Whale."

THE WHITENESS OF THE WHALE

"But how can I hope to explain myself here," says Ishmael: "and yet, in some dim, random way, explain myself I must, else all these chapters might be naught" (*Moby Dick*, 187). The matter that needs explaining is how in the whiteness of the whale there could be felt, simultaneously or alternately, a spiritual beauty and a "nameless horror."

What is hard to understand is how the color white can arouse in the beholder two absolutely different sets of feelings. These feelings correspond to the two tendencies in human nature, or the two influences exerted upon humanity from beyond its own nature, that we are attempting to characterize.

In the first instance, white is the color of divinity.

> In the higher mysteries of the most august religions it has been made the symbol of the divine spotlessness and power; by the Persian fire worshippers, the white forked flame being held the holiest on the altar; and in the Greek mythologies, Great Jove himself being made incarnate in a snow white bull.... (*Moby Dick*, 187-8)

Yet for all its association with "celestial innocence and love," there "lurks an elusive something in the innermost idea of this hue, which strikes more of panic to the soul than that redness which affrights in blood." Here, says Melville, we are dealing with a matter "so mystical and well nigh ineffable" as almost to defy rational understanding: "subtlety appeals to subtlety, and without imagination no man can follow another into these halls" (*Moby Dick*, 191).

We must be imaginative and subtle, but we must also be exact at this point, lest Melville himself lead us away from understanding. The question is not which of the two aspects of whiteness, the glorious or the grisly, is the real one. The goal is not to convince ourselves that the innocent kind of whiteness is youthful illusion, behind which, if we have enough grown-up courage to push on, we shall discover the frightful nature of what white "really" is—even though this is the course taken by Ishmael's reflections. We are dealing not with illusion and truth but rather with two illusions, which is to say with two mutually opposed aspects of human experience, neither of which represents complete and balanced truth.

White stands for light, and the first aspect of light that is under consideration here can be associated, as we have suggested, with Lucifer. It gives him his name. This whiteness speaks for the super-earthly; it draws us back toward earlier stages of spiritual development before humanity had taken on the weight of matter. It awakens the longing to escape from the earth: the desire to retreat into the white dress of untempted purity, or at least to don the priestly vestments of untouchable dignity and sacred esteem.

If this first kind of light or whiteness may be linked with any and all of the religions of ancient time, we must associate the second kind with the sterility of our modern laboratories and operating rooms, the abstractness of our postmortem science. Melville, speaking through Ishmael, in his attempt to explain the coldness and emptiness of a certain kind of white light, builds toward just this conclusion.

> It cannot well be doubted, that the one visible quality in the aspect of the dead which most appalls the gazer, is the marble pallor lingering there; as if indeed that pallor were as much like the badge of consternation in the other world, as of mortal trepidation here. (*Moby Dick*, 190-1)

The pallor of death, whether it appears on the face of a corpse or in the "eternal, frosted desolateness" of solitary peaks in mountain fastnesses or in the boundless, blizzard-swept graveyard of Antarctic ice-fields, is chilling. It is frightening. "Not yet," says Ishmael, "have we solved the incantation of this whiteness."

> Is it that by its indefiniteness it shadows forth the heartless voids and immensities of the universe, and thus stabs us from behind with the thought of annihilation...? Though in many of its aspects this visible world seems formed in love, the invisible spheres were formed in fright. (*Moby Dick*, 194)

That is, they were formed in chill abstraction, apart from wisdom or love or even purpose. The beauty and warmth that naive people think they are encountering in nature and in destiny are but appearances. They may seem to be present everywhere, but this proves only that illusions enwrap us on all sides. The reality that lies behind them is not beautiful, because it is not warm, not colored, not odorous, not sounding. At least, we shall be convinced that this is the case if we accept what many scientists have had to tell us about the nature of all our sensory perceptions.

Newton did as much as anyone to tear away the veil human beings had always seen as "the starry heavens," and to expose the universe as purely a mechanism. And by the time *Moby Dick* was published, Darwin had begun the explanation of how plants, animals, and human beings develop in such a universe: by a fight to the death of all against all, with advantage falling to this one or that according to the heartless, unthinking chances of purely random mutations.

Before both Newton and Darwin, it was Galileo who laid the epistemological foundation for their mechanistic approaches. He established a fundamental distinction between what he called the primary, or real, and the secondary, or only apparent, attributes of things. Secondary are heat, light, color, sound, taste, odor. All these are subjective: that is, they exist only in the supposition of the beholder who prefers to make believe that they are there. Primary and real attributes are such featureless, unimaginable, alien abstractions as mass-energy, and velocity. Though such concepts are everywhere accepted by the philosophers of science, and though they account for the faithless outlook of the modern world, the average layperson of today still ignores them. Out of a healthy instinct to protect ourselves—through ignorance if necessary—against things frightful, we keep such ideas away from our feeling-life. But for a poet, a bold soul and partly a morbid one, such as Melville, they strike home in the heart.

If Newton's idea of color be true, thought Melville, and Galileo's distinction between the *reality* of unseen, mechanical abstractions and the *unreality* of our most clearly received, most comforting, and inspiring human perceptions, then "the palsied universe lies before us a leper." The soul who has courage to look facts in the face, take off "colored and coloring glasses," and see the workings of the world as they really are, is likely to become snowblind and stonecold. The concluding paragraph of the chapter on the whiteness of the whale is worth quoting almost in its entirety:

> Or is it, that as in essence whiteness is not so much a color as the visible absence of color, and at the same time the concrete of all colors; is it for these reasons that there is such a dumb blankness, full of meaning, in a wide landscape of snows—a colorless, all-color of atheism from which we shrink? And when we consider that other theory of the natural philosophers, that all other earthly hues—every stately or lovely emblazoning— ... all these are but subtle deceits, not actually inherent in substances, but only laid on from without; so that all deified Nature absolutely paints like the harlot, whose allurements cover nothing but the charnel house within; and when we proceed further, and consider that the mystical cosmetic which produces every one of her hues, the great principle of light, for ever remains white or colorless in itself, and if operating without medium upon matter, would touch all objects, even tulips and roses, with its own blank tinge—pondering all this, the palsied universe lies before us a leper; and like willful travellers in Lapland, who refuse to wear colored and coloring glasses upon their eyes, so the wretched infidel gazes himself blind at the monumental white shroud that wraps all the prospect around him. And of all these things the Albino Whale was the symbol. Wonder ye then at the fiery hunt? (*Moby Dick*, 194-5)

When Coleridge had studied Newton's *Optics* thoroughly, he exclaimed, "Everything fits so perfectly; the reasoning is faultless! It *must* be wrong." Goethe, however, saw in Newton's *Optics* simply an example of one way of interpreting the phenomena of nature. He considered that way in certain respects useful but nevertheless fatally reductionist and therefore fundamentally unreal. He believed that if scientific inquiry were to continue to explain qualitative phenomena in this style, it would lay waste the entire world, not only for inner human experience but also ultimately in its practical consequences. "May God us keep from single vision and Newton's sleep!" wrote Blake in a letter to Thomas Butts.

Out of their instinct for reality, Coleridge, Goethe, and Blake rejected the mechanistic world view that held a morbid fascination for Melville. They saw it as illusion, because it was the product of a one-sided application of human intelligence. Melville personified this maimed, unnatural, and inhuman outlook in the older Ahab. The dire captain comes before us perhaps not as one-eyed in his vision, but certainly as one-legged in his understanding.

In what we have called his second phase even though the story opens with him already in this condition, Ahab represents the highest intellectual development pushed on by audacious, relentless will.

> "What is it, what nameless, inscrutable, unearthly thing is it; what cozening, hidden lord and master, and cruel, remorseless emperor commands me; that against all natural lovings and longings, I so keep pushing, and crowding, and jamming myself on all the time; recklessly making me ready to do what in my own proper, natural heart, I durst not so much as dare? Is Ahab, Ahab?" (*Moby Dick*, 534-5)

Ahab attacks life and nature in this manner, and in the mirror that life holds up to him he sees a certain kind of monster on the counterattack. This monster is the image of his own attitude. But his own attitude is borrowed in turn from concepts of the nature of the universe we live in that scientific materialists of the nineteenth century had put forth: brute power and mechanism that have somehow managed to spawn men and women of tenderest feelings and noblest aspirations and that beguile humankind with illusions of beauty, truth, and goodness only to wipe them out with complete indifference—if such a thing be imaginable; or, if not, with "inscrutable malice." Is it any wonder that the smoldering pride in Ahab should be enraged?

> "All visible objects, man, are but as pasteboard masks. But in each event—in the living act, the undoubted deed—there, some unknown but still reasoning thing puts forth the moldings of its features from behind the unreasoning mask. If man will strike, strike through the mask! How can the prisoner reach outside except by thrusting through the wall? To me the white whale is that wall, shoved near to me.... I see in him outrageous strength, with an inscrutable malice sinewing it. That inscrutable thing is chiefly what I hate; and be the white whale agent, or be the white whale principal, I will wreak that hate upon him. (*Moby Dick*, 162)

Ahab in his deep longings, his spiritual ambition, his will to glory, is antique: a Prometheus, a Lucifer. But in his thwarted longing and wounded pride he succumbs to a modern inspiration. He himself enters upon the ruthless will to power that is served by the cold-blooded intellect. He is assimilated by a principle that stands in complete contrast to Lucifer. As Lucifer is comparatively a spirit of warmth and light, though also a one-sided tempter, this other being is a spirit of chill and frosty darkness. Ahab does not, of course, recognize this spirit as coming out of his own character, but he sees it attacking him from outside through Moby Dick. This is the spirit of "all truth with malice in it; all that cracks the sinews and cakes the brain":

> That intangible malignity which has been from the beginning; to whose dominion even the modern Christians ascribe one-half of the worlds; which the ancient Ophites of the east reverenced in their statue devil;—Ahab did not fall down and worship it like them; but deliriously transferring its idea to the abhorred White Whale, he pitted himself, all mutilated, against it. (*Moby Dick*, 183)

"I AS PERSIAN"

To gain a clearer idea of who it is that pulls mankind in the opposite direction from Lucifer, we must take account of a too-little-noticed feature of *Moby Dick*, namely, of the fact that it is through and through a story in the mood of ancient Persia. In *Mardi*, Melville had said: "My memory is a life beyond birth," and "Zoroaster whispered me before I was born."[5] In *Moby Dick*, we start out with the observer-narrator Ishmael, a Persian name. Captain Ahab's personal whaleboat crew and harpooneer are all Parsee, that is, Persian fire-worshippers. This crew lurks below decks in the afterhold—which for our purpose means deep in the subconscious—where Ahab is seen mysteriously visiting them in the dark of night. The Parsee leader, Fedallah, is from beginning to end the inspiring, controlling spirit behind Ahab, his prophetic voice of doom. "Though it come to the last," Fedallah says, "I shall still go before thee thy pilot" (*Moby Dick*, 491).

> At times, for longest hours, without a single hail, they stood far parted in the starlight; Ahab in his scuttle, the Parsee by the mainmast; but still fixedly gazing upon each other; as if in the Parsee Ahab saw his forethrown shadow, in Ahab the Parsee his abandoned substance. (*Moby Dick*, 527)

Melville goes to considerable lengths to make of Fedallah an almost disembodied being, a shadow who never sleeps and who is almost infinitely old—whose origin lies far back in time. He was felt by the ship's crew to be the devil himself.

As the chase is driving towards its climax off Japan, the *Pequod* runs into a typhoon.

> When darkness came on, sky and sea roared and split with thunder, and blazed with lightning.... All the yardarms were tipped with pallid fire; and touched at each tri-pointed lightning-rod-end with three tapering white flames, each of the three tall masts was silently burning in that sulphurous air like three gigantic wax tapers before an altar. (*Moby Dick*, 495-7)

Ahab seizes the mainmast lightning-rod links in his left hand, places his foot on the prostrate Parsee, raises his eyes and right hand upward to the white flames, and utters these words:

> "Oh! thou clear spirit of clear fire, whom on these seas I as Persian once did worship, till in the sacramental act so burned by thee, that to this hour I bear the scar; I now know thee, thou clear spirit, and I know now that thy right worship is defiance. To neither love nor reverence wilt thou be kind; and e'en for hate thou canst but kill; and all are killed." (*Moby Dick*, 499)

In some way the mysterious but compelling story of *Moby Dick* is rooted in the religious concepts and world-conception of ancient Persia. Before offering what I think Melville himself believed about this fact, I should like to say a word about the religion of Persia, founded many thousand years before the time of Christ by Zarathustra or Zoroaster. This inspirer of Persian culture, and through it indirectly of the Hebrew and Greek cultures, taught that world-reality is divided into two aspects, the light and the dark. The prince of darkness and falsehood he called Angra Mainyu, or Ahriman. The spirit of light and truth, the great aura of the sun, he called Ahura Mazdao, or Ormazd. The spirit of the depths of darkness was conceived as working to entangle human beings in matter. Ahura Mazdao was revered as the primordial spirit of creative goodness, but perhaps the conception of his nature also included unrecognized elements of the Luciferic. At any rate, the particular spirit of death and evil with which Ahab in his later phase identified Moby Dick was clearly defined. Let us call him, as the Persians did, Ahriman.

In terms of present-day experience, we could say that Lucifer holds us aloof from the common lot and common sense of humanity on earth; he makes of us visionaries and earth-estranged, overheated spiritualists. Ahriman, however, pulls us too deeply into the earth experience; he makes of us shrewd, heartless, and power-seeking materialists. What Melville sought was the Golden Mean, the way that lies between them. But to balance the forces of light and darkness, as he unsuccessfully strove to do, a triadic rather than a dualistic world view is needed. The third reality, the reconciling, harmonizing, truly human factor, is to be looked for in or through the heart. This inspiration of the center, which stands in freedom between the polar opposites that draw us off balance, Melville thought to find—as he acknowledged at the conclusion of his earlier book, *Mardi*—in the one who was both Son of Man and Son of God. In *Mardi*, Melville calls Christ "Alma," and the Mardian who in that book represented highest wisdom felt his search had led aright when he found Alma. But Taji, the Ishmael of *Mardi*, remained unreconciled. Something in him demanded that the quest be continued and intensified, though it lead to death itself.[6] The result we have in *Moby Dick*.

Returning to the last passage quoted: "Oh! thou clear spirit of clear fire whom on these seas I as Persian once did worship ... ," we can perhaps visualize something in

Ahab's nature as being disposed to approach the spirit of light "Persian-style." But how shall we understand *"I as Persian once"*? Shall Ahab have been in fact Persian "once upon a time"—which, according to Melville's view, would have been in an earlier life—or do we have to do with Ahab in an earlier stage of his present life, behaving as a Parsee of old might have done? Perhaps there is something to be said for both interpretations; but what about: *"till in the sacramental act* so burned by thee, that to this day I bear the scar"?*

In *Moby Dick* mystery opens into mystery. I base my own interpretation of what the author intended concerning Ahab's deeper motivation upon Melville's numerous references in this book and others to the idea of repeated earth lives (see for example Chapter 98, "Stowing Down and Clearing Up"). The suggestion is unmistakably made in the early chapter where Melville first describes Ahab's relation to Moby Dick. In this chapter, after we have been shown how the whale represents the whole force of darkness and evil operating both in cosmic nature and in human destiny, and after we are persuaded that Ahab was obsessed by his resentment of the whale, both for its personal injury to him and for its portents of hurt to all humans—after all this, how shall we account for the first sentence in the very next paragraph?

---

*A close reader of *Moby Dick* might object that in Chapter 28 the question raised by Ahab's apostrophe to the lightning is answered through the testimony of an old Gayhead Indian, who claimed that at an earlier time, when Ahab was about forty years of age, he had been struck and branded by lightning in a storm at sea. But this explanation of Ahab's "vivid scar," which is obviously more a spiritual symbol than a physical reality, is acknowledged to be a superstitious guess, rather than a statement of fact. Besides, if Melville really had in his own mind that Ahab's earlier encounter with cosmic light and fire had been simply a matter of being struck during a bad storm, even if vengefully struck, it seems most unlikely that he would have referred to the event as a "sacramental act." One cannot visualize that Ahab's mood was one of worship at such a time, or that he was performing sacred acts. Still less does the Gayhead Indian's assertion explain the phrase "I as Persian."

> This is much, yet Ahab's larger, darker, deeper part remains unhinted. (*Moby Dick*, 184)

How, indeed, can we account for the entire paragraph, which goes on to supply the mysterious hint that is to outweigh everything that has yet been said? We are asked to visualize the situation. All that has been said of Ahab's relationship to the whale is not more, says Melville, than the description of a grand and wonderful "Hotel de Cluny" such as was the architectural and artistic wonder of the European Middle Ages. Melville has permitted us to enter this great building and penetrate to its heart, but he now invites us to start the descent from this very heart into the deeper foundations upon which the whole edifice rests. Make this descent through time, "ye nobler, sadder souls," and you will approach the real secret of what you want to know! Observe that you are now carried back to an earlier age. The medieval Hotel de Cluny rests upon Roman foundations, built to supply heat for the Roman baths that were once here.

> [In these halls,] far beneath the fantastic towers of man's upper earth, his root of grandeur, his whole awful essence sits in bearded state; an antique buried beneath antiquities, and throned on torsoes! so with a broken throne, the great gods mock that captive king; so like a Caryatid, he patient sits, upholding on his frozen brow the piled entablatures of ages. (*Moby Dick*, 184-5)

Melville suggests that what is true of Ahab is equally true of any soul that feels within itself a deep ego-problem, a baffling life-riddle. Every such soul must go back in time, to find the real secret of its destiny.

> Wind ye down there, ye prouder, sadder souls! question that proud, sad king! A family likeness! aye, he did beget

ye, ye young exiled royalties; and from your grim sire only will the old State secret come.

According to the teaching of reincarnation, which Melville felt to be confirmed by his own inner experience, the positive fruits of one life on earth are carried over in some form into the next. One can work with them and build upon them—a supposition that could go far to explain how a twenty-eight to thirty-year old youth of very little education could write, quite out of the blue, such books as *Mardi* and *Moby Dick*. But incomplete or negative experiences are also carried over, and these too must be further dealt with. This is the idea Melville advances as the key of keys to Ahab's quest—Ahab standing no doubt for a single aspect of Melville himself.

One has the impression that in the present life, when he appears on the horizon of our present story, Ahab is to a large extent a man of his time. That is, he is an aggressive, intellectual, godless exploiter of nature; he follows Ahriman. But at heart he is still bemused by Lucifer. One can speculate, however, that it was in a past life of critical importance that his destiny received its characteristic stamp. Permitting ourselves to think freely for the moment in the idiom of ancient Persia, we may imagine him as an overly zealous disciple, or even priest, of some mystery school, fanatical in his devotions, let us say, but motivated too much by ambition. Walking the path he presumed to be that of spiritual development, he stumbled at a certain stage. Because he was already far along, his fall was more than an ordinary failure. Having confused imperious personal ardor with the true devotion that is patient and never personal and having therefore been rejected of the spirit, his soul was deeply confounded. And if his fault was even the cause of his death—a possibility not to be discounted when we consider the absolute rigor of the ancient practices—so that he was struck down in his embittered condition while still far from any thought of making amends, we must suppose that in a following life his struggle to regain self-assurance would take him through the most uncertain and tempestuous conditions. We can believe that he would start out with the feeling that he had been maimed, but for unknown reasons. He would bear a grudge against life that could not be explained on contemporary grounds. He would feel that joy in living, and success, had been taken from him by a hand he could not identify, and according to a logic he could not feel to be justified. He would have lost his footing, been left with only one leg to stand on.

Such a man would be hard put to appreciate the workings of "divine Providence." A part of him would be tempted instead to believe that the course of events was more malevolent than meaningless. This part of his soul would wander through life as an outsider, rejected, and rejecting. And with its fiery temperament, it would rage against the unfair treatment fate had accorded it.

If our scenario for Ahab is accepted as it is meant, as admittedly pure fiction, yet an attempt to picture the causative *principle* behind Ahab's profound alienation, we shall not find it strange that his next life should to some extent have to repeat the mistakes of the earlier one.* One can perhaps imagine that in the earlier time, he failed because his devotion to the spirit had too much of personal ambition in it. In the present life, he fails because his vaunted independence is built too much upon antagonism and opposition. He is *against* something outside himself, but *for* nothing of his own. His original ambition, his first attempt, as it were, to curry favor with the spirit had shown a lack of self-dependence. When out of disappointment, ambition now turns to blame and hate, the mistake might seem to be

* Let me emphasize, if emphasis be needed, that my suppositions have not been intended as a way of trying to arrive at truth by guesswork. They are meant only to dramatize and bring alive a riddle we cannot solve, but that we can also not ignore. Not the *fact* but the *style* of the matter is of concern here.

of a different kind, yet it is still the same old failure in self-dependence. Though he proclaims proud defiance of gods and men, he is in no sense his own man. He cannot be quiet, cannot make sound judgments, cannot enjoy, cannot create. He is completely beside himself. The secret of human freedom, on which love is based, and the secret of love, on which true freedom is based, he has yet to learn.

> ... all loveliness is anguish to me, since I can ne'er enjoy. Gifted with the high perception, I lack the low enjoying power; damned, most subtly and most malignantly! damned in the midst of Paradise! (*Moby Dick*, 166)

The implications of the above hypothesis for Melville himself are that he may well have felt that the past he suggests for Ahab was actually an aspect of his own. Perhaps he has this very kind of mistake to do penance for, and this very lesson to learn. As a writer, he could project and objectify the problem of spiritual pride and ambition in the character of Captain Ahab and thus advance his understanding of something in his own nature so as to consider how to overcome it.

FATAL LONGING

In the remarkable chapter entitled "The Lee Shore," Melville epitomizes much of what we have attributed to him, and to Ahab as an aspect of himself, in the matter of temperament, motivation, and problematic destiny. He pictures a man who cannot rest on the land of conventional truth, including conventional religious beliefs, but must again and again drive outward from all safe harbors into the unknown perils of the sea. On the one hand, this man is a spiritual hero, because he spurns every comfort of the "treacherous, slavish shore"; in his quest for ultimate truths he prefers to brave "the lashed sea's landlessness" even though this brings him to a tempestuous death.

> As in landlessness alone resides the highest truth, shoreless, indefinite as God—so better is it to perish in that howling infinite, than be ingloriously dashed upon the lee, even if that were safety! For worm-like, then, oh! who would craven crawl to land! (*Moby Dick*, 105-6)

The person we have called a heaven-stormer, a metaphysical plunger, is always led beyond himself. The courage he praises himself for may be actually a fatal conceit. Such a person never finds what he is looking for. He is led, or forced, upon one wild goose chase after another, by something in himself that remains unrecognized. Melville says that "all deep, earnest thinking is but the intrepid effort of the soul to keep the open independence of her sea," but the compulsive plunger enjoys no such open independence. His presumptuous longings let him be sucked into the howling infinite, battered and beaten by it, until he and his are destroyed. His ambition is simply suicidal. And though Melville, in this particular case, ends by saying: "Take heart, take heart.... Up from the spray of thy ocean-perishing—straight up, leaps thy apotheosis!" one cannot agree that willfulness is strength, and foolhardiness a higher form of courage. What leaps straight up from the fallen man is not himself as a god but Lucifer in triumph at the destructive success he has wrought and handed over to Ahriman.

Inordinate desire, even for the spiritual, disturbs the balance that is demanded by what Blake called "the human Form divine." Ambitious desire pulls us away from what is harmonious and integral in ourselves, leaving us not more but less than human. Melville spoke more truly when in the later chapter entitled "Brit" he named the briny deep for what it is—for what the premature challenger will find it to be:

No mercy, no power but its own controls it. Panting and snorting like a mad battle steed that has lost its rider, the masterless ocean overruns the globe. (*Moby Dick*, 275)

The ocean of morbid, driven introspection has nothing to do with the apotheosis of courage and independence. On the contrary, it unhorses every willful rider, and by its "universal cannibalism" swallows all that is best in him or her.

Consider all this; and then turn to this green, gentle, and most docile earth; consider them both, the sea and the land; and do you not find a strange analogy to something in yourself? For as this appalling ocean surrounds the verdant land, so in the soul of man there lies one insular Tahiti, full of peace and joy, but encompassed by all the horrors of the half known life. God keep thee! Push not off from that isle, thou canst never return! (*Moby Dick*, 276)

It is because Ahab represents the part of Melville himself that did not want to heed this sound advice that the author could say of him:

As touching all Ahab's deeper part, every revelation partook more of significant darkness than of explanatory light. (*Moby Dick*, 461)

And Ahab said of himself:

"So far gone am I in the dark side of earth, that its other side, the theoretic bright one, seems but uncertain twilight to me." (*Moby Dick*, 519-20)

Though Ahab in his youth, or in another life, may have sought transcendental light, when we encounter him as Captain of the *Pequod*, he is sailing into the oceanic darkness of his own subconsciousness.

"Yet dost thou dark half, rock me with a prouder, if a darker faith. All thy unnameable imminglings float beneath me here...." (*Moby Dick*, 490)

And meet it is, that over these sea-pastures, wide-rolling watery prairies and Potters' Fields of all four continents, the waves should rise and fall, and ebb and flow unceasingly; for here, millions of mixed shades and shadows, drowned dreams, somnambulisms, reveries; all that we call lives and souls, lie dreaming, dreaming, still; tossing like slumberers in their beds; the ever-rolling waves but made so by their restlessness. (*Moby Dick*, 478)

It is worth noting at this point, in a book where all is parable, that the meditative waters in which Moby Dick is hunted are not fresh but salt. Of fresh water Thoreau had earlier written, "A lake ... is the earth's liquid eye.... There it lies all the year, reflecting the sky—and from its surface there seems to go up a pillar of ether, which bridges over the space between earth and heaven.... Across the surface of every lake there sweeps a hushed music."[7] And in the chapter "The Prairie," Melville compares the "clear, eternal, tideless mountain lakes" to human eyes, or at least to the eyes of geniuses who gaze upon the eternal, and he imagines "antlered thoughts descending there to drink" (*Moby Dick*, 345). Melville's observation coincided with Thoreau's: namely, that fresh springs and lakes serve the earth as senses, through which it vividly perceives the cosmos. But the sea is salty, and if we think of the earth as a living cosmic being, as Melville said it was, and possessed of vital organs and functions, as he believed, the salt seas must resemble the abdomen more than the head. In the great oceans, the earth is withdrawn into its own metabolism, somnolent rather than awake, and the thoughts that course through its waters are dreams that grow progressively darker, the more deeply we penetrate into them.

> ... to and fro in the deeps, far down in the bottomless blue, rushed mighty leviathans, sword-fish, and sharks; and these were the strong, troubled, murderous thinkings of the masculine sea. (*Moby Dick*, 531)

A CREW OF ISOLATOES

The kind of hunt Ahab embarked on could not succeed, for

> in pursuit of those far mysteries we dream of, or in tormented chase of that demon phantom that, some time or other, swims before all human hearts; while chasing such over this round globe, they either lead us on in barren mazes or midway leave us whelmed. (*Moby Dick*, 237)

In the end, a self-defeating strategy brought the *Pequod*, its captain, and all its crew except Ishmael, the observer, to ruin. We have already suggested some of the lessons Melville was teaching himself as an individual by the writing of this tragedy. It remains to ask why many commentators have felt that the parable of Ahab and the whale has dimensions that go far beyond the moral development of a single individual. Why, indeed, should it be studied for prophetic clues to the destiny of the West, particularly America?

In order to test the hypothesis that *Moby Dick* is in a real sense the epic of America, which sets the pace for Western culture, let us begin by assuming it. The *Pequod* then becomes the American ship of state. Aboard is a polyglot mixture of nationalities, starting from a "mongrel" base of renegades and castaways symbolized by the anonymous crew, and rising through several grades of those who begin to carry responsibility, as personified in the petty officers, Flask, Stubb, and Starbuck. The whole is commanded by one whose overweening, obsessive, ever-intensifying purpose either enlisted or swept aside all other wills. The good ship America carries a proletariat, a petit bourgeoisie, and an upper-middle, cultured, ruling class. It includes so-called advanced peoples, who do not distinguish themselves (the mates), and peoples called primitive because they remain closer to the origins of life (the harpooneers), who do comport themselves with distinction.

Fittingly, Melville characterizes the dramatic personnel in this epic of the modern Western consciousness as "Isolatoes all"; that is, each has his own reason for being cut off from the normal health of mind that reflects a sure bond with fellow human beings, with nature, with destiny. Each is alienated; each is an ego fallen "out of the hands of God." Ahab, the egomaniac, would of course be in charge of such a crew.

Just below Captain Ahab is the first mate, Starbuck. Starbuck is the finest kind of American, shrewd and sound, industrious and skillful, practical and pious. He has the instinct of goodness, is moderately well educated, is courageous but not crazy. Why is Starbuck so helpless before Ahab? Why does Ahab's purpose so completely dominate both Starbuck, as the most advanced type of responsible, idealistic, good-hearted American, and the primitive harpooneers (the red man, Tashtego; the black, Daggoo; the brown, Queequeg; even the "tawny," Fedallah)? The answer in the case of the harpooneers is simply that they do not participate in the structure of authority. In the case of Starbuck, however, the answer is that his "mere unaided virtue or right-mindedness" is but a relic or residue of religious morality as passed down through ever more secular generations, in an ever more attenuated and anemic form. Starbuck's state of virtue is no match for the Luciferic-Ahrimanic drive of the demonic Ahab.

Here, then, was this grey-headed, ungodly old man, chasing with curses a Job's whale round the world, at the head of a crew, too, chiefly made up of mongrel renegades, and castaways, and cannibals—morally enfeebled also, by the incompetence of mere unaided virtue or right-mindedness in Starbuck, the invulnerable jollity of indifference and recklessness in Stubb, and the pervading mediocrity in Flask. Such a crew, so officered, seemed specially picked and packed by some infernal fatality to help him to his monomaniac revenge. How it was that they so aboundingly responded to the old man's ire—by what evil magic their souls were possessed . . . —all this to explain, would be to dive deeper than Ishmael can go. (*Moby Dick*, 186)

Let us suppose that the reason the whole ship's company could be swept along by Ahab and take his mad quest as their own is that all are partly moved by the spiritual principle that threatens to capture our own time, and that Ahab centrally *represents* this same spirit. How shall we identify the quality of being and striving that dominates Western civilization and carries all before it regardless of the fears or hopes that may at times make some of the passengers want to jump ship? Is it not a predatory pride of intellect that is bent upon harnessing and exploiting nature through the instrumentality of an ever more godless science and an ever more rapacious technology? When science becomes all brain, and technology becomes all will, and both leave out the heart; when this combination no longer allows itself to be taught by art or religion; and when the training of intelligence and enterprise asks for no corresponding progress in moral and human development; then an Ahab mentality rules—then Ahriman, behind Ahab, is in charge.

So in dreams, have I seen majestic Satan thrusting forth his tormented, colossal claw from the flame Baltic of Hell. (*Moby Dick*, 376)

"Pure intellect." said Emerson, "is the pure devil."[8] Contemptuously, the godless intellect extends its sway, bringing all into subjection. Captain Ahab, compassion squeezed from his heart under the pressure of urgencies and adversities he had called upon himself, became all intellect. He abandoned his human conscience toward his wife and child at home, toward his crew, toward the legitimate goals of his whaling voyage. He found himself offended by even the scientific quadrant inasmuch as this represented to him the aspect of earthly science that still needs to take its bearings from heaven: "I trample on thee, thou paltry thing that feebly pointest on high; thus I split and destroy thee!" The harpoon he fashioned for Moby Dick was quenched in human blood, and baptized in the name of the devil: "Ego non baptizo te in nomine patris, sed in nomine diaboli!" (*Moby Dick*, 484)

There can be no question but that cold-blooded technical thinking, pure abstract brainwork, aspires to become captain of the modern ship of state, especially in the West. Blind to qualitative values, it tends to be impatient of the rights of individuals and to trample on the rights of nature. Through Ahab, Melville shows us how "That certain sultanism of his brain . . . became incarnate in an irresistible dictatorship" (*Moby Dick*, 144). It is not far-fetched to believe that the practical, prophetic instinct in Melville discerned over a hundred years ago how swiftly the modern world is moving toward dictatorship, an unprecedented dictatorship not only over the externalities of life but over the private mind and will as well. The artists, ministers, teachers, scientists, businessmen, and statesmen of the last century have proven quite unable to halt this fatal trend. At their best, they are Starbucks: "morally enfeebled" in their "mere unaided virtue and right-mindedness."

The key words here, of course, are "mere unaided." In our time what is unaided becomes mere. Ahab is filled alternately with the inhuman and antihuman impulses first of Lucifer and then of Ahriman. He is thereby robbed of his true identity and any hope for genuine love or happiness. But his power is not mere. It is aided in the sense that superhuman agents work in and through him. Moby Dick was prophetic in showing that times were coming when humanity must once again reckon with the supernatural. To use the appropriate mythic analogy, those who would fight Leviathan, the dragon-whale power, should pray for inspiration and courage from Marduk-Michael, wielder of the sacred sword and spear.

JONAH AND THE WHALE

Melville has told us that he dreaded that his story might be taken for "a monstrous fable, or still worse and more detestable, a hideous and intolerable allegory" (*Moby Dick*, 204). Allegories are arbitrary intellectual constructions, and Melville knew that what he had to say was controlled by an instinct for truth that lay deeper than intellect can dive. He knew that a true myth, and not a fancied fable, was working itself out in his imagination, and that it unfolded according to a necessity rooted in the very nature of things. He embellished it from time to time, from this aspect and that, with such comments as might serve to hint its depths; but he did not presume to give it any final interpretation, for he sensed that the meaning of the whale went beyond Ahab's personal destiny. The overtones and undertones of the myth that inspired him sounded, like those of every true symbol, on many levels, cosmic as well as human. The riddle of humanity's relationship to the cosmic whale, after all, is at least as old and as enigmatic as the story of Jonah, which Melville made the prelude to his own rendering.

What was there about Jonah's whale that made it the symbol of all that meant most to the early Christians? It was, of course, the greatest of "fishes"; but why in any case did a fish become the symbol of Christ? The Greek name for fish is *ichthys*, the first syllable of which, *ich*, in the German tongue means "I," the ego. These same three letters are also the initials of the name given to the Son of Man. But surely these first Christians were not merely playing with language when they made themselves secretly known to each other by tracing in the sand the figure of a fish.

Perhaps it is not far-fetched to think of the greatest fish as the earth itself, the earth Christ came to redeem, and with which he united himself. Melville pictured the earth as swimming and browsing through the cosmic ether-ocean, yet it is the dwelling place of the human community. We human beings, whose origin is on high, find ourselves consigned to the earth for a term, for its sake and our own. To be swallowed up, as it were, into this whale's belly leaves us either so bewildered, frightened, and misled as to forget our origin altogether, or it provokes us mightily to remember and realize it. Out of the fish's belly, we pray with Jonah:

> Out of the belly of hell cried I, and thou heardest my voice. For thou hadst cast me into the deep, in the midst of the seas; and the floods compassed me about; all thy billows and thy waves passed over me. Then I said, I am cast out of thy sight; yet I will look again toward thy holy temple. The waters compassed me about, even to the soul: the depth closed me round about, the weeds were wrapped about my head. I went down to the bottoms of the mountains; the earth with her bars was about me for ever: yet hast thou brought up my life from corruption, O Lord my God. (Jonah 2:2-6)

The whale can carry us down and down, or it can rise with us to deliver us safely. The early Christians, who were themselves forced to live below ground in the catacombs, inscribed on their walls the sign of Jonah. Were they remembering that Christ, after his crucifixion, descended into the underworld for three days—the same length of time that Jonah spent in the whale's belly—in order to bring his redemption into the earth itself? Did it seem to them that the meaning of history lies in the choice humanity faces, to live its life on earth either with or without Christ? Did they believe that the free choice of humankind would one day permit Christ to achieve what Jonah, as representative of the still unaided human ego, could only augur but not accomplish with human powers alone; namely, the upward transformation, the spiritualization, of the great earth-whale?

Following the implications of this possibility, we come to see in the whale the symbol of the earth's mighty abundance, its beauty, its strength, and its danger. We imagine that when humanity—every individual of it a Jonah—remains true to that light within itself that comes from beyond the earth, the living earth rejoices. Its creatures and energies become ever more harmonious and mutually helpful. But when we forget the light, the earth-experience darkens for all creatures as it does for us; that is, the whale dives to blackest depths.

Ahab, in the earlier form of his egoism, had perhaps coveted more to possess than to serve the light. Frustrated in his assault upon the heights, he became bitter, even as Jonah in his spiritual pride had done. Of Jonah at a later stage it was said that he was exceedingly displeased and very angry with the Lord for the way he had managed things. And when the Lord asked him, "Doest thou well to be angry?" Jonah replied, "I do well to be angry, even unto death" (Jonah 4:4,9). While Jonah became suicidal in simply deciding to withdraw from life, Ahab's suicidal impulse took the form of a violent attack. When Lucifer had not brought him the heavenly victory he sought, he abandoned himself to Ahriman's power in the vain hope to gain at least an earthly triumph of vengeance. Torn between Lucifer and Ahriman, and spurning the hints of salvation held out to him through the humble simplicity of Pip, and the pious integrity of Starbuck, Ahab could not find the true victor, the true friend of mankind and of the earth. His second error inevitably proved as disastrous as his first.

PROPHETIC WARNING

Through the voyage of the *Pequod*, Melville shows what happens when we set out, under the command of a ruthless intelligence and an arrogant will, to dominate and exploit the earth that was given to us for quite another purpose. The *Pequod* set itself to hunt down the creature who, as we have suggested, of all beings on earth best symbolizes the innocence and abundance of nature's spiritual energy. The hunting, killing, stripping, and boiling down with its own fire of the ever-diminishing whale population, is as exact a picture as one could find for the main task so-called productive—actually consuming—modern civilizations set before themselves. Once upon a time there were many whales and few whalers, even as in the Arctic there have always been many caribou and some wolves. A symbiotic relationship favorable to both sides could possibly be maintained. But as we grow smart, bold, greedy, and uncaring, we invent technical improvements to kill whales faster and with less effort. The whales grow scarcer; the hunt intensifies. Technology now dominates the operation of whaling. The whole fishery can no longer be seen as a humane working in and with nature; certainly not as humanity on the side of nature, but clearly as humanity against nature, with no holds barred.

> Now, then, thought I ... here goes for a cool, collected dive at death and destruction, and the devil fetch the hindmost. (*Moby Dick*, 228)

In the mirror that life itself holds up to us, we see technological civilization—which is to say, many aspects of modern

America as exemplified in the ship *Pequod* under Captain Ahab—advancing against the living earth in a predatory, merciless, and coldly cruel manner. The image that advances therefore from within the mirror of imaginative experience, namely, the vicious whale, symbolizes the changed aspect of nature as she may be expected henceforth to present herself. As attackers, we can expect increasingly to be met by the threats of nature grown malignant, nature gone berserk.

If we wonder how such a phenomenon could happen, we should ask those who study weather, nutrition, public health, and ecology. We should observe that actual loss of fertility follows the overuse of chemical fertilizers; that as fruits and vegetables are brought to merely external perfection they lose in nutritive value; that intensive use of pesticides and antibiotics results in more virulent pests and disease organisms; that "triumphs" of irrigation often result in salinization of the earth and lowered water tables. We should note that the victories over infectious diseases, of which we are so proud, are accompanied by an increase of all types of degenerative diseases: cardiac, muscular, skeletal, glandular, nervous. We should consider, in other words, what may be called the paradoxes of technical "progress."

A civilization that prefers quantity to quality and substance to form may expect to meet its nemesis in cancerous overgrowths of all kinds, whether of bodily tissues, of population, of government, of cities, of corporations, of automobiles, or of money. A civilization that honors only matter will be overwhelmed by its own refuse and pollution. Believing only in the physical senses, it will fall prey to eroticism, gluttony, and the like. Excessively mental, it will wear itself out in the race to be as instantaneous as thought. Growing all to head, it will have no way to escape the fatal deposits of chalk in artery and joint. A civilization built upon a coldly technical attitude that seeks many kinds of testimony but never that of the heart, will be struck down typically by heart failure.

America suffers acutely from all of these paradoxes, and we know that in particular it is one of the most unhealthful nations in the world for the human heart. In Melville it found a prophet whose own constitution prepared him to speak from and for the human being of heart and lungs. "I stand for the heart," he wrote.[9] Melville's genius is connected with the heart—with the failed heart. And questions of heart, taking "heart" in its highest symbolic meaning as well as physically, are the issue for America.

The heart strives to equilibrate and harmonize what occurs above in cerebral-cognition with what occurs below in visceral-volition. Even so, Melville, a prophetic representative of America itself, lived always as one torn between these two worlds; his greatness came to deep intuitions of both, but did not suffice to reconcile them. He perceived how our experience of the world alternates, as the heart itself beats, between form and force, coldness and warmth, death and life; yet he could not discover how to convert this perpetual conflict between opposites into a loving, rhythmic collaboration in which thinking and doing, self and world, heaven and earth, idealism and realism might find a creative outlet in unequivocal wisdom, in well-tempered happiness, and in the sure mastery of circumstances. His difficulty in achieving this solution made Melville all the more a specialist in the problems that concern the heart. It enabled him to foretell most forcefully what must happen to a people who advance in both intellectuality and power, but who fail to develop the heart that can make them truly creative and creative of truth.

It is well known that in the end Ahab loses his life to the whale, who also rams and sinks the Pequod. We are led to see that if it comes to a showdown, cosmic nature will yet surely humble human willfulness. Nature will rebel; our predatory arrogance will find itself crushed by a great power that only we ourselves make relentless. But the precise picture that Melville gives us of this last event is worth remembering. As the stove ship subsides into the remorseless sea, her three masts are still for a moment visible, topped by the three pagan harpooneers. As we watch the American Indian, Tashtego, strike a last blow to nail Ahab's torn flag back to the top of the mainmast, we see a swooping, intercepting sky-hawk—"the bird of heaven" who may be the Pacific Ocean's nearest representative of the American Eagle—caught beneath the hammer and carried down with the ship. The prophecy is fatal, but only for an America that would allow itself to be commandeered all the way into the future by a mentality that values power above love.

* * *

Turning to the next chapter, we shall find that what Walt Whitman sought to infuse into the soul of his native land was, indeed, love.

NOTES

1. Herman Melville, *Moby Dick* (New York: Random House, 1950), 3. Page numbers for all further references to this books will be given in the text.
2. Henry David Thoreau, *Journal*, 1840.
3. Ralph Waldo Emerson, "The Poet," *The Complete Essays and Other Writings of Ralph Waldo Emerson*, Brooks Atkinson, ed. (New York: Random House, 1950), 332. Page numbers for all further references to these essays will be given by essay title in the text.
4. Walt Whitman, "I Sing the Body Electric," in *The Portable Walt Whitman*, Mark Van Doren, ed. (New York: Viking Press, 1960), 160. Page numbers for all further references to these essays will be given by poem title in the text.
5. Herman Melville, *Mardi: And a Voyage Thither* (New York: New American Library of World Literature, 1964), 305.
6. Ibid., Chapter 189.
7. Thoreau, *Journal*, 1840.
8. B. Perry, ed., *The Heart of Emerson's Journals* (New York: Houghton Mifflin, 1926), 207.
9. From a letter to Nathaniel Hawthorne in the spring of 1851, quoted in Eleanor Melville Metcalf, *Herman Melville: Cycle and Epicycle* (Cambridge: Harvard University Press, 1953), 109.

4

WALT WHITMAN: POET OF DEATH AND LIFE

WHITMAN's first volume of twelve poems in ninety pages, set in print largely by the poet himself, appeared on a July day in 1855. But of course it was not written in a day. On a later occasion, the author indicated that he had rewritten the manuscript at least five times and that it had been in active gestation for about seven years. When Emerson, aged fifty-two, received the complimentary copy of *Leaves of Grass* sent him by Whitman, his famous letter of thanks had this to say:

> Dear Sir—
>
> I am not blind to the wonderful gift of *Leaves of Grass*. I find it the most extraordinary piece of wit and wisdom that America has yet contributed. I am very happy in reading it, as great power makes us happy....
>
> I give you joy of your free and brave thought. I have great joy in it. I find incomparable things said incomparably well....
>
> I greet you at the beginning of a great career, which yet must have had a long foreground somewhere, for such a start.[1]

What Emerson meant by a long foreground we do not know, and probably he was not definite about it in his own mind. He obviously meant, however, to suggest something more than a mere seven years: perhaps a spiritual biography reaching into the far past, or an extraordinary mystical deepening in the present life, or both.

In 1855, Whitman was thirty-six. In the few years just before he brought out this first testament, he had been earning his living primarily as a house builder and carpenter. Earlier, he had spent years moving from printer to journalist to editor of several small newspapers. Though as a youth he had taught school for a time on Long Island, his own education never went beyond high school. Nothing in Whitman's preparation, nothing he had previously written or done—nothing, indeed, in the literary culture of his time—gave any hint of what was to come in *Leaves of Grass*.

To account for the spiritual vitality, assurance, and abundance Whitman put into his unique masterpiece, scholars assume that at around the age of thirty he must have undergone some great inner change that they cannot pinpoint as to either time or content, but that summoned depths of unknown origin in him. Henry Bryan Binns, the Englishman whose unusually perceptive biographical interpretation, appearing thirteen years after Whitman's death, could still build upon the memory of personal friends of the author, spoke for all students who marvel at Whitman's inspiration when he called the poet "a man of special and exceptional character, a new type of mystic or seer," one who "belongs to the order of the initiates."[2]

Whitman's own "Song of Myself" leads one to the loftiest conception of his standpoint, resources, and motives.[3] Such lines as the following clearly do not speak as the scribes and Pharisees, but as the utterance of one having authority—and yet as one, too, who has found his authority where it is equally available to everyone: in what knows itself to be unborn as well as undying.

I pass death with the dying, and birth with the
new-wash'd babe, and am not contain'd between
my hat and my boots. ("Song of Myself," 35)

I know I am deathless,
. . . .
And whether I come to my own today or in ten
thousand or ten million years,
I can cheerfully take it now, or with equal
cheerfulness I can wait.

To be in any form, what is that?
(Round and round we go, all of us, and ever come
back thither.) ("Song of Myself," 58)

And as to you Life I reckon you are the leavings of
many deaths,
(No doubt I have died myself ten thousand times
before.) ("Song of Myself," 91)

I am an acme of things accomplish'd, and I an
encloser of things to be. ("Song of Myself," 83)

This day before dawn I ascended a hill and look'd
at the crowded heaven,
And I said to my spirit *When we become the enfolders
of those orbs, and the pleasure and knowledge of
every thing in them, shall we be fill'd and
satisfied then?*
And my spirit said No, we but level that lift to
pass and continue beyond. ("Song of Myself," 87)

The fact that such words, though scattered everywhere through this first volume of poems, had not been hinted in Whitman's previous writings, seems to suggest a parallel to the awakening experienced by St. Francis and other spiritual guides—a sudden irruption of spiritual fire into a prepared but sleeping soul. There is much reason to accept this view, and little to doubt it. It accords with Whitman's own testimony that he nevertheless experienced premonitions of such an awakening long before the traditional age of thirty.

THERE WAS A CHILD

The poet started in life with childhood's normal impressionability greatly heightened.

> There was a child went forth every day,
> And the first object he look'd upon, that object he became,
> And that object became part of him for the day or a
>   certain part of the day,
> Or for many years or stretching cycles of years.
> . . . .
> These became part of that child who went forth
>   every day, and who now goes, and will always
>   go forth every day.
>   ("There Was a Child Went Forth," 372-4)

In time, sheer impressionability, the gift to identify himself wholly with the other, became in Whitman a capacity for wonder as well. Wonder eventually became love, and out of love arose creativeness.

It may be that "Out of the Cradle Endlessly Rocking" (256-62) recalls, or at least typifies, the happening that awakened young Walt's first consciousness of those powers in the world and in himself that were to become the basis of his lifework. This transformation took place when he still enjoyed the innocence of childhood, yet could be roused, by a seemingly simple experience, to feel a passion of sympathy for the mysteries of external nature, and a passionate wonder at the mystery of his own soul.

The poet remembers himself as a boy on the shores of Long Island in the month of May. He tells how it was that his awakener to the secret Life of life was—death.

> A man, yet by these tears a little boy again,
> Throwing myself on the sand, confronting the waves,
> I, chanter of pains and joys, uniter of here and hereafter,
> Taking all hints to use them, but swiftly leaping
>   beyond them,
> A reminiscence sing.

Two small birds, "guests from Alabama," had built their nest near the beach. On the nest of "four light-green eggs spotted with brown" crouched the female, with the male ever near at hand.

> And every day I, a curious boy, never too close,
>   never disturbing them,
> Cautiously peering, absorbing, translating.

Suddenly one day young Walt observed that the female bird had vanished, never to return. Perhaps she had been killed. Henceforward through the long summer by the sea, in the evening and at night under moon and stars, he occasionally caught glimpses of the solitary remaining bird, and strained to catch the meaning of his song.

> I, with bare feet, a child, the wind wafting my hair,
> Listen'd long and long.

The bird's aria brought to the surface of the boy's soul deeply hidden questions that found their answer eventually in a message rising from the waves of the ever-pulsing seas.

> Demon or bird! (said the boy's soul,)
> Is it indeed toward your mate you sing? or is it

> really to me?
> For I, that was a child, my tongue's use sleeping,
>   now I have heard you,
> Now in a moment I know what I am for, I awake,
> And already a thousand singers, a thousand songs,
>   clearer, louder and more sorrowful than yours,
> A thousand warbling echoes have started to life
>   within me, never to die.

In this moment the innocent peace of childhood ended for Whitman: "the fire, the sweet hell within, the unknown want" began; and with it at the same time the oppressive, exhilarating sense of what was to be his task on earth.

The young Whitman turns from the bird's plaint to the deeper message the sea itself seems waiting to impart:

> A word then, (for I will conquer it,)
> The word final, superior to all,
> Subtle, sent up—what is it?
> . . . .
> Whereto answering, the sea,
> Delaying not, hurrying not,
> Whisper'd me through the night, and very plainly
>   before daybreak,
> Lisp'd to me the low and delicious word death,
> And again death, death, death, death,
> Hissing melodious, neither like the bird nor like
>   my arous'd child's heart,
> But edging near as privately for me rustling
>   at my feet.

The ardent boy was moved by the ineffable. Part of him reached out beyond ocean's shore and sky. Yet another part held its focus upon the love story of the two small feathered guests from Alabama. The tragic end of this story deepened his experience, and the immediacy of the song by which the he-bird transmuted its love and suffering into sheer beauty taught him what a human soul, his own soul, could eventually do with such experiences.

Yet at the same time it was not enough to know that love exists, and tragedy; and that through song these passionate events can become beauty. The child's soul sought something more. Reverting from focus to unfocus, it rose from the small drama of the twin birds to the universal setting in which it took place.

The boy felt the meaning of the events he had witnessed somehow distilled out of the embracing whole. The sea spoke for that whole. The spirit of the sea was remote and yet near; vast yet inclusive. It receded to unknown distances, yet touched his very heart.

By the grace of his inner awakening, young Whitman felt something approach him from behind-yet-within the mysterious ocean waters and ocean sky. This something was tenderness, and so he could call it sweet; it was balm, and so he could call it delicious. He felt it as the spirit of divine love: hoping all things, assuring all things, fulfilling all things. Its breath was triumph and joy for one in the midst of life; and yet with equal certainty he felt and knew that the name of this all-absolving, all-enlivening spirit was death. Life's ultimate greatness, fullness, and freedom, then, lay in death!

Now, the youth felt, he had what he had sought! Not only does divine love enfold those passing through the seeming tragedy of extinction here on earth, but that same absolute light and warmth also surround, pervade, and guarantee every detail of ordinary life itself. From this moment until his own death after long illness at the age of seventy-two, Whitman began to sing, as very few have ever done, Praise Songs to Death. He never ceased trying to help his listeners realize that the dread Nothing is more truly to be known as the creative ALL—not an emptiness but a fullness, not an end but a beginning, and not a Beyond only, but especially a

WALT WHITMAN: POET OF DEATH AND LIFE

Here-and-Now. At every stage of his life, Whitman sought to show that as the mystery of the eternal cosmic ONE is opened in human hearts by the right appreciation of death, this same recognition in turn awakens love for the multiplicity of earthly life itself. It offers, indeed, the only sure key to happiness on earth.

Whitman said of himself,

> For I bestow upon any man or woman the entrance to
> all gifts of the universe. ("To Rich Givers," 282)

Evidently he felt himself to be one whom the knowledge of the meaning of death had prepared to be a spokesman for the eternal Spirit.

> I do not think Life provides for all and for Time and
> Space, but I believe Heavenly Death provides for all.
>   ("Assurances," 454)

THE RIDDLE

In the collection of poems entitled *From Noon to Starry Night*, Whitman included what he called "A Riddle Song." (480-2) This riddle has to do with the secret of both life and death.

> That which eludes this verse and any verse,
> Unheard by sharpest ear, unform'd in clearest eye or
> cunningest mind,
> Nor lore nor fame, nor happiness nor wealth,
> And yet the pulse of every heart and life throughout
> the world incessantly,
> Which you and I and all pursuing ever miss,
> Open but still a secret, the real of the real,
> an illusion,
> Costless, vouchsafed to each, yet never man the owner.

Whitman says that "two little breaths of words" comprise this mystery that can be neither seen nor heard, nor yet grasped by the intellectual mind.

Two words, yet all from first to last comprised in it.

Two words that yet are one: one that is "the pulse of every heart and life throughout the world incessantly."
Without attempting as yet to specify these two words precisely, we shall certainly not be far wrong if we think that they were intimately related in Whitman's mind with what he calls Heavenly Death, or what, during the same period of his life, he apostrophizes elsewhere as "Santa Spirita."

> Santa Spirita, breather, life,
> Beyond the light, lighter than light,
> . . . .
> Essence of forms, life of the real identities,
>   permanent, positive, (namely the unseen,)
> Life of the great world, the sun and stars, and of man,
>   I, the general soul.
> Here the square finishing, the solid, I the most solid,
> Breathe my breath also through these songs.
>   ("Chanting the Square Deific," 541)

This all-creative, all-imbuing spirit that lights up or comes to consciousness authentically within the individual human being is nothing other than the Self of all selves. Whitman indicates as much in the very first words of the final, inclusive edition of his *Leaves of Grass*:

ONE'S-SELF I sing . . .

The two words that the reader has been searching for—so original and so final—are surely indicated by the capitalized ONE'S SELF. But though this indication is explicit and emphatic enough, it is still abstract. ONE'S SELF lacks the fire that truly inspires the poet in the present instance. It bespeaks the human personality, indeed, but does not bring us close to it. More decisively individual, yet nonetheless universal, are the two words that can never be applied to oneself from outside by any other person. It is in them that the self really awakens to itself.

Evidently, the riddle lies in the rarely sensed and still more rarely fathomed relationship between "I am" and "I AM." The former is spoken habitually and carelessly by the unawakened self. The latter is spoken by God within the self. It was the name uttered by the One who spoke to Moses out of the burning bush. It was spoken of himself by the One who said of himself: "I Am the light of the world; he that followeth me shall not walk in darkness, but shall have the light of life." (Jn. 8:12) "Before Abraham was, I AM." (Jn. 8:58) The relationship between these two words gives the clue needed for an understanding of Whitman's concept of how Life is related to death.

Hidden in the riddle of the "I" is the possibility of our participation as individuals in the self-existent, self-sustaining Spirit that underlies all of creation. Religious tradition has held that "I AM" is the name of God. It is this realization of eternal, creative Self-existence, which can arise within the consciousness of the individual, that Whitman sees completing "the Square Deific." For while this essence of Spirit is the source and substance of life, action, and evolution of any kind whatever, it begins to become conscious of itself only in us. Only we, in our feeble, preliminary way, begin to speak the "I." Not the stones, nor the plants, nor the animals, but only the fourth member of the "square" of earthly kingdoms has this ability. Only in human beings has the Deity raised up the possibility of a "solid," or awakened consciousness of Selfhood.

Thus, though almost all human beings are capable of saying "I" to themselves, few have any real sense of how this ability brings the whole of the natural creation to its climax. They do indeed say "I," but they tend to imagine this "I" as based upon, as arising from, and more or less identical with, their physical bodies. And because physical bodies disintegrate when life ends, such people cannot but fear death. But Whitman knew that in laying low the body, death exalts the soul. It does not obliterate but intensifies the triumphant, eternal aspect of "I."

THE MYSTERY OF DEATH

For Whitman, death is just about synonymous with spirit; and, as Emerson said, "Spirit hath life in itself." Thus Whitman conceived of death as the renewal of ever-evolving spiritual forces in the individual. For him, it had nothing to do with static conceptions of either final bliss or last Judgment. Death, he felt, should be seen as a necessary, and a welcome, stage in the eternal development of every human soul. While earthly life calls upon us to awaken, to care, and to do, for the most part our awakening is sleepy, our caring is shallow and desultory, and our deeds rarely go beyond hints of the possible. After death, all spiritual strivings, however timid and tentative, are as seeds whose time of germination has come at last. They are drawn forth into the light to grow further toward perfection. What may not have been able to advance beyond a hope or a desire of the soul during life in the physical body, advances in the body-free existence after death to become ability. The arrows of intention and hope that earth-life has, as it were, but aimed, are carried to the mark by death.

Conceptions of this kind are needed, if one is to appreciate lines such as the following:

> O I see now that life cannot exhibit all to me, as the day cannot,
> I see that I am to wait for what will be exhibited by

death. ("Night on the Prairies," 457)

(Life, life is the tillage, and Death is the harvest
according.)
("As I watched the Ploughman Plowing," 459)

There is a great difference between traditional Western ideas of immortality and Whitman's. His were dynamic and progressive. He regarded life after death as, in fact, preparation for a new life on earth. As often as the individual soul hungers for an outbreathing into the universal, so often is this hunger followed eventually by its opposite; the soul that has become universalized seeks once again to be individualized.

Whitman could not have agreed with Nietzsche's caustic observation that apparently "The purpose of waking is to sleep well"—meaning that, as religiously viewed, the purpose of life on earth is to secure an eventual dead-end bliss in heaven, even though that be in the bosom of the Father. Whitman felt that our long-term task is not to withdraw from the earth, but to enter ever more deeply into it, until all that is cold here shall have been warmed and all that is opaque and dark shall have been made transparent and luminous. Immortal life does not lead those who actually live it to condemn material reality; rather, it inspires and equips them to assist lovingly in the further evolution and complete spiritualization of earthly existence.

Perhaps we may say that Whitman was Eastern in his recognition that all of material existence derives from high spiritual beginnings, but he was Western in emphasizing that the opposite is also true: that spirituality continues to evolve in, through, and by means of the physical-earthly.

Through thy idea, lo, the immortal reality!
Through thy reality, lo, the immortal idea!
("Thou Mother With Thy Equal Brood," 461)

It was his especially Western gift to sense the spirit as a futurity that is potential in the present of all beings. The contemplation of spiritual life pointed him always forward.

> I have press'd through in my own right,
> I have sung the body and the soul, war and peace
>   have I sung, and the songs of life and death,
> And the songs of birth, and shown that there
>   are many births. ("So Long!," 505)

FROM DEATH TO LIFE, FROM SOUL TO BODY

Whitman's vision of death provides just the leaven of spirituality his readers need, to lift the burden of materiality heaped upon them by the catalogs his poems tend to become. Some pages of *Leaves of Grass* remind one of an "auctioneer's inventory of a warehouse," and as Thoreau told Harrison Blake, "by his heartiness ... he puts me into a liberal frame of mind prepared to see wonders ... stirs me well up, and then—throws in a thousand of brick."[4]

We must assume that for Whitman himself, "plain" facts were much less plain than for most of his readers. "Plain divine facts" he once called them, for "unadorned" reality was, for his seeing eyes, always self-adorning. For him, no sensory fact was ever mere prose; even to list such facts was already poetry and therefore enough to awaken love. One is reminded of Emerson's observation:

> For the world is not painted or adorned, but is from the beginning beautiful; and God has not made some beautiful things, but Beauty is the creator of the universe.[5]

For Whitman, physical objects, events, and processes, above all the human body, were all beautiful and heartwarming because creative spirit expressed itself through all. His special relationship with "heavenly death" had opened his heart to embrace the most prosaic aspects of so-called "ordinary" earthly life. But we may come even closer to Whitman's apprehension of these two aspects of reality if we shift, as he often does, from the vocabulary of death and life to the parallel language of body and soul.

> I am the poet of the Body and I am the poet of the Soul.
> ("Song of Myself," 49)

This is even-handed, certainly. It presents no obvious difficulties and leaves usual habits of thought undisturbed. One is accustomed to try, after all, to give due credit to both body and soul. But Whitman's approach is complex and by no means usual.

> I believe in you my soul, the other I must not abase itself to you, And you must not be abased to the other.
> ("Song of Myself," 32)

To honor the soul and not wish to see it dominated and misled by mere bodily appetites is still a not uncommon attitude. But what about the humble body not abasing itself before the honored soul? Should not the lower be subjected to the higher?

Whitman's answer to this question would be affirmative: Yes, the lower must honor and serve the higher. But which is higher? While it is true that the soul, as the seat of consciousness and therefore of moral responsibility, is clearly more advanced and thus should hold the upper hand over the dumb body, which without the soul would be useless, it is also true, though less usually observed, that the soul, compared to the body, is in many ways unstable and imperfect. The chaos of impulsive, mutually contradictory desires that inhabits the soul cannot be compared for either form or function with the harmonious perfection of balanced organic relationships that constitutes the body. Seen against the wondrous artifact that serves as our body, our soul is quite formless and comparatively ill-assorted.

> If any thing is sacred the human body is sacred.
> ("I Sing the Body Electric," 103)

> Whoever you are, how superb and divine is your body,
>   or any part of it!
> ("Starting from Paumanok," 23)

For Whitman, the body is higher as well as lower than the soul. Both are worthy of reverence, but not one more than the other.

> I have said that the soul is not more than the body,
> And I have said that the body is not more than the soul.
> ("Song of Myself," 89)

> And I will make the poems of my body and of mortality,
> For I think I shall then supply myself with the poems of
>   my soul and of immortality.
> ("Starting from Paumanok," 17)

> Behold, the body includes and is the meaning, the main concern and includes and is the soul.
> ("Starting from Paumanok," 23)

Whitman is drastic because he wants to be unmistakable. As late as 1888, three years before his death, in a letter to W. S. Kennedy in which he wished to underline his difference from Emerson, he repeated this formulation: *"Leaves of Grass's* word is the body, *including all,* including the intellect and the soul."[6]

Taken at face value, the poet's words could seem to suggest that the human soul is but a bodily epiphenomenon, a vapor generated and given off by the body. Many who think along natural scientific lines will perhaps tend to agree with this supposition. But then there can be no avoiding the logical conclusion that when the body disintegrates at death, the soul must disappear with it. In that case, how could one who believed as Whitman did in the soul's life after bodily death, imagine that the body is "the meaning and the main concern," or that it "includes and is" the soul?

It is clear that Whitman wanted to speak very strongly against moralistic or otherworldly outlooks that would have the human soul hover in the heavenly abstract, through contempt for things earthly such as the body. These views assume what is not to be assumed, namely, that the soul comes from above and is therefore to return on high, while the body that seems to come from below shall be cast off and abandoned to the dishonor of decay. It was not that Whitman saw no justification for the usual view of the matter. That he could and did is evident in this line:

> Myself discharging my excrementitious body to be
> burn'd, or render'd to powder, or buried . . .
> ("A Song of Joys," 188)

But there was something quite different that he felt to be of greater importance. He expressed this other truth in the lines that immediately follow the ones above.

> My real body doubtless left to me for other spheres,
> My voided body nothing more to me, returning
> to the purifications, further offices, eternal uses
> of the earth. (188)

"Body" obviously means two different things to Whitman. It is a vessel filled out by matter, which deserves to be discarded in time, but more fundamentally, the vessel itself is a purely spiritual *form*, whose essence and origin lie beyond time and beyond the earth. The first kind of body is indeed material substance, the second is Idea—not abstract "idea," but living, creative Idea. The latter is fully as spiritual as the soul itself, and perhaps even antedates it. Of this ideal, *im*material body Whitman had an especially vivid sense:

> Proved to me this day beyond cavil that it is not my
>   material eyes which finally see,
> Not my material body which finally loves, walks,
>   laughs, shouts, embraces, procreates. (186)

It is with the same meaning that Whitman speaks of "The real life of my senses transcending my senses and flesh," and it is this *real* life of the senses of which we must remind ourselves when we encounter such self-characterizations as these:

> Walt Whitman, a kosmos, of Manhattan the son,
> Turbulent, fleshy, sensual, eating, drinking and
>   breeding.... ("Song of Myself," 52)

> I believe in the flesh and appetites....
>   ("Song of Myself," 54)

While without doubt expressing something other than spirituality in such passages, the poet, even at his most rowdy and equivocal, is conscious of being inspired mainly by something chaste. He immediately goes on to add: "Seeing, hearing, feeling are miracles, and each part and tag of me is a miracle." This sense of the miraculous spiritualizes all else.

> O the joy of my soul leaning pois'd on itself,
>   receiving identity through materials and loving
>   them, observing characters and absorbing them,
> My soul vibrated back to me from them....

> The real life of my senses and flesh transcending my
> senses and flesh. ("A Song of Joys," 186)

TRANSIENT SUBSTANCE, ENDURING FORM

In "Crossing Brooklyn Ferry," Whitman gives beautiful expression to the relationship between the wide world of physical appearances and the receptive soul that has learned to distinguish between transient substance and enduring form. Such a soul looks at the passing scene with "free" senses and sees it in the light of eternity. It is indeed typical of Whitman that this poem could as well have been entitled "Sub Specie Aeternitatis." Observing the myriad commonplaces of an ordinary ferry-crossing, the poet is filled with a vivid sense that whatever in the scene is of form—the Idea, the spirit—rather than of material substance, is accessible to and provides nourishment for his soul. It will therefore endure as long as his own soul endures. In this mood he addresses the beloved sights and sounds of the East River.

> The impalpable sustenance of me from all things at
> all hours of the day.
> . . . .
> The glories strung like beads on my smallest sights
> and hearings, on the walk in the street and the
> passage over the river,
> . . . .
>
> Appearances, now or henceforth, indicate what you are,
> You necessary film, continue to envelop the soul,
> About my body for me, and your body for you, be hung
> out divinest aromas,
> Thrive, cities—bring your freight, bring your shows,
> ample and sufficient rivers

> Expand, being than which none else is perhaps more
> spiritual,
> Keep your places, objects than which none else is more
> lasting.
>
> You have waited, you always wait, you dumb,
> beautiful ministers,
> We receive you with free sense at last, and are
> insatiate henceforward,
> . . . .
> We use you, and do not cast you aside—we plant
> you permanently within us,
> We fathom you not—we love you—there is
> perfection in you also,
> You furnish your parts toward eternity,
> Great or small, you furnish your parts toward the
> soul. (163-9)

This ideal-real nature of any and every object* can stand out and be known only within the human soul. Whitman perceives that objects are waiting for this fulfillment, this chance, through the love of an attentive human being, to arrive at last and be recognized in the sense of their permanent reality. Objects depend upon human beings to give them voice, to complete their manifestation—and thus to anchor them in eternity.

On the other hand, as Whitman makes plain, the human soul needs the objects of the world as much as they need it. They are its indispensable nourishment; without them, it would be impoverished to the vanishing point. They enlarge the soul by inviting it always to grow beyond itself. They have the further function of concentrating the soul, enabling it to realize its own powers and to know its own

---

*"Nature is transcendental, exists primarily, necessarily, ever works and advances, yet takes no thought for the morrow. Man owns the dignity of the life which throbs around him, in chemistry, and tree, and animal, and in the involuntary functions of his own body. . . . " Emerson in "The Transcendentalist."[7]

mind. Without them, the soul would remain but a featureless latency of meanings that would never become actually known, because they would never be called into use. In beholding and tallying the objects of the natural environment—in loving them—the soul comes, indeed, progressively to its larger Self.

> You air that serves me with breath to speak!
> You objects that call from diffusion my meanings and
>   give them shape!
> . . . .
> I believe you are latent with unseen existences, you are
>   so dear to me.
>   ("Song of the Open Road," 152)

> And I will not make a poem nor the least part of a
>   poem but has reference to the soul,
> Because having look'd at the objects of the universe,
>   I find there is no one nor any particle of one but has
>   reference to the soul.
>
> Was somebody asking to see the soul?
> See, your own shape and countenance, persons,
>   substances, beasts, the trees, the running rivers,
>   the rocks and sands.
>
> All hold spiritual joys and afterwards loosen them;
> How can the real body ever die and be buried?
>   ("Starting from Paumanok," 22)

We return to the question of the "real" body, or, as the poem "Eidólons" calls it,

> Thy body permanent,
> The body lurking there within thy body,
> The only purport of the form thou art, the real I myself,
>   an image, an eidólon.

St. Paul speaks of the body natural and the body spiritual. We can believe that Whitman's affinity for the body natural was strong. Yet in the final edition of *Leaves of Grass*, he placed "Eidólons" at the very beginning, as an introductory statement meant to be revealing for all that followed. This placement shows that his abiding joy in the contemplation of physical bodies of whatever kind lay in his awareness of them as archetypal form, as living Ideas, as creative "eidólons." His statement of this conception deserves longer quotation.

> I met a seer,
> Passing the hues and objects of the world,
> The fields of art and learning, pleasure, sense,
> To glean eidólons.
>
> . . . .
>
> Lo, I or you,
> Or woman, man, or state, known or unknown,
> We seeming solid wealth, strength, beauty build,
> But really build eidólons.
>
> . . . .
>
> All space, all time,
> . . . .
> Fill'd with eidólons only.
>
> The noiseless myriads,
> The infinite oceans where the rivers empty,
> The separate countless free identities, like eyesight,
> The true realities, eidólons.
>
> Not this the world,
> Nor these the universes, they the universes,
> Purport and end, ever the permanent life of life,
> Eidólons, eidólons.
>
> . . . .

> Unfix'd yet fix'd,
> Ever shall be, ever have been and are,
> Sweeping the present to the infinite future,
> Eidólons, eidólons, eidólons. (5-7)

THE MYSTERY OF SEX

In love, above all, and in sex as an integral expression of love, Walt Whitman found the very center of the mystery of how natural and supernatural, or spiritual, are related to each other. For him, sex was peculiarly the touchstone for all else. It was unmistakable to him that those who praised most of his poems but could not abide his *Children of Adam* or *Calamus* did not really understand the essential of what he had to say. They had never gotten to the bottom of it. He saw sex as the radical test of whether or not he had succeeded in his aim of transvaluing all values. Only readers who were truly with him could be glad for his celebration of sexual love. They alone could appreciate that the essence of what he offered was as far from selfish physical appetite as it was from the psychic guilt so often aroused by the mere mention of sex.

During his last years at Camden, Whitman said to Horace Traubel: "Calamus needs clear ideas: it may be easily, innocently distorted from its natural, its motive, body of doctrine."[8] Perhaps because he was a poet, not a philosopher, he himself was in no hurry to supply these clear ideas. He realized that in some ways his poems were equivocal or at least obscure, but he made no apologies for this. But when his English admirer John Addington Symonds had pressed him for explanations of *Calamus*, he did admit to Traubel: "I maybe do not know all my own meanings: I say to myself, 'You, too, go away, come back, study your own book, see what it amounts to.'"[9] He was, however, clear enough about his meaning to know that ordinary concepts and reactions could not grasp it. He knew he had a secret, and though he avoided trying to formulate it, he knew at what depth it lay.

> Whoever you are holding me now in hand,
> Without one thing all will be useless,
> I give you fair warning before you attempt me further,
> I am not what you supposed, but far different.
> ("Whoever You Are Holding Me Now in Hand," 118)

And will you be a follower? he asks. Will you declare yourself a candidate for my love and teaching about love? I must warn you that

> The way is suspicious, the result uncertain, perhaps
>   destructive,
> You would have to give up all else, . . .
> Your novitiate would even then be long and exhausting,
> The whole past theory of your life and all conformity to
>   the lives around you would have to be abandon'd,
> Therefore release me now before troubling yourself
>   any further. . . .
> ("Whoever You Are Holding Me Now in Hand," 119)

Whitman warns of the danger that his teaching will either confuse the life of the admiring reader and would-be follower, or mislead it entirely by arousing impulses that carry him or her away from the goal rather than toward it.

> But these leaves conning you con at peril,
> For these leaves and me you will not understand,
> They will elude you at first and still more afterward . . .
> . . . .
>
> For it is not for what I have put into it that I have
>   written this book,

> Nor is it by reading it you will acquire it,
> ....
> Nor will my poems do good only, they will do just as
>   much evil, perhaps more,
> For all is useless without that which you may guess
>   at many times and not hit, that which I hinted at;
> Therefore release me and depart on your way.
>   ("Whoever You Are Holding Me Now in Hand," 120)

Even when Whitman is coming to the very edge of the clear ideas he declares to be necessary, he draws back from going further. He gives hints of two quite different, even contradictory, kinds. He sings of passionate life, yet shows himself passionately devoted to death. The hint we most need for the understanding of *Calamus* is perhaps to be found indirectly in the poem immediately preceding it. That hint, once again, concerns death and the essential meaning death imparts to all aspects of life, especially to love.

To the extent that sexual love becomes a means for the expression of what survives death, what is eternal in men and women, it is spiritualized. As we have seen, what Whitman means by "death" is precisely this eternal life that makes true love possible.

> O I think it is not for life I am chanting here my
>   chant of lovers, I think it must be for death,
> For how calm, how solemn it grows to ascend to the
>   atmosphere of lovers,
> Death or life I am then indifferent, my soul
>   declines to prefer,
> (I am not sure but the high soul of lovers welcomes
>   death most). ("Scented Herbage of My Breast," 117)

Whitman conjures the presence of an intensified spirituality that can be seen, on the one hand, as glorifying sexual experience or, on the other, as radically purging it.

> Clear and sweet is my soul, and clear and sweet is
> all that is not my soul. ("Song of Myself," 30)

* * *

By comparison with Whitman, both Emerson and Thoreau represented what we may call the more ascetic side of spiritual striving. Their goal, like his, was insight into the conditions of life, and they knew that clear vision is granted only to souls of purity. In Emerson's words, "The sublime vision comes to the pure and simple soul, in a clean and chaste body."[10] Their strategy of spiritual development, therefore, led through a purification of the senses and a curbing of sensual willfulness and desire—the very things that Whitman almost seems to flaunt! Had the latter's avowed physicality been really so physical, however, neither Emerson nor Thoreau would have found him attractive or believable. Obviously he must have satisfied them that not only his theoretical purpose but his full-bodied presence was graced by the Ideal, and that it was indeed "clean."

In a letter written shortly after the first appearance of *Leaves of Grass* and his own meeting with Whitman, Thoreau recorded his firsthand impressions. As concerns the apparent rampancy of egoism in the *Leaves*, he has this to say:

> Since I have seen him, I find that I am not disturbed by any brag or egoism in his book. He may turn out the least of a braggart of all, having the better right to be confident.

And then, regarding his emphasis on sex:

> But even on this side he has spoken more truth than any American or modern that I know. I have found his poem exhilarating, encouraging. As for his sensuality—I do not

so much wish that those parts were not written, as that men and women were so pure that they could read them without harm.[11]

In the chapter in *Walden* entitled "Higher Laws," Thoreau explored the relationship between physicality and spirituality, that is, between sensual and ideal experience. Though Whitman's temperament and experience could at times seem to contrast drastically with the moral standards Thoreau set for himself, in essence they shared the same understanding.

> Who knows what sort of life would result if we had attained to purity? If I knew so wise a man as could teach me purity I would go seek him forthwith.... Yet the spirit can for the time pervade and control every member and function of the body, and transmute what in form is the grossest sensuality into purity and devotion. The generative energy, which, when we are loose, dissipates and makes us unclean, when we are continent invigorates and inspires us. Chastity is the flowering of man and what are called Genius, Heroism, Holiness, and the like, are but various fruits which succeed it. Man flows at once to God when the channel of purity is open.[12]

For his part, Emerson recognized that it is spiritualized thinking that lifts the power of love completely out of animal instinct:

> Thought makes everything fit for use.... What would be base or even obscene, to the obscene, becomes illustrious, spoken in a new connection of thought. The piety of the ancient Hebrew prophets purges their grossness.[13]

The reader, as it happens, finds a good deal in Whitman that reminds him of the Hebrew prophets. But there can be no denying that in the young poet an element of willful grossness arose out of egoism and sensuality:

> Who goes there? hankering, gross, mystical, nude ...
> ("Song of Myself," 48)

Of this aspect of Whitman, Emerson wrote ruefully enough in a letter to a woman friend: "Our wild Whitman, with real inspiration but choked by Titanic abdomen...."[14] Yet these passages are comparatively rare. They are boastful, and we remember that boastfulness generally indicates some feeling that is less than sure of itself. We may well believe that in lines such as the one above, the poet is not describing the actuality of physical behavior but is, for special purposes, conjuring pictures intended to affirm his uncritical solidarity with the common man whom he so much wished to represent.

Whitman's strength lay in the fact that he was touched in the very bowels of compassion by sacred love. His love did not absorb light, but rather gave it off. It was an inspired religious force of sympathy that linked him intimately with the whole surrounding world and supplied him to overflowing with the resources of hope and love that he spent so prodigally upon his human brothers and sisters.

So-called profane "love" inevitably tends to contract into the cruelty of heedless, heartless desire. Captured by greed for selfish pleasure, it becomes an exploitative rather than a generous and productive kind of passion. When it is truly profane, nothing like Whitman's kind of compassion—his so abundant "milk of human kindness"—flows from it. Since it excludes infinitely more than it includes, there is actually far more of antipathy in it than of sympathy. While Whitman's far-reaching sympathy embraces perhaps even this kind of love, it was never typical of his own nature. That he loved things for their own sake was no pose; his idea of love is really the opposite of self-gratifying lust.

Let a man seek pleasure everywhere except in himself.
Let a woman seek happiness everywhere except in
 herself. ("Reversals," 364)

Such an ideal is neither licentious nor perverse, but rather pure, even as the unconscious, unegoistic necessities of nature's beings are pure. Beyond that, it is pure also as a conscious impulse of the human soul.

The continence of vegetables, birds, animals,
The consequent meanness of me should I skulk or find
 myself indecent, while birds and animals never once
 skulk or find themselves indecent,
The great chastity of paternity, to match the great
 chastity of maternity,
The great oath of procreation I have sworn....
 ("Spontaneous Me," 109)

THE GREAT OATH

What is this "great oath of procreation"?

From that of myself without which I were nothing,
From what I am determin'd to make illustrious,
 even if I stand sole among men...
 ("From Pent Up Aching Rivers," 94)

Of course, Whitman is speaking here of his male sexuality. A few lines further on, he says he is singing "the song of procreation." But what exactly does he wish to make illustrious, and why should this undertaking threaten to leave him standing alone among men? He is determined to raise to the level, not of mere respectability, but of highest honor, the very part that is most condemned by society in general. He sees just this part as serving the most intuitive as well as the most creative goals of the human soul and spirit. Thus he focuses upon what he conceives to be the integral connection between the lowest and the highest in human nature.

Whitman recognized that by ignorance of the true nature of what is called the lower man, modern humanity has, by its dark concepts and practices, been sabotaging inherent, high possibilities. He entertained, however, a mighty hope for the future. His oath of procreation refers to his determination to help realize this hope.

For Walt Whitman, virility and femininity are not some kind of low beginnings only. They are shining future goals for the complete and perfect development of men and women alike. What Goethe called the "eternal feminine" in *all* human beings draws them ever upward toward higher forms of beauty, goodness, and truth. What might be called the "heroic masculine" is that in *every* human being which masters circumstance to enact and establish these same ideals. As Whitman showed so plainly in his own development, the interplay between the masculine spirit and the feminine soul is something that altogether transcends physical sexuality since it takes place in both sexes. The two factors are but phases, on different levels, of the complete individuality of each human being.

Whitman's contention was that whatever is wrong with raw sexuality can be mastered and transmuted into true creativity by nothing less than love itself. To promulgate that doctrine and establish the example of such love, he felt himself both called and gifted.

Whitman's daimon permitted him no compromises; first of all, when it came to directing the light and warmth of open sunshine upon what had hitherto been held secret and dark: namely, the simple actuality of the bodily organs and acts of normal sex. This done, he had to evoke with convincing power the spiritual reality that lies behind these bodily symbols. By an inpouring of body-free love, he had to spiritualize sex. His task, therefore, implied two seemingly opposite purposes: out of the spirit, to draw down new health into the bodily function itself; and then to lift up from out of the body that eternal essence for which the body serves here on earth only as symbol and instrument. Whitman's songs of life had the first purpose; his songs of death, the second.

COURAGE TO BE

Whitman takes sex as the symbol of love and himself as the comprehensive symbol of sex. In affirming himself, he affirms the potency that he means to make illustrious. But the real power he celebrates is that of *the courage to be*, which shows itself primarily in the will—the will that supports free initiative and impregnates the world process creatively with what proceeds from the depths of the human spirit.

The male principle individualizes, and it is precisely the spirit of individuality that Whitman means to exemplify and hopes to awaken in those who come under his influence.

> The sky up there—yet here or next door,
>   or across the way?
> The saints and sages of history—but you yourself?
>   ("Song of Myself," 81)

He celebrates the female principle too, of course, and feels that he represents it equally well in his own soul. This is the principle that establishes rapport and builds community and that is receptive to the Idea, surrounding it with faithful memory and trusting love—with hopeful warmth to nurture and flesh it out over the course of time.

> The female contains all qualities and tempers them,
> She is in her place and moves with perfect balance,
> She is all things duly veil'd, she is both passive
>   and active,

> She is to conceive daughters as well as sons, and sons as
>   well as daughters.
> . . . .
>
> ———
>
> The male is not less the soul nor more, he too is in his
>   place,
> He too is all qualities, he is action and power,
> The flush of the known universe is in him,
> . . . .
> Knowledge becomes him, he likes it always,
>   he brings every thing to the test of himself.
>   ("I Sing the Body Electric," 101)

Whitman's single-minded dedication to rescuing the spiritual import of sex certainly placed him at times in danger. Yet the course of his life as a whole shows that he never lost sight of his essential purpose, for his message of grace grew ever clearer and stronger. The mood of his younger years, which had often been so emphatically physical, underwent a beautiful transformation as time went on. This change is apparent in the following passages; the first, from *The Children of Adam*, was written before he was forty, and the second, from his conversations with Traubel in Camden, at the age of sixty-nine:

> To be surrounded by beautiful, curious, breathing,
>   laughing flesh is enough,
> . . . .
> I do not ask any more delight, I swim in it as in a sea.
> There is something in staying close to men and women
>   and looking on them, and in the contact and odor
>   of them, that pleases the soul well,
> All things please the soul, but these please the
>   soul well. ("I Sing the Body Electric, " 99-100)

———

How many's the time I've just lived for days and days
    practically on my affections alone—the sight of my
    friends, the sky: thinking life away from, outside,
    all appetites.[15]

Whitman's great oath to celebrate "procreation" may well have taken form during the mystical deepening that occurred in his early thirties. On the whole, however, it remained decisive for him. The extraordinary immediacy of the ties he felt linking him—by the very nature of the constitution destiny gave him—with "the armies of those I love," placed upon him a sacred obligation to "respond" with his best.* He felt called on for the uniquely procreative deed that he identifies in the very first stanza of "I Sing the Body Electric":

They will not let me off till I go with them,
    respond to them,
And discorrupt them, and charge them full with the
    charge of the soul. (103)

The male sperm is of itself procreative, but more men

---

*While Whitman did not mean by these "armies" anything actually military, it is not to be overlooked that during the Civil War, as he himself recounts in *Specimen Days*, he spent untold strength of compassion in visiting sick, wounded, and dying soldiers.[16]

In my visits to the hospitals I found it was in the simple matter of personal presence, and emanating ordinary cheer and magnetism, that I succeeded and help'd more than by medical nursing, or delicacies, or gifts of money, or anything else. . . .

During those three years in hospital, camp or field, I made over six hundred visits or tours, and went, as I estimate . . . among from eighty thousand to a hundred thousand of the wounded and sick, as sustainer of spirit and body in some degree, in time of need. These visits varied from an hour or two, to all day or night; for dear or critical cases I generally watch'd all night. Sometimes I took up my quarters in the hospital, and slept or watch'd there several nights in succession. Those three years I consider the greatest privilege . . . and, of course, the most profound lesson of my life. I can say that in my ministerings I comprehended all, whoever came in my way, northern or southern, and slighted none. It arous'd and brought out and decided undreamt-of depths of emotion. It has given me my most fervent views of the true ensemble and extent of the States.

have sperm than are either masculine or creative. In any case, Whitman was not interested in adding to the physical population of his beloved "States," but rather in the starting of "countless immortal lives with countless embodiments." ("I Sing the Body Electric," 103) Within the souls that already exist, he said, there lie sleeping "greater heroes and bards." ("A Woman Waits For Me," 107) These souls should be awakened to their immortal possibilities. They need to be impregnated with the quickening flame of the eternal spirit. This fire was the intended substance of his poems, which are nothing less than distilled love—a germinal force, a power of creative will great enough, he imagined, to serve the whole nation. Clearly this is what is intended by the following typical line:

> I shall demand perfect men and women out of my love-spendings. ("A Woman Waits For Me," 107)

IN CONCLUSION

With considerable justice perhaps, one may accuse Whitman of overdoing a good thing. Yet that is more likely to be the judgment of people who have not yet seen quite into the heart of his great Ideal. Visionaries tend, indeed, to a certain monomania, but they should be forgiven it. The tempering that their impulse may need will come not from inhibitory strictures laid upon them by convention, but from further evolution of the living truth that originally possessed them and that they hoped to share with as many other human beings as possible. The dialectic of the free soul's own demand to become whole can be depended upon to discover and bring forward from within itself the truly appropriate counterbalance.

Walt Whitman felt that he had a sacred duty to perform, and he did it as best he could. There were moments when he knew full well, and painfully, the limitations of his own vision and power. In *Sea Drift*, he tells how one day in later life, while he was walking the shores of his native "Paumanok," the "electric self out of the pride of which I utter poems" suffered a confrontation with the same "fierce old mother," still "hoarse and sibilant," who had whispered the song of death to him in his childhood.

> As I wend to the shores I know not,
> As I list to the dirge, the voices of men and women wreck'd,
> As I inhale the impalpable breezes that set in upon me.
> As the ocean so mysterious rolls toward me closer and closer, I too but signify at the utmost a little wash'd-up drift,
> A few sands and dead leaves to gather,
> Gather, and merge myself as part of the sands and drift.
>
> O baffled, balk'd, bent to the very earth,
> Oppress'd with myself that I have dared to open my mouth,
> Aware now that amid all that blab whose echoes recoil upon me I have not once had the least idea who or what I am,
> But that before all my arrogant poems the real Me stands yet untouch'd, untold, altogether unreach'd
> Withdrawn far, mocking me with mock-congratulatory signs and bows,
> With peals of distant ironical laughter at every word I have written,
> Pointing in silence to these songs, and then to the sand beneath.
>
> I perceive I have not really understood any thing, not a single object, and that no man ever can,
> Nature here in sight of the sea taking advantage of me to dart upon me and sting me,

Because I have dared to open my mouth to sing at all.
("As I Ebb'd ... ," 263-4)

Walt Whitman knew his limitations, but he remained convinced of the fruitfulness of regarding the world-process as he did: that is, from the viewpoint of the creative force, divine in both origin and destination, that underlies all that exists and eternally evolves. In this force, essentially a force of *spiritual will that flowers in conscious love,* he saw concentrated the element of futurity that carries the living seeds of development through and past death itself.

* * *

In what follows, our attention will focus upon another distinguishing aspect of the poet's nature, namely, his extraordinary feeling of identification with the destiny of this American land and its people.

NOTES

1. "Emerson and Whitman," in *The Shock of Recognition*, Edmund Wilson, ed., 2 vols. (New York: Grosset and Dunlap, 1955), 247.

2. Henry Bryan Binns, *A Life of Walt Whitman* (New York: Haskell House, 1969), vii-viii.

3. Walt Whitman, "Song of Myself," *Leaves of Grass* (New York: Aventine Press, 1931), 35. Page numbers of further references to this book will be given by poem title in the text.

4. Wilson, *The Shock of Recognition*, op. cit., vol. 1, 265.

5. Ralph Waldo Emerson, "The Poet," *The Complete Essays and Other Writings of Ralph Waldo Emerson*, Brooks Atkinson, ed. (New York: Random House, 1950), 321. Hereafter referred to as *Essays*.

6. Wilson, *The Shock of Recognition*, op. cit., 289.

7. Emerson, "The Transcendentalist," *Essays*, 92.

8. Horace Traubel, *With Walt Whitman in Camden*, (New York: Rowman and Littlefield, 1961), vol. 1, 74.

9. Ibid., 76-7.

10. Emerson, "The Poet," *Essays*, 333.

11. Thoreau, in *The Shock of Recognition*, op. cit., 264-5.

12. Henry David Thoreau, "Walden," *Walden and Other Writings of Henry David Thoreau*, Brooks Atkinson, ed. (New York: Random House, 1950), 197.
13. Emerson, "The Poet," *Essays*, 327.
14. Emerson, as quoted in *The Shock of Recognition*, op.cit., 266.
15. Traubel, *With Walt Whitman in Camden*, op. cit., vol. 1, 172.
16. Whitman, "Specimen Days," *The Portable Walt Whitman*, Mark Van Doren, ed. (New York: Viking Press, 1960), 522 and 583-4.

5

WALT WHITMAN: THE NEW COLUMBUS

The scope and spirit of your paper on Democracy delight and satisfy me beyond all expectation, and I write without compliment or reserve to the man, the American Columbus, whose sagacity has thus sounded adventurously the sea of our Social Chaos and anchored his thought securely in the soil of the newly discovered Atlantides about which Grecian Plato died dreaming.
—Amos Bronson Alcott to Walt Whitman

BARD OF THE GREAT IDEA

WALT WHITMAN felt that as an American he was given a special awareness of what it means to be an individual. He wanted to make his country aware of its historically unique function and advantage in this respect. He would have America find its reason for existence in this secret of individuality. Yet he realized, of course, that the essential human individuality is not to be found in nationality, and this, too, he would have America know.

Can one think of another relationship to America as personally impassioned as Walt Whitman's? There are and have been wonderfully patriotic souls, loyal in the best sense to their country, among them statesmen and soldiers who with foresight and high purpose have placed their lives in its service; indeed, countless men and women who have loved, prayed, and worked for its welfare. But is there another who presumed to speak for its very soul, who felt himself destined to be its living conscience, and believed in his unique power to fructify it? Is there another personality who assumed such a privileged relationship?

Somehow the poet felt it was appropriate that the spirit of America should call upon him to give it voice, a voice not otherwise to be heard, for he saw himself as effectively "incarnating his land, attracting it body and soul to himself ... his spirit surrounding his country's spirit."

> By blue Ontario's shore,
> As I mused ...
> A Phantom gigantic superb, with stern visage
>   accosted me,
> *Chant me the poem*, it said, *that comes from*
>   *the soul of America* ...
> *And sing me ... the song of the throes of Democracy.*[1]

Whitman realizes of course that there will and must be others who will also undertake to speak for America:

> I listened to the Phantom by Ontario's shore,
> I heard the voice arising demanding bards.
> . . . .
> For the great Idea, the idea of perfect and free
>   individuals,
> For that, the bard walks in advance, leader
>   of leaders.
> . . . .
> Bards of the great Idea! ... You by my charm I invoke.
>   ("By Blue Ontario's Shore," 353, 355, 364)

But whoever you are, he continues, you must "surely be questioned beforehand by me with many and stern questions: "Who are you indeed who would talk or sing to America? ... What is this you bring my America? Is it uniform with my country?" ("By Blue Ontario's Shore," 356-7) For he asks of the American Spirit, "Who except myself has yet conceiv'd what your children en-masse really are?" ("Long, Too Long America," 320)

Starting from Paumanok, Long Island, where he was born, the poet means, in unmistakable terms, to set an example of the *individual* human being who has become conscious of his or her unique worth in the cosmic scheme. Whitman will have his native land, this New World, impregnated with the new spirit that properly belongs to it.

> Solitary, singing in the West, I strike up for a New
>   World.
> . . . .
> See, projected through time,
> For me an audience interminable.
> . . . .
> . . . Americanos, a hundred millions,
> One generation playing its part and passing on,
> Another generation playing its part and passing on in
>   its turn,
> With faces turn'd sideways or backward toward me
>   to listen,
> With eyes retrospective toward me.
>   ("Starting From Paumanok," 14-15)

Obviously this "me," to which millions of ears in future generations are imagined to be listening as though to receive their clue, and toward which all eyes are seen to be turning, is not merely Walt Whitman, the physical person of a certain brief moment in time. It is something more, something timeless, typified or represented by that person. For this "solitary" individual thinks of himself as really only the voice of the national spirit, the national conscience, which requires of its citizens that they learn to accept at last the duty of moral self-determination, reminding each separately that he or she has indeed been made in the image of divinity. And it proclaims therefore that the national purpose of America shall be to advance the cause of creative freedom, which is none other than the cause of Individuality.

This principle, as Whitman means it, deserves the capital letters he gives it; for he feels that it is precisely this "great Idea" that is seeking to impregnate the human race in the New Age. It is the evolutionary unfolding of this new consciousness that has characterized the whole modern era, beginning with the famous explorers, discoverers, and inventors of the Renaissance—beginning, indeed, with the time when a Genoese mariner opened up the New World.

> Give me to sing the songs of the great Idea,
>   take all the rest.
> . . . .
> I swear I begin to see the meaning of these things,
> It is not the earth, it is not America who is so great,
> It is I who am great or to be great, it is You up there,
>   or any one,
> It is to walk rapidly through civilizations,
>   governments, theories,
> Through poems, pageants, shows, to form individuals.
>
> Underneath all, individuals,
> I swear nothing is good to me now that ignores
>   individuals,
> . . . .
> The whole theory of the universe is directed
>   unerringly to one single individual—namely
>   to You.
>   ("By Blue Ontario's Shore," 358,360)

Whitman would sing the modern individual as "a simple, separate person." But this person is to be celebrated only to make him aware of something in himself that is far from simple and far from separate. For in every human form there dwells the soul, and in the soul, the spirit—the unlimited, all-embracing, all-perfecting Universal.

> Come said the Muse,
> Sing me a song no poet yet has chanted,
> Sing me the universal.
>
> In this broad earth of ours,
> Amid the measureless grossness and the slag,
> Enclosed and safe within its central heart,
> Nestles the seed perfection.
> . . . .
>
> And thou America,
> For the scheme's culmination, its thought
>   and its reality,
> For these (not for thyself) thou hast arrived.
> . . . .
> Embracing carrying welcoming all, thou too by
>   pathways broad and new,
> To the ideal tendest.
> . . . .
> Only the good is universal.
>
>   ("Song of the Universal," 234-6)

Whitman feared that unless this secret of destiny—the truth of what constitutes the goodness of Individuality or the truly free spirit—could be brought to consciousness among his fellow Americans, the nation would remain asleep, continuing to flounder in materialism, blundering forward without purpose or compass, expending its magnificent energies pointlessly, too often with results both ugly and destructive. These concerns he set forth plainly in his *Democratic Vistas* (see Chapter Eight).

The poet believed the time had come for his nation to discover its real reason for being and to awaken to its moral and spiritual purpose in the mind of the God of nations. This discovery had no doubt to be made first by exceptional men and women in their own souls; from them it would then pass into the nation as a whole. But among those chosen to be such discoverers and representatives of the great Idea, no doubt one would stand out as foremost. One would be, as Alcott said, America's new Columbus.

Whitman originally sensed this "new Columbus" in his compatriot Emerson, because it was Emerson who first shocked him awake to himself. "I was simmering, simmering, simmering; Emerson brought me to a boil."[2] In the second edition of his *Leaves of Grass*, which appeared in 1856, Whitman printed his reply to the encouragement he had received earlier from Emerson.

> Of course, we shall have national character, an identity.... Such character ... is to stand compact upon that vast basis of the supremacy of Individuality—that new moral American continent. Those shores you found. I say that none has ever done, or ever can do, a greater deed for the States, than your deed.... [It] is yours to have been the original true Captain who put to sea, intuitive, positive, rendering the first report....[3]

The older man had awakened Whitman to what it meant to be truly an individual, a divine average human being. But Emerson's "intellectual Declaration of Independence" (in the words of Oliver Wendell Holmes) was based upon *spiritual self-discovery*. "In self-trust all the virtues are comprehended," was his quiet affirmation.[4] Perhaps most who read Emerson today will pass by such a sentence without a tremor, or they may be beguiled by a mistakenly simplistic, egoistic interpretation of it. But for Whitman, this pronouncement must have come like a bolt of lightning; its penetration must have been profound and its reverberations prolonged. Every further line of Emerson's gospel added to the blaze kindled by such words. Again and again, Emerson was sounding the very notes his nation most needed to hear—notes that Whitman felt himself destined to carry further on his own. Then, too, in a passage like the following, he seemed to be hearing the very accents of his own voice. He must have encountered in these sentiments, in this orientation, a mandate for himself—not only surprising, but profoundly congenial to his own genius, disposition, and awakening intuition.

> I ask not for the great, the remote, the romantic; what is doing in Italy or Arabia; what is Greek art, or Provencal minstrelsy; I embrace the common. I explore and sit at the feet of the familiar, the low. Give me insight into today, and you may have the antique and future worlds.... The meal in the firkin; the milk in the pan; the ballad in the street; the news of the boat; the glance of the eye, the form and gait of the body; show me the ultimate reason of these matters; show me the sublime presence of the highest spiritual cause lurking, as always it does lurk, in these suburbs and extremities of nature....[5]

THE NEW COLUMBUS

In 1882, the year of Emerson's death, Whitman wrote again of the one whom he had earlier addressed as "Master." But this time his reference to Emerson as the literary Columbus of America had undergone a sea change. After complaining that so much of the world's literature "seems at its best some little fleet of boats, hugging the shore of a boundless sea, and never venturing, exploring the unmapp'd—never, Columbus-like, sailing out for New Worlds, and to complete the orb's rondure," he went on to qualify his judgment of Emerson. The Concord sage, he said, writes frequently "in the atmosphere of this thought, and his books report one or two things from that very ocean and air...." His words are "more legibly address'd to our age and American polity than by any man yet."[6] But there is little doubt that with the passage of time, though Whitman continued to esteem and love his great friend as warmly as ever and still thought of him as "Columbus-like," he came eventually to feel that he himself was actually much closer to the Admiral of the Ocean Sea.

In what follows, I must ask the reader's trust, for my purpose in dwelling in some detail upon the powerful affinity that existed in Whitman's feeling, between himself and Columbus, may not at first be clear, and it requires us to make something of a detour. In my view, making this detour should help us to introduce important aspects of the poet's nature that reach beyond what has been suggested in the foregoing chapter. It may have the further, if parenthetical, advantage of broadening our theme, "American Heralds of the Spirit," to include—on this 500th anniversary of America's historical beginning—the discoverer himself. Whitman, one feels, would have thought this most appropriate.

Historical interpretation presently tends to identify Columbus with the greedy and heartless rapacity of many of the conquistadors who followed him. Instances of unsavory treatment of this new land's inhabitants are being cited. Certainly he was a man of his time, and our later, presumably more enlightened age views with abhorrence behavior that was commonplace then. Yet I see little to be gained and much to be lost by overemphasizing the limitations of this adopted national hero, when so much good can come from remembrance of what was heroic and may even have been holy about him. Whitman encourages us to feel that high destiny did indeed inspire and guide the Admiral's ocean-crossing. And he felt that it was from this same spirit that he himself as a poet sought inspiration and guidance for the America of his own time.

It is therefore not surprising to find that one of the greatest poems of Whitman's mature years was "Passage to India," and one of his most moving, written at about the same time, was his "Prayer of Columbus." In a telling passage, his early biographer, Henry Bryan Binns, calls attention to the importance for the poet of his ever more deeply felt relationship to the mariner.

> Simple and direct, the "Prayer of Columbus" breathes the religious spirit in which it is conceived. Lonely, poor and paralyzed, battered and old, upon the margin of the great ocean of death, [the poet] pours out his heart and tells the secret of his life; for, as Whitman himself confessed, it is he who speaks under thin historical disguise.[7]

We shall return to these two poems, which powerfully attest to the spirituality of the bond Whitman felt for Christopher Columbus. But similarities in the two men's psychology underlie this bond and therefore also deserve mention. First and basic among the dispositions Whitman shared with Columbus was, obviously, the poet's lifelong affinity for the sea and its ships.

> Everything that belonged to the sea exercised a spell over him. The first vision that made him desire the gift of words was that of a full-rigged ship; and the love of ships and shipping remained a passion with him to the end; so that when he sought to describe his own very soul it was as a ship he figured it.[8]

But O the ship, the immortal ship!
O ship aboard the ship!
Ship of the body, ship of the soul, voyaging
    voyaging, voyaging.
("Aboard at a Ship's Helm," 260)

Whitman was of course no ocean sailor, but in *Specimen Days* he looks back to his love for ferries:

> What oceanic currents, eddies, underneath—the great tides of humanity also, with ever-shifting movements. Indeed, I have always had a passion for ferries; to me they afford inimitable streaming, never-failing poems.[9]

The carry-over from love of the sea to the quality of his poetic themes and lines was inevitable and deeply satisfying to the poet. He wrote of his poetry:

> The want for something finished, completed, and technically beautiful will certainly not be supplied by this writer, as it is by existing esthetic works.... Its likeness is not the solid stately palace, nor the sculpture that adorns it, nor the paintings on its walls. Its analogy is the Ocean. Its verses are the liquid, billowy waves, ever rising and falling, perhaps sunny and smooth, perhaps wild with storm, always moving, always alike in their nature as rolling waves, but hardly any two exactly alike in size or measure (meter), never having the sense of something finished and fixed, always suggesting *something beyond*. (Emphasis added)[10]

SOMETHING BEYOND

It is this sense of the spiritual "something beyond," which he ever affirmed and toward which he felt ever drawn, that lies at the root of Whitman's feeling for the sea, as well as of Columbus' extraordinary adventures. Was not the latter also really seeking something beyond? His marine explorations are usually thought of as physical in motive as well as in fact; yet behind them may there not somehow have reigned a higher, if unconscious, purpose, namely, the role the new continent was to play in opening up the modern age? The discoverer, of course, could have had no real conception of this future destiny, in either practical or theoretical terms; yet one can imagine it as somehow an obscurely inspiring force within him. Was it not part of his extraordinary faith and courage? Whitman, one believes, would have said Yes. While the seas he sailed were metaphysical rather than physical, they were equally untraveled, equally perilous. The stubborn resolve they demanded of him could be regarded as very similar, though in a different dimension, to that which sustained the great navigator. The markers of his own adventure into the unknown were not exploratory leagues traveled but poems written. Very many of those poems he drew from the sea, and all were tuned to it.

> *Here are our thoughts, voyagers' thoughts,*
> *Here not the land, firm land, alone appears . . .*
> *The sky o'erarches here, we feel the undulating*
>   *deck beneath our feet,*
> *We feel the long pulsation, ebb and flow of endless*
>   *motion,*
> *The tones of unseen mystery, the vague and vast*
>   *suggestions of the briny world, the liquid-flowing*
>   *syllables,*
> *The perfume, the faint creaking of the cordage,*
>   *the melancholy rhythm,*
> *The boundless vista and the horizon far and dim*
>   *are all here,*
> *And this is ocean's poem.*
>
>   ("In Cabin'd Ships at Sea," 2-3)

The poet chose the above lines, italicized by him, to open the final edition of his often revised and enlarged *Leaves of Grass*. He concluded the work of a lifetime with the following oceanic contemplation:

> Grand is the seen, the light, to me—grand are
>   the sky and stars,
> Grand is the earth, and grand are lasting time and space,
> And grand their laws, so multiform, puzzling,
>   evolutionary;
> But grander far the unseen soul of me,
>   comprehending, endowing all those,
> Lighting the light, the sky and stars, delving
>   the earth, sailing the sea,
> (What were all those, indeed, without thee,
>   unseen soul? of what amount without thee?)
> More evolutionary, vast, puzzling, O my soul!
> More multiform far—more lasting thou than they.
>   ("Grand is the Sun," 561)

Whitman's was a ship of the soul. His destination was what lies invisibly "beyond" the manifest. But to assert that the same, germinally at least, may also have been the case with Christopher Columbus is to depart from what American children are taught in school. Students are usually led to imagine that the aim Columbus had set himself was simply economic (and even, eventually, a plundering expedition). He sought to find a shorter sea route for European ships seeking trade with the Far East. Viewed in this way, he would seem, in marked contrast to Whitman, to have been of an eminently practical mind: one, perhaps, which was spurred primarily by worldly ambition, encouraged in turn by shrewd new calculations as to the curvature of the physical earth.

In Columbus' time, the student is told, the Far East was beginning to be known through adventurous spirits who traveled overland eastward from Europe, but sailors avoided traveling too far to the West by sea, lest they come upon the fearsome Abyss at the end of the world. To the far West lay terrible dangers, a realm unknown but certainly fatal to human beings. But of this paralyzing supposition Columbus was apparently skeptical. One is asked to picture him as an adventurer who simply trusted in his five senses, his cool reason, his own derring-do, and perhaps his acquisitive instinct. If he harbored any higher purpose beyond the commercial one with its promise of fame and riches, we are asked to suppose that it was precisely the desire to dispel the fears based on ignorance and religious superstition.

Perhaps it is right to think of Columbus' travels as being inspired not by any mystical, Whitmanesque urge to pass beyond known material limits into the beckoning spiritual Unknown. His may have been a contrary will: to release his contemporaries from a frightening "spiritual" Unknown that was blocking the material benefits that await those who have the audacity to trust in scientific calculations. Undeniably, such an attitude may have played a part in his motivation; and if so, it would sharply contrast with what inspired Whitman. But many of Columbus's own words sound a different note. Consider, for example, his own translation of a favorite passage from Seneca's play, *Medea*. In these lines, he obviously saw his own destiny prefigured.

> There will come a time after many years when the Ocean will loose the chains that fetter things, and the great world will lie revealed, and a new mariner, like unto him who was Jason's pilot ... will reveal a new world, and then Thule will not be the most extreme of all lands.[11]

Evidently, Columbus was captivated at least as much by the spirit of prophecy as by the motives of either commercial or scientific enterprise. His own *Book of Prophecies*, written about 1500, was a collection of all the passages to be found in Scripture that he could regard as having predicted his discovery of the New World. In introducing this work to his Sovereigns, he explained that the ultimate purpose of his voyaging was to recapture the Holy Sepulchre for the Holy Church.

Columbus begins his introduction by describing his extensive experience as a mariner and goes on to tell of how God gave him gifts that further prepared him for his great feats of navigation: a grasp of the tools of astrology, geometry, and arithmetic as well as the techniques of accurate mapping. He emphasizes, however, that mere knowledge and experience of this kind could never have enabled him to achieve his goal, for it was not *with* the counsel of worldly learned men that he had to proceed, but *against* it. The real force that propelled him at all times, the star that guided him throughout, he claimed to have found in the prophetic testimonies of the Old and New Testaments and in the twenty-three Epistles of the Holy Apostles.

As a biographer informs us, "He goes on to say that he learned to forget all his earlier knowledge and experience and to put his whole trust in Holy Scripture and in certain prophecies of holy men" (*Columbus*, 155).

> It is possible that Your Highnesses and any others who know me, and who might come to see this document, may privately or publicly find fault with me on various grounds, and say that I am not a man of learning, and call me a half-crazed mariner, a mere layman, etc. I swear in the words of St. Matthew: "I thank thee, O Father, Lord of heaven and earth, because thou hast hid these things from the wise and prudent, and hast revealed them unto babes."

In such sentiments, Columbus portrays himself not as learned or shrewd beyond other men, but as a babe in the trusting simplicity of his aims and his faith in guidance from that higher Source for whom human knowledge is but folly. He continues:

I will speak of one [prophecy], because it is connected with my enterprise, and it gives me peace and bestows contentment upon me whenever I think of it.... *I have already said that neither reason nor mathematics nor maps of the world were of any help to me, that I should fulfill the enterprise of the Indies. But the words of Isaiah were completely fulfilled,* and this is what I wish to write here, that it may be firmly set in Your Highnesses' minds. [Emphasis added]

"Listen, O isles, unto me: and hearken, ye people from afar; The Lord hath called me from the womb; from the bowels of my mother hath he made mention of my name .... I will also give thee for a light to the Gentiles, that thou mayest be my salvation unto the end of the earth.... Surely the isles shall wait for me, and the ships of Tarshish first, to bring thy sons from afar, their silver and their gold with them.... For, behold, I create new heavens and a new earth...." (*Columbus*, 155)

Of course, if one consults the book of Isaiah itself, there is no doubt that its prophecies all centered, not on the awaited discoveries of a future Genoese sailor, but on the advent of the Savior, Christ Jesus. That the great navigator should have lifted a sentence here and another there out of the original text, so as to piece together a favorable prophecy concerning his own achievement, is certainly cause for wonder. Was he willfully fooling himself or trying to beguile his royal sponsors?

Perhaps there is an element of truth in both charges. Yet though we may conceive of his time, in certain aspects, as devoutly gullible to a fault and religiously naive perhaps, neither he nor his patrons were stupid. It is hardly conceivable that the original meaning of Isaiah's prophecies could have been unknown to either party. Indeed, it is hard to imagine how Columbus' presumption in arrogating to himself this particular scripture could have seemed anything less than sacrilegious in the eyes of pious believers.

"I CELEBRATE MYSELF"

Columbus' interpretation of Isaiah may be compared with many of Whitman's proclamations concerning himself and his task. The same enigma appears in both, namely, unlimited boasting that yet is not meant as boasting. The "Song of Myself," for example, may be seen as a lengthy exercise in self-glorification. It celebrates what the poet finds uniquely in himself, but it does so only because what he finds there stands for what waits to be found equally by others in themselves.

In "Song of Myself" Whitman spends many pages recounting instances of his gift for identifying himself completely with all manner of other human beings in their joys, trials, battles, sicknesses, and sufferings. Then comes this canto that readers may tend to pass over because it is certainly difficult, and can at first seem incredibly presumptuous. Whitman seems to identify himself with the One who suffered torture and ignominy upon the cross, yet overcame death and rose again to secure eternal life for all humanity. Yet, who accomplished this? Not the man Jesus, but the God in him who represents what all people have in common in their ultimate depths, if they will but recognize it.

> Enough! enough! enough!
> Somehow I have been stunn'd. Stand back!
> Give me a little time beyond my cuff'd head,
>   slumbers, dreams, gaping,
> I discover myself on the verge of a usual mistake.
> That I could forget the mockers and insults!
> That I could forget the trickling tears and the
>   blows of the bludgeons and hammers!
> That I could look with a separate look on my own
>   crucifixion and bloody crowning.
> I remember now,
> I sense the overstaid fraction,

> The grave of rock multiplies what has been confided
>   to it, or to any graves,
> Corpses rise, gashes heal, fastenings roll from me.
> I troop forth replenish'd with supreme power,
>   one of an average unending procession,
> Inland and sea-coast we go, and pass all
>   boundary lines,
> Our swift ordinances on their way over the whole earth,
> The blossoms we wear in our hats the growth of
>   thousands of years.
>
>   ("Song of Myself," 74-5)

After further difficult and seemingly extravagant passages of a similar kind, Whitman relents with this mitigating confession and pledge:

> I know perfectly well my own egotism,
> Know my omnivorous lines and must not write any less,
> And would fetch you whoever you are flush with myself.
>
>   ("Song of Myself," 80)

It becomes apparent that the poet was not a megalomaniac, after all, but rather a participating witness of the drama of Selfhood's experience on earth, exemplified by the Passion of Jesus. In considering the analogy between Columbus' self-advertisement and Whitman's, it is possible to conceive that the mariner in his apparent arrogance is also basing himself upon a large-hearted rather than a purely egoistic understanding of his relationship to divinity. In applying to himself prophecies meant originally for Another, could he perhaps have justified or excused himself somewhat in this manner? "You who read my *Book of Prophecies*, trouble not yourselves about the undisputed first meaning of these passages, but read attentively nevertheless, with an open attitude. Do you not find remarkable the many ways in which each of these prophecies, as by coincidence, even in details, applies faithfully also to the ventures that have fallen to my lot? Is it not permissible, indeed, to view especially what touches the life of the Son of Man—the life of the Savior—as the prototype and foreshadowing of developments in the diverse lives of all human beings who take Him as their model?"

All allowances having been made, one must still grant that there remains a distinct sense of hubris in the posture of Columbus, a self-pride closely resembling Whitman's. This quality I shall not try to characterize further, except to suggest that while it may have been essentially innocent in both cases, it may also have been one of the factors most responsible for the dismissal and rejection they encountered in their own time, which both men suffered as the bitter fruit of all their labors.

Whatever may have been the complex motives behind the *Book of Prophecies* Columbus so assiduously compiled, there can be no doubt about his reverence for prophetic utterances and his feeling for himself as a man of destiny. Such an orientation is not that of one who trusts primarily in his own personal abilities. It indicates, rather, an enthusiastic and visionary outlook on life, one that believes in revelation as a valid source of guidance for earthly undertakings. How open Columbus himself was to seek and to receive at firsthand such guidance from a higher source is apparent in the story his son Ferdinand tells of a great storm at sea his father confronted and seemingly quelled. The same is demonstrated as well in the father's own account of still another major crisis suffered off the coast of the New World.

First, we have Ferdinand's record of this event, as quoted and supplemented by Samuel Eliot Morison:

"Besides these divers terrors there occurred one no less dangerous and wonderful, a waterspout which on Tuesday December 13 passed by the ships, the which had they not dissolved by reciting the Gospel according to St. John, it would have swamped whatever it struck without a doubt; for, it draws water up to the clouds in a column thicker than a water-butt, twisting it about like a whirlwind." It was the Admiral who exorcised the waterspout. From his Bible he read an account of that famous tempest off Capernaum, concluding, "Fear not, it is I!" Then, clasping the Bible in his left hand, with drawn sword he traced a cross in the sky and a circle around his whole fleet.[12]

Obviously, Columbus did not content himself with merely pouring over Holy Writ, for in practical exigencies he applied his religious conviction with full force. That he was also capable of his own mystical experiences appears from this account, written to his Sovereigns in 1502:

> I was outside and all alone on this very dangerous coast, with a high fever and greatly exhausted. There was no hope of rescue. In this state ... groaning with exhaustion, I fell asleep, and I heard a most merciful voice saying: "O fool, so slow to believe and to serve thy God, the God of all! What more did He do for Moses or for his servant David: He has had thee in His care from thy mother's womb. When He saw thee a grown man, He caused thy name to resound most greatly over the earth. He gave thee the keys to the gates of the Ocean, which were held with such great chains. Thou wast obeyed in many lands, and thou hast won a mighty name among Christians. What more did He do for the people of Israel when He led them out of Egypt, or for David, that shepherd boy whom He made a king in Jewry? Turn thyself to Him, and acknowledge thy sins. His mercy is infinite. Thine old age shall not prevent thee from achieving great things, for many and vast are His domains. ...
>
> Thou criest for help, with doubt in thy heart. Ask thyself who has afflicted thee so grievously and so often: God or the world? The privileges and covenants which God giveth are not taken back by Him. Nor does He say to

them that have served Him that He meant it otherwise, or that it should be taken in another sense; nor does He inflict torments to show His power. Whatever He promises He fulfills with increase; for such are His ways. Thus have I told thee what thy Creator has done for thee, and for all men. He has now revealed to me some of those rewards which await thee for the many toils and dangers which thou hast endured in the service of others." I heard all this as if in a trance, but I could find no reply to give to so sure a message, and all I could do was to weep over my transgressions. Whoever it was that had spoken, ended by saying: "Fear not, but have faith. All these tribulations are written upon tablets of marble, and there is reason for them." (*Columbus*, 172-3)

We may detect in this account a number of statements and sentiments calculated to touch Queen Isabella in her piety so as to exert a certain influence upon her. Plain is the discoverer's hope of being restored to favor at court and granted once again those powers and privileges that he thought had been promised and were now, unjustly, being denied him. But we have no grounds for supposing the experience essentially falsified.

There are others who confirm the piety and faith of Columbus' own life-habits. His son Ferdinand, for example, relates that "in matters of religion he was so strict that for fasting and saying the canonical offices he might have been taken for a member of a religious order." And Las Casas, the son of an associate close to the Admiral, testifies to what he heard from his father as well as from Columbus himself:

> In matters of the Christian religion, without doubt he was ... of great devotion.... [He] was most devoted to our Lady and to the seraphic father St. Francis; seemed very grateful to God for benefits received from the divine hand,

wherefore, as in the proverb, he hourly admitted that God had conferred upon him great mercies.... And he was especially affected and devoted to the idea that God should deem him worthy of aiding somewhat in recovering the Holy Sepulchre.[13]

MEN OF DESTINY

In seeking to compare the life-gestures, the styles, of the two men, Whitman and Columbus, I have suggested that in the latter's *Book of Prophecies*, as in the narration of his mystical experience, there is a strain that reminds us strongly of Whitman. While Whitman was generally modest and unassuming in his social relationships, when it came to his feeling for the high destiny he believed himself called to serve and to his drive to ensure what he conceived to be the advancement of this great life-work, he was notoriously capable of both "brag" and cunning. Over the years, many a glowing newspaper advertisement and review of the poet's work seems to have been penned by the poet himself. As an experienced journalist and editor, he knew how such things could be managed. He is said himself to have written a major portion of John Burrough's admiring *Whitman: A Study*. Especially in his early maturity he was ever ready to present himself in grand terms and to hear his *Leaves of Grass* spoken of fulsomely. No doubt he felt justified by his conviction that he represented a much more important cause than his own personality. No doubt he conceived that it was up to him personally to proclaim his impersonal significance at every turn, because he felt both that his role *was* unique and that he knew its worth better than any other person could. That Walt Whitman may conceivably have reasoned thus to himself need not, of course, prevent our perceiving something a little excessive in the trend to self-glorification that characterized both him and the Discoverer to whom he looked as to a kindred soul.

A contemporary of Columbus has left us his account of the unfavorable impression Columbus sometimes made upon those to whom he sought to recommend his cause. He describes a scene in which the mariner was petitioning the King of Portugal for aid:

> The king, as he observed this *Christovao Colom* to be a big talker and boastful in setting forth his accomplishments, and fuller of fancy and imagination with his Isle of Cypango [Japan] than certain whereof he spoke, gave him small credit.[14]

Son Ferdinand, however, as might perhaps be expected, viewed his father's presentation of himself more charitably:

> For the Admiral, being a man of generous and lofty thoughts, would covenant [bargain? demand?] to his great honor and advantage, in order to have his own reputation and the dignity of his house conform to the grandeur of his work and of his merits.[15]

Whitman made an essentially similar claim upon the future. He wanted to be recognized uniquely for having been the one to declare and champion America's special destiny, setting it apart from all that had gone before. The main difference between the two men lies not in the degree of their self-promotion, but in the quality of the reward they expected. Columbus showed the greater concern for worldly values, even though in his mind these were also linked with the spiritual. He sought to assure himself and his heirs of all the honor, authority, and a good share of the revenue that he imagined must certainly in time accrue from his great discovery. This eventuality, of course, was not to be and could not have been; yet for these things he "covenanted" stubbornly to the end, believing such to have been promised him. Though honorific titles were held out to him—Admiral of the Ocean Sea, Viceroy, Governor—he recognized that these of themselves had small practical significance, and, indeed, it was complete deprivation and dishonor, even to the point of prison and chains, he would be required to endure.

MODESTY, MODERATION, AND PATIENT FORBEARANCE

To balance the self-assertion exhibited by both these men, the other and more endearing side of their characters should be given its due. Bishop Las Casas did not deny that Columbus was "eloquent and boastful in his negotiations"; but he took no offense from this observation. Rather, he was at pains to round out the picture, which, here again, can remind us of Whitman. Christopher Columbus, wrote Las Casas,

> was serious in moderation, affable with strangers, and with members of his household gentle and pleasant, with modest gravity and discreet conversation; and so could easily incite those who saw him to love him. In fine, he was most impressive in his port and countenance, a person of great state and authority and worthy of all reverence. He was sober and moderate in eating, drinking, clothing and footwear....
>
> He was a gentleman of great force of spirit, of lofty thoughts, naturally inclined (from what one may gather of his life, deeds, writings and conversation) to undertake worthy deeds and signal enterprises; patient and long-suffering ... and a forgiver of injuries, and wished nothing more than that those who offended against him should recognize their errors, and that the delinquents be reconciled with him; most constant and endowed with forbearance in the hardships and adversities which were always occurring and which were incredible and infinite; ever holding fresh confidence in divine providence.[16]

Descriptions of the poet that we have from his friends and followers bear a marked resemblance to that given of the Admiral by Las Casas. Dr. Richard Maurice Bucke, for example, who had ample opportunity to make physical and psychological observations of the mature Whitman, sketched his findings in the book *Cosmic Consciousness*:

> The habitual expression of his face is repose, but there is a well-marked firmness and decision. I have never seen his look, even momentarily, express contempt, or any vicious feeling. I have never known him to sneer at any person or thing, or to manifest in any way or degree either alarm or apprehension, though he has in my presence been placed in circumstances that would have caused both in most men.
>
> Walt Whitman's dress was always extremely plain ... he dressed in a substantial, neat, plain, common way ... indeed, an exquisite aroma of cleanliness has always been one of the special features of the man; ... and no one could know him for an hour without seeing that it penetrated his mind and life, and was in fact the expression of a purity which was physical as much as moral, and moral as much as physical. Walt Whitman, in my talks with him at that time, always disclaimed any lofty intention in himself or his poems. If you accepted his explanations they were simple and commonplace. But when you came to think about these explanations, and to enter into the spirit of them, you found that the simple and commonplace with him included the ideal and the spiritual.[17]

Bucke's appraisal of the man may have been idealized; yet it is substantially confirmed by Binns, the discerning biographer:

> His love of silence, his spiritual caution, his veracity and simplicity of speech, his soul-sight, and the practical balance of his mysticism—that temperance of character upon which his inspirational faculties were founded—and,

finally, the equal democratic goodwill he showed all men; these qualities speak the original Quaker type [though to the Society of Friends Whitman never nominally belonged].[18]

Not to be overlooked is the affinity with St. Francis exhibited by both Columbus and Whitman. The special devotion of Columbus to the saint, as witnessed by Bishop Las Casas, is similar to the relationship suggested in the case of Whitman. The intimate spiritual kinship with all natural beings that comes to expression in Francis' "Hymn to Brother Sun" could stand as the prototype of the poet's whole experience of nature.

In the simplicity of his life-habits, in his ever-deepening religious commitment, and in his charity and power of human sympathy, the poet—despite conspicuous differences in certain respects—might be regarded as a disciple of whom the saint would have been proud. Passages, such as the following, on the themes of religion, nature, and humanity show how close in sentiment they were.

> I say the whole earth and all the stars in the sky
>   are for religion's sake
> I say no man has ever yet been half devout enough,
> . . . .
> Know you, solely to drop in the earth the germs of a
>   greater religion,
> The following chants each for its kind I sing.[29]
>   ("Starting from Paumanok," 19-20)

> I have loved the earth, sun, animals, I have despised
>   riches,
> I have given alms to every one that ask'd, stood up for
>   the stupid and crazy, devoted my income and labor
>   to others, . . .
>   ("Song of Myself," 54)

Not till the sun excludes you do I exclude you,
Not till the waters refuse to glisten for you and the
   leaves to rustle for you, do my words refuse to
   glisten and rustle for you.
                              ("To a Common Prostitute," 394-5)

And I know that the spirit of God is the brother
   of my own,
And that all the men ever born are also my brothers,
   and the women my sisters . . .
And that a kelson of the creation is love.
                              ("Song of Myself," 33)

I am he attesting sympathy. ("Song of Myself," 51)

Agonies are one of my changes of garments,
I do not ask the wounded person how he feels,
   I myself become the wounded person.
                              ("Song of Myself," 69)

Of course, we know far less about the sentiments of Columbus than about those of Whitman, but Ferdinand's observations concerning his father have attested to comparable Francis-like traits.

FAITH AND SUFFERING IN TWO LIVES

Walt Whitman's own conception of the man with whom he so closely identified himself in sickness as in health, in failure as in success, in old age as in youth, comes to vivid expression in his "Prayer of Columbus." He pictures the Admiral "near the close of his indomitable and pious life—on his last [fourth] voyage, when nearly 70 years of age. . . ." (Actually, Christopher Columbus was about fifty-two at this time, and Whitman about fifty-four when he composed his "Prayer." At fifty-three, the poet had suffered a stroke that left him partially paralyzed for the remaining eighteen years of his life.)

In the prayer, Whitman speaks for Columbus, whom he visualizes being shipwrecked on Jamaica, "where laid up for a long and miserable year—1503—he was taken very sick, had several relapses, his men revolted, and death seemed daily imminent; though he was eventually rescued, and sent home to Spain to die, unrecognized, and neglected and in want...."[19] As Bucke comments: "The prayer is in reality, of course, Walt Whitman's own and all the allusions in it are to his own life, work, and fortunes—to himself."[20]

> A batter'd, wrecked old man,
> Thrown on this savage shore, far, far from home,
> Pent by the sea and dark rebellious brows, twelve dreary months,
> Sore, stiff with many toils, sicken'd and nigh to death,
> I take my way along the island's edge,
> Venting a heavy heart.
>
> I am too full of woe!
> Haply I may not live another day;
> I cannot rest O God, I cannot eat or drink or sleep,
> Till I put forth myself, my prayer, once more to Thee,
> Breathe, bathe myself once more in Thee, commune with Thee,
> Report myself once more to Thee.
>
> Thou knowest my years entire, my life,
> My long and crowded life of active work, not adoration merely;
> Thou knowest the prayers and vigils of my youth,
> Thou knowest my manhood's solemn and visionary meditations.
> Thou knowest how before I commenced I devoted all to come to Thee,

Thou knowest I have in age ratified all those vows and
 strictly kept them,
Thou knowest I have not once lost nor faith nor
 ecstasy in Thee,
In shackles, prison'd, in disgrace, repining not,
Accepting all from Thee, as duly come from Thee.

All my emprises have been fill'd with Thee,
My speculations, plans, begun and carried on in
 thoughts of Thee,
Sailing the deep or journeying the land for Thee;
Intentions, purports, aspirations mine, leaving
 results to Thee.

O I am sure they really came from Thee,
The urge, the ardor, the unconquerable will,
The potent, felt, interior command, stronger than
 words,
A message from the Heavens whispering to me even
 in sleep,
These sped me on.

. . . .

By me the hemispheres rounded and tied, the
 unknown to the known.
The end I know not, it is all in Thee,
Or small or great I know not. . . .

. . . .

One effort more, my altar this bleak sand;
That Thou O God my life hast lighted,
With ray of light, steady, ineffable, vouchsafed of Thee,
Light rare untellable, lighting the very light,
Beyond all signs, descriptions, languages;
For that O God, be it my latest word, here on my knees,
Old, poor, and paralyzed, I thank Thee.

> My terminus near,
> The clouds already closing in upon me,
> The voyage balk'd, the course disputed, lost,
> I yield my ships to Thee.
>
> My hands, my limbs grow nerveless,
> My brain feels rack'd, bewilder'd,
> Let the old timbers part, I will not part,
> I will cling fast to Thee, O God, though the waves
>   buffet me,
> Thee, Thee at least I know.
>
> ("Prayer of Columbus," 427-9)

The whole orientation of this poem portrays a Columbus strikingly different from the one some writers now would urge upon us: namely, the Admiral as a man linked with and even representative of the greed and cruelty that so closely followed him. That incidents of violent inhumanity certainly occurred during the Admiral's expeditions cannot be denied. Yet neither, it seems to me, can we discount the far nobler picture Whitman offers in his "Prayer."

TWO PASSAGES TO INDIA

Ill health, poverty, loneliness, and the apparent negation of all his dreams and hopes made Walt Whitman feel a vital kinship with Christopher Columbus in the latter's dark hour. But when the poet's mood was wholly positive, his sense of affinity with the mariner remained no less vivid. Christopher had accomplished what he had meant to be a passage to India and had opened the New World with it. Walt could imagine no closer analogy to what he himself was trying to do. He, too, would make his own "passage" and open a world he would help to make truly new.

The first voyage of discovery was undertaken at the time when European civilization was awakening to the opportunities the physical world offered to people of scientific prowess and daring. Whitman saw that what had been intended by the early explorers of the sea, among whom the deed of Columbus stands first, was only now in his own time being fully realized. To open his own saga, he would celebrate the Suez Canal, the Union Pacific Railroad, the transatlantic cable just laid under the ocean, all attesting to the triumph of scientific acumen and practical courage over the barriers of physical geography. The planet had been rounded, and people brought close together. A basis had been established for unity at last: for understanding as well as commerce between East and West. The material benefits promised to be extraordinary, far, indeed, beyond all treasures of gold and silver. What remained to do?

In Whitman's conception, destiny now required that merely physical exploits and benefits be placed in the context that alone could give them higher life and meaning. This was the task upon which he saw himself engaged. The time had come for a second and more greatly conceived "Passage to India," as he named the poem in which he set forth his vision and intention, calling for a new kind of explorer and for still greater courage. The commerce now to be opened up was no longer between one physical continent or nation and another, but between the whole planet—all of humanity, with all of nature—and that spiritual ground of Being which alone gives invulnerable security and genuine happiness to life on earth.

The "Passage" so devoutly longed for and ardently intended by Walt Whitman for himself and for the country he wished to serve led from the material plane to the spiritual. His "India" lay in the realm of Spirit.

Once the earth has been physically circled, and humanity, through swift travel and instant communication, been drawn tightly together and woven into a single fabric, a certain kind of question becomes ever more pressing for all: What will come at last of this inexorable drive toward physical union? What do we human beings in our hearts really live for? Is there something we truly seek above all? What can give harmony, peace, and creative joy to this life that we shall be forced to live in such pressing closeness?

Walt Whitman felt that behind, beneath, within, and above the enigmas of material existence are divine wisdom, love, beauty, and strength. He asked only to participate in these realities at firsthand. To this end, he wished release from the limitations, the blindness, the hard-heartedness, of merely earthbound understanding. He would expand into worlds of light and love. In "Passage to India," his soaring inpiration; his faith and courage; his whole compassionate, hopeful, adventurous nature, come powerfully to expression. It therefore should be allowed to sound the last note here. But since this requires a longer extract from the lengthy masterpiece than can be comfortably accommodated in the present chapter, about half of the poem will be found in Appendix B, to which readers are encouraged to turn.

> Away O soul! hoist instantly the anchor!
> Cut the hawsers—haul out—shake out every sail!
> ("Prayer of Columbus," 425)

* * *

It does not surprise us that the very last poem written by Whitman, though not included in his final *Goodbye My Fancy*, was addressed to Columbus.[21] As we pass now from Whitman to Emerson, we may take this last avowal of the poet as an opportunity to remind ourselves once more of what it was that the figure and example of Columbus stood for in his own mind when, at the beginning of his career, he first corresponded with Emerson. His words are worth repeating:

> Of course we shall have national character, an identity.... Such character ... is to stand compact upon that vast basis of the supremacy of Individuality—that

new moral American continent without which, I see, the physical continent remained incomplete, may-be a carcass, a bloat.... [It] is yours to have been the original true Captain who put to sea, intuitive, positive, rendering the first report."

For Whitman, Columbus represented the modern spirit of Individuality as it was seeking to emerge in humanity's evolution, in order to inaugurate not only a New World but a New Age. Because Whitman saw the danger that America might mistake egoistic self-concern and self-will for genuine individuality, his own evolving effort moved always toward setting an example of the real thing, which in freedom and with love works to unite rather than to separate human beings. In Emerson he found one who was perfectly clear that the source of genuine individuality does not lie in the surface traits and abilities that distinguish one person *from* another, often settting them at odds. True individuality for both lies in the spiritual depths they share, where they are not many but one. For Whitman, the champion of the Middle Atlantic seacoast, Emerson, the sage of Concord, was an intrepid and beloved fellow-warrior who fought in his own way, with perfect understanding and integrity, the battle that both men foresaw to be more crucial than any other for the future of their country.

NOTES

Perhaps my effort to compare Columbus and Whitman, to draw them into meaningful connection with each other, may have raised questions in the minds of some readers. Questions such as: "What exactly are you trying to prove? Are you spinning out a fantasy, or are you serious? If the latter, in what sense? Could you be suggesting that the earlier man reappeared in the later?"

My motive in writing this chapter has been more than fanciful, for I am convinced that there *is* something important about the relationship between these two men. Though I cannot see as far into it as it seems to deserve, I have tried in various ways to characterize its reality. The effort to do so has at least persuaded me of one thing, namely, that such a juxtaposition of Whitman and

Columbus tends to make us more fruitfully thoughtful about both men than we would otherwise have been.

Concerning the idea itself of reincarnation, chapter two will have made clear that Whitman believed in it as strongly as did Alcott, Thoreau, Melville and many contemporaries. Yet in no place, as far as I know, did he, despite his deep feelings of affinity, ever state that he thought himself actually to be the same identity or entelechy that had once lived as Columbus. My own approach to the question is this: I, too, take reincarnation to be a fact of life, a reality underlying all our lives. But I do not at all favor guessing or theorizing about this mystery, on the basis of mere similarities or coincidences. These but lead curious minds into a forest of illusions. The reality of the matter is well hidden, for what I think are good reasons, from ordinary investigation such as mine has been.

1. Walt Whitman, "By Blue Ontario's Shore," *Leaves of Grass* (New York: Aventine Press, 1931), 347. Page numbers for further references to this book are given by poem title in the text.

2. "Emerson and Whitman," in *The Shock of Recognition*, Edmund Wilson, ed., 2 vols. (New York: Grosset and Dunlap, 1955), vol. 1, 270.

3. Ibid., 263.

4. Ralph Waldo Emerson, "The American Scholar," in *The Complete Essays and Other Writings of Ralph Waldo Emerson*, Brooks Atkinson, ed. (New York: Random House, 1950), 57.

5. Ibid., 61.

6. Whitman, quoted in *The Shock of Recognition*, op. cit., 285-6.

7. Henry Bryan Binns, *A Life of Walt Whitman* (New York: Haskell House, 1969), 254.

8. Ibid., 60.

9. Whitman, "Specimen Days," in *The Portable Walt Whitman*, Mark Van Doren, ed. (New York: Viking Press, 1960), 489-90.

10. Horace Traubel, *With Walt Whitman in Camden* (New York: Rowan and Littlefield, 1961), vol. 1, 414.

11. Bjoern Landstroem, *Columbus* (New York: Macmillan, 1966), 10. Page numbers for further references to this book are given in the text.

12. Samuel Eliot Morison, *Admiral of the Ocean Sea* (Boston: Little, Brown, 1942), 618-9.

13. Ibid., 44-6.

14. Joao de Barros, as quoted in ibid., 71.

15. Ferdinand Columbus, as quoted in ibid., 72.

16. Ibid., 45-6.

17. Richard Maurice Bucke, *Cosmic Consciousness* (New York: Dutton, 1929), 216-8, 224-5.

18. Binns, *A Life of Whitman*, op. cit., 180.

19. Whitman, in his preface to the poem as printed in *Harper's Monthly*, 1875. Quoted in Gay Wilson Allen, *The Solitary Singer* (New York: Macmillan, 1955), 458.

20. Bucke, *Cosmic Consciousness*, op. cit., 232-3.

21. Binns, *A Life of Walt Whitman*, op. cit., 340.

6

EMERSON'S CHRISTIANITY

*God builds his temple in the heart on
the ruins of churches and religions.*
—Emerson, *Journals*

*There was never so great a thought laboring in the breasts of men
as now. It almost seems as if what was aforetime spoken fabulously
and hieroglyphically was now spoken plainly, the doctrine, namely,
of the indwelling Creator in man.* —Emerson, *"The Times"*

DECLARATION OF INDEPENDENCE

FROM birth, Ralph Waldo Emerson seemed destined for the ministry, for he came from a long line of ministers. In 1829, at the age of twenty-six, he was in fact ordained and installed as assistant pastor, soon to be pastor, of "Old North," the Second Church, in Boston.

Yet only three years later, the frank expression of his view of such a central feature of Christian worship as the rite of Holy Communion had forced his withdrawal from the Church. And though, upon invitation, he continued for a time to preach actively here and there, he never thereafter accepted another permanent appointment.

In a sermon of 1832 before his congregation in the Second Church, Emerson had said of the Communion ritual that "an importance is given by Christians to it which never can belong to any form."

> This mode of commemorating Christ is not suitable to me. That is reason enough why I should abandon it. If I believed it was enjoined by Jesus on his disciples, and that he even contemplated making permanent this mode of commemoration, every way agreeable to an Eastern mind, and yet on trial it was disagreeable to my own feelings, I should not adopt it.[1]

That Emerson's views on Christian doctrine and practice remained controversial may be seen by the reaction of many of the clergy in Boston to an address he was asked to make in 1838 to the senior class of Harvard's Divinity School. Officials of the School were sufficiently distressed by his testimony to disclaim all responsibility for the thoughts he had sought to impart, and nearly thirty years passed before Harvard could feel ready to welcome him back. As he himself wrote not long afterward in his journal, "It is plain from all the noise that there is atheism somewhere; the only question is now, which is the atheist?"[2] In his address Emerson had spoken with his customary gentle and charitable eloquence, but his heartfelt words were certainly uncompromising.

> Historical Christianity has fallen into the error that corrupts all attempts to communicate religion. As it appears to us, and as it has appeared for ages, it is not the doctrine of the soul, but an exaggeration of the personal, the positive, the ritual. It has dwelt, it dwells, with noxious exaggeration about the person of Jesus. The soul knows no persons.... One would rather be "A pagan, suckled in a creed outworn," than to be defrauded of his manly right in coming into nature and finding ... even virtue and truth foreclosed and monopolized.... You shall not own the world; you shall not dare and live after the infinite Law that is in you, and in company with the infinite Beauty which heaven and earth reflect to you in all lovely forms;

but you must subordinate your nature to Christ's nature; you must accept our interpretations, and take his portrait as the vulgar draw it. ("Divinity School Address," 73)

It is important to note that when, on this occasion, the speaker confessed to the Divinity School students his distaste for the Church's portrayal of Christ, and his vital disagreement with many of its interpretations of Christ's life and message, he was not thereby trying to dissuade his hearers from entering the Christian ministry. Quite the contrary, he was pleading with them to restore legitimacy to the act and place of religious worship in the name of Christ.

To this holy office you propose to devote yourselves. I wish you may feel your call in throbs of desire and hope. The office is the first in the world.... And it is my duty to say to you that the need was never greater of new revelation than now. ("Divinity School Address," 75)

Emerson made an emphatic distinction between "the doctrine of the soul," which is valid for all humanity for all time, and the Church's glorification of Jesus in parochial ways.

In how many churches, by how many prophets, tell me, is man made sensible that he is an infinite Soul; that the earth and heavens are passing into his mind; that he is drinking forever the soul of God? ("Divinity School Address," 76)

The real Christ, Emerson felt, pointed always to the universal soul in which all human beings participate, and his example represents the highest ideal for every human life. In Emerson's view, Christ "felt respect" for the revelations once given by Moses and the prophets, but he always placed first "the eternal revelation in the heart" of living human beings.

Thus was he a true man. Having seen that the law in us is commanding, he would not suffer it to be commanded. Boldly, with hand, and heart, and life, he declared it was God. Thus is he, as I think, the only soul in history who has appreciated the worth of man. ("Divinity School Address," 72-3)

In this address Emerson meant, as he said, to contrast the Church with the soul. To the former he attributed "the universal decay and now almost death of faith in society."

In the soul then let the redemption be sought. . . . It is the office of a true teacher to show us that God is, not was; that He speaketh, not spake. The true Christianity—a faith like Christ's in the infinitude of men—is lost. ("Divinity School Address," 80)

How, then, were the speaker's young hearers to prepare themselves to deliver the doctrine of the soul?

Let me admonish you, first of all, to go alone; to refuse the good models . . . and dare to love God without mediator or veil. ("Divinity School Address," 81)

Thus we find ourselves circling around the root of Emerson's objection to the "Christian" Church, as well as the basic element in his doctrine of the soul. He was profoundly convinced that human beings must begin at last to practice "self-reliance," and that whatever would persuade or compel them away from this practice must be regarded as the enemy of true religion.

When Emerson delivered the address entitled "The American Scholar" before the Phi Beta Kappa Society at Harvard in 1837, Oliver Wendell Holmes called it "our intellectual Declaration of Independence." More recently, Brooks Atkinson has observed that "what statesmen had already accomplished in the sphere of politics, Emerson applied to culture . . . by exhortation and radiance."

What were the clarion calls to freedom that Emerson sounded and what was the aura of independence that radiated from his example? They all were only evidences of the radical individualism, the self-determining individuality he represented in his own life. They were the outcome of self-reliance. "Insist on thyself," was his counsel. "Trust thyself!"

> I see not any road of perfect peace which a man can walk, but after the counsel of his own bosom. ("Heroism," 259)

> I will so trust that what is deep is holy, that I will do strongly before the sun and moon whatever inly rejoices me and the heart appoints. ("Self-Reliance," 160)

Within the depths of the individual's own being, within his own heart, is to be found "the absolutely trustworthy." There and nowhere else.

> What your heart thinks great, is great. The soul's emphasis is always right. ("Spiritual Laws," 197)

> Nothing is at last sacred but the integrity of your own mind. . . . No law can be sacred to me but that of my nature. . . . The only right is what is after my constitution; the only wrong what is against it. ("Self-Reliance," 148)

> In self-trust all the virtues are comprehended. ("The American Scholar," 57)

We are forced, of course, to make an all-important distinction. For the soul's emphasis that moves us so powerfully at a certain moment may partake more of self-will than of the self-trust Emerson had in mind when he advised his hearers to "act singly" ("Self-Reliance," 153). It may not be the true center of our unified soul that is clamoring for attention. So often we do what we prefer or are persuaded to do; yet in so acting, we do not necessarily believe in our hearts that what we are doing is right. We do not actually approve of it. We are indulging rather than trusting ourselves, and so we come to feel out of sorts with ourselves. Even when we defend our impulsiveness or carelessness against criticism coming from others, we suspect they may be right. We are therefore no longer integral, self-identical, or "single," but of two (or more) minds.

Scripture advises that when the eye is single, the whole body will be full of light. Yet in truth, to act singly is something we seldom achieve. Emerson pointed both to our profound need for, and the sure availability of, the one light that makes "single " activity and "virtue" the same thing.

Thus we are led to Emerson's concept of "virtue," which takes account of the word's Latin origin, going back apparently to *vis* or *vir* or perhaps to an even earlier source in which the two are closely connected. *Vis* denotes power or worth; *vir* stands for "man." Considered in this light, virtue is that essential power or worth that makes for true humanity or "manhood." When an individual acts with integrity, being fully present and entirely committed in his or her spiritual humanity, there comes the realization that "virtue" and "man's" own being are one and the same. Therefore, as human beings, we should never aspire to being called virtuous by others who judge according to external standards. Our proper goal is simply to be fully awake, caring, and self-active; in other words, to be virtue itself. There is humor as well as his customary rigor in the way Emerson develops this thought.

> Virtues are, in the popular estimate, rather the exception than the rule. There is the man and his virtues. Men

do what is called a good action, as a piece of courage or charity, much as they would pay a fine in expiation of daily non-appearance on parade. Their works are done as an apology . . . [for] their living in the world—as invalids and the insane pay a high board. Their virtues are penances. I do not wish to expiate but to live. . . . I wish [my life] to be sound and sweet, and not to need diet and bleeding. I ask primary evidence that you are a man, and refuse this appeal from the man to his actions. I know that for myself it makes no difference whether I do or forbear those actions which are reckoned excellent. I cannot consent to pay for a privilege where I have intrinsic right. Few and mean as my gifts may be, I actually am, and do not need for my own assurance or the assurance of my fellows any secondary testimony. ("Self-Reliance," 149-50)

That there must be far-reaching and possibly disturbing implications to be drawn from this "doctrine of the soul" is obvious.

It is easy to see that a greater self-reliance must work a revolution in all the offices and relations of men; in their religion; in their education; in their pursuits; their modes of living; their association; in their property; in their speculative views. ("Self-Reliance," 162)

Indeed, said Emerson,

truly it demands something godlike in him who has cast off the common motives of humanity and has ventured to trust himself for a taskmaster. High be his heart, faithful his will, clear his sight, that he may in good earnest be doctrine, society, law, to himself, that a simple purpose may be to him as strong as iron necessity is to others! ("Self-Reliance," 161)

THE NEW COVENANT

At present, as we focus upon Emerson's relation to Christianity, it is only the religious implications of his principle of self-reliance that are of concern. But that there is a significant issue here seems plain enough; for what starker contrast can there be than that between the absolute "Trust thyself!" of the Concord sage and St. Paul's equally unconditional "Not I, but Christ in me!"?

For Emerson, the reality of the true Self in human beings, that which makes them human, is "God." He speaks more readily of God than of Christ. "Either God is there," he says, "or he is not there." ("Spiritual Laws," 191)

> Let us stun and astonish the intruding rabble of men and books and institutions by a simple declaration of the divine fact. Bid the invaders take their shoes from off their feet, for God is here within. ("Self-Reliance," 159)

Emerson maintains that any person who thinks of his or her ordinary self as capable of "possessing" no matter what virtue or virtues, is self-deluded, and his or her seemingly good intentions will surely miscarry. Our supposedly good methods will eventually produce bad results. All good that is truly good is but the presence and present action of the true I Am, the Self of the self. Emerson addresses this being as the Over-Soul, or even simply as the Soul.

> What we commonly call man, the eating, drinking, planting, counting man, does not, as we know him, represent himself, but misrepresents himself. Him do we not respect, but the soul, whose organ he is, would he let it appear through his action, would make our knees bend. When it breathes through his intellect, it is genius; when it breathes through his will, it is virtue; and when it flows through his affection, it is love. And the blindness of the

intellect begins when it would be something of itself. The weakness of the will begins when the individual would be something of himself. ("The Over-Soul," 263)

What Emerson calls the Soul, or Over-Soul, however, he identifies not directly with Christ, but rather with that in which he conceived that Christ himself had perfect faith, and that for which Christ Jesus stands out before and above all others on the plain of history. In addressing the Harvard students, he said:

> The true Christianity—a faith like Christ's in the infinitude of men—is lost. None believeth in the soul of man, but only in some man or person old and departed. ("Divinity School Address," 80)

In such utterances, which abound throughout his writings, Emerson throws down his challenge to the prevailing doctrines and practices of the Church. Is it I, he asks, who am untrue to Christ, or perhaps you? You deify one man, Jesus. I believe that Christ came to show that all human beings should be deified, that is, that they should be brought to recognize, awaken, obey, and become the Deity in themselves.

> Jesus Christ belonged to the true race of prophets. He saw with open eye the mystery of the soul.... He lived in it and had his being there. Alone in all history he estimated the greatness of man. One man was true to what is in you and me. He saw that God incarnates himself in man. ("Divinity School Address," 72)

> We know that all spiritual being is in man.... As there is no screen or ceiling between our heads and the infinite heavens, so there is no bar or wall in the soul, where man, the effect, ceases, and God, the cause, begins.... We lie

open on one side to the deeps of spiritual nature, to the attributes of God. ("The Over-Soul," 264)

For Emerson, the Christhood of Jesus simply made explicit what is implicit in every human being. One can believe it was in this sense that he read St. John's teaching: All things came forth, in the beginning, through the Word of God. "*In the Word was Life, and the Life was the Light of men...and that was the true Light, which lighteth every man that cometh into the world.*" Christ Jesus lived from this Light, was filled by it, and represented it most perfectly. "Thus was he [Jesus] a true man," said Emerson, for he more than any other pointed all men to "the eternal revelation in the heart" ("Divinity School Address," 72). In the form prophesied by Jeremiah, this revelation was certainly familiar to the one-time minister:

> Behold the days come, saith the Lord, that I will make a new covenant with the house of Israel.... This shall be the covenant that I will make with the house of Israel: After those days, saith the Lord, I will put my law in their inward parts, and write it in their hearts, and will be their God, and they shall be my people. And they shall teach no more every man his neighbor, and every man his brother, saying, Know the Lord; for they shall all know me, and from the least of them unto the greatest of them, saith the Lord.... (Jer. 31:31-4)

Emerson himself tried to live by this covenant and to read God's revelations in his own heart, and he felt the deepest respect and a profound love for the example set by Jesus Christ. It would seem, however, that this prophecy—which he felt was corroborated in his own experience, and equally valid for all truly modern souls—specified that it could be only "after those days" that the new covenant between God and human beings would come to pass. The phrase seemed clearly to indicate a turning-point that was yet to come. Between then and now, the moment of this radical change in human history must have occurred. When was that decisive moment, and by what or whose agency was it made possible?

Did Emerson wrestle with these questions, as posed in this way? Quite possibly he may have; yet he seems never to have identified the problem as being of greatest importance for his own conception of the nature and mission of Christ. Had he been asked what caused the change from the old covenant to the new and what was the historical moment, if any, of this change, one senses that he would have been reluctant to center it precisely in the life, death, and resurrection of Christ Jesus, as God become flesh. He did not think it reasonable to imagine that all of history could be set on a completely new course by the gift of a single life, no matter how great. Nor did he suppose that, *absent* such a uniquely transforming and empowering gift to the earth from on high, no human being would have been able to experience the kind of spiritual self-certainty that he felt deeply and justifiably rooted in himself. Herein, of course, lies the difference between his teaching and Church doctrine. Herein, from the Church's point of view, Emerson's recognition of the unique contribution of Jesus Christ must seem to fall short, for it fails to identify him specifically as the unique Savior of mankind.

The question may nevertheless be asked: Who is closer to the real purpose of Christ's mission on earth? Is it those who "confess" Jesus Christ as their personal Savior and Redeemer, ever reciting their allegiance to him and seeking to convert the rest of humanity to his worship, but who in practice may be listening too seldom for the silent prompting of the inner word that sounds in the stillness of their own hearts? Or, contrastingly, is it those who actually follow the advice of Jesus himself, as they seek the kingdom of God within rather than outside themselves;

and who counsel their fellow mortals to trust the I AM revealed within their own "I am," telling them, as Emerson did, that "only by coming to themselves, or to God in themselves, can they grow forevermore" ("Divinity School Address," 74)?

The answer to this question, in Emerson's case, requires that we visualize clearly just what he had in mind as the relationship between the lesser self and the greater Self. What was it in the soul of a human being that he thinks deserving of absolute trust, and how does he distinguish it from so much in every soul that is misleading? In his essay "Self-Reliance," he himself asks: "Who is the Trustee? What is the aboriginal Self, on which a universal reliance may be grounded?"

> The inquiry leads us to that source, at once the essence of genius, of virtue, and of life, which we call Spontaneity or [spiritual] Instinct. We denote this primary wisdom as Intuition, whilst all later teachings are tuitions. In that deep force, the last fact behind which analysis cannot go, all things find their common origin. For the sense of being which in calm hours rises, we know not how, in the soul, is not diverse from things, from space, from light, from time, from man, but one with them and proceeds obviously from the same source whence their life and being also proceed. ("Self-Reliance," 155)

In so saying, Emerson indicates once more the distance he is at pains to establish between his view of the universal or cosmic Divine Spirit that underlies and inheres in all natural beings and processes, and those religious views that focus too narrowly, as it seems to him, upon the earthly life of a particular human being who is alleged to have embodied the perfection of Divinity for all time, yet who obviously entered and accepted the limits of the human condition, unprecedentedly few as in his case these limits may have been.

The soul knows no persons. It invites every man to expand to the full circle of the universe, and will have no preferences but those of spontaneous love. ("Divinity School Address," 73)

THE ISSUE OF FREEDOM

In trying in various ways to ascertain the essential in Emerson's concept of self-reliance as a moral-religious absolute, we confront what was the central issue for him. This issue is freedom. Shall the human soul be freely self-determining, or must it always be derivative and dependent? On this issue, the radical champion of freedom always expressed himself in terms that were as courageous as they were reverent.

> When good is near you, when you have life in yourself, it is not by any known or accustomed way; you shall not discern the footprints of any other; you shall not see the face of man; you shall not hear any name; the way, the thought, the good, shall be wholly strange and new. It shall exclude example and experience. You take the way from man, not to man. All persons that ever existed are its forgotten ministers.... Why then do we prate of self-reliance? Inasmuch as the soul is present, there will be power not confident but agent. To talk of reliance is a poor external way of speaking. Speak rather of that which relies because it works and is. ("Self-Reliance," 158)

I find in my own soul the very ground and source of Being, Emerson asserted, and place my whole trust in that. When in the primordial spirituality of the world itself I can recognize at the same time the essence of my own self, and find in its will what I myself acknowledge with love as my own heart's desire, then obviously I am God-centered, God-prompted, and indeed God-existent.

> Self-existence is the attribute of the Supreme Cause, and it constitutes the measure of good by the degree in which it enters into all lower forms. ("Self-Reliance," 159)

But the choice as to whether this recognition and realization actually come to pass in me is not God's but mine, and that makes all the difference.

Emerson would probably not have disagreed with Augustine's pronouncement, "In slavery to God is perfect freedom." But he would want it clear that only that individual could say this honestly who felt and knew, as did Christ Jesus, that in the moment of decision to serve, "The Father and I are one."

Such were Emerson's experience and belief. But in pursuing his quest for freedom of the human soul, he says he remembers

> an answer which when quite young I was prompted to make to a valued adviser who was wont to importune me with the dear old doctrines of the Church. On my saying, "What have I to do with the sacredness of traditions, if I live wholly from within?" my friend suggested—"But these impulses may be from below, not from above." I replied, "They do not seem to me to be such; but if I am the Devil's child, I will live then from the Devil." ("Self-Reliance," 148)

Characteristically, just a few paragraphs earlier he had written: "God will not have his work made manifest by cowards."

> The whole course of things goes to teach us faith. We need only obey. There is guidance for each of us, and by lowly listening we shall hear the right word. ("Self-Reliance," 194)

Does it seem paradoxical that this champion of freedom—which he understood to be *spiritual self-activity*—should speak so much of obedience? Certainly, *obedience* to the self-sought, self-heard, self-welcomed, and self-embraced voice of the spirit within, was for Emerson the essence of freedom.

> All reform aims in some one particular to let the soul have its way through us; in other words, to engage us to obey. ("The Over-Soul," 264)

> Who has more obedience than I masters me, though he should not raise his finger. Round him I must revolve by the gravitation of spirits. ("Self-Reliance," 158)

In the case of Jesus, Emerson recognized the will to perfect obedience: "Jesus speaks always from within, and in a degree that transcends all others" ("The Over-Soul," 272). Is this the reason why so much of humanity is drawn, by the very gravitation of spirits, into orbiting round his central sun? Something in Emerson resisted pursuing his thought to all the implications of this conclusion. Presumably he felt that while the extraordinarily obedient and faithful soul of Jesus could well be the sun around which countless human lives would, to their immense benefit, thereafter gladly revolve, there must nevertheless remain a distinction between the man himself and the divine principle to which he was obedient. It was this principle, this Sun, not this man as such, he felt, that deserves worship.

Emerson himself would not have called this Sun "Christ." For him, Christ would seem to have been a name signifying only that the man Jesus was one anointed in high degree to serve God. There was God, and there was Jesus. God he could not personify, and especially not in an exclusive way. "To personify God is to exclude him from my consciousness," he said.[3] Only because God is as universal as light itself, and as formless, can every individual feel him as the very principle of his or her own life. As for Christ, Emerson may have thought of him as exemplifying the condition of blessing that comes to rest in a certain measure upon every truly enlightened one, rather than as signifying the only Son of God.

When it comes to the question of Jesus Christ being both human and divine, Emerson's view, as we have seen, was that the same can be said in varying degrees of all of us. Human beings are all, in some measure, both sons of man and Sons of God. The blending of two aspects, with the complete penetration and transformation of the lower by the higher, may have been consummated in Jesus Christ so that his humanity was raised to the divine and his divinity became completely humanized. But it seemed to Emerson that though Jesus may well be accounted unique in the matter of degree, he was not so in kind. In his view, all who recognize that their apparent "I am's" are but aspects of the one and only real I AM, and all who therefore strive in this sense to become *truly* themselves, are in their potentiality even as Jesus. According to John himself, such are born not simply of an hereditary line, nor of carnal desire, nor even of parental plans and purposes, but directly of God. They, even as Jesus, are newly "begotten" of the Father (John 1:13)

> It is one light which beams out of a thousand stars. It is one soul, which animates all men. ("The American Scholar," 59)

THE SPIRIT OF TRUTH

Does Emerson overestimate human powers? When he capitalizes "Man," does he, in effect, confuse the human being with God? Is there at least a puffing up of the human ego?

Not arrogance but obedience was Emerson's teaching and example. "The man who renounces himself, comes to himself" ("Divinity School Address," 69). It is in kneeling before what is above us that we descend; yet in this very obeisance we rise, for inevitably we become what we admire.

> The simplest person who in his integrity worships God, becomes God. ("The Over-Soul," 275)

> If a man is at heart just, then in so far is he God: the safety of God, the immortality of God, the majesty of God do enter into that man with justice. ("Divinity School Address," 68-8)

Can that aspect of divinity with which Emerson sought to put himself in tune, the aspect he so genuinely loved and celebrated, be given a name? He felt free to call it "God," but we may still inquire: What aspect of God? In addressing the Divinity School students, was he not, in answering this question, characterizing at the same time the role he had from the beginning chosen for himself?

> Yourself a newborn bard of the Holy Ghost, cast behind you all conformity, and acquaint men at first hand with Deity.... Live with the privilege of the immeasurable mind. ("Divinity School Address," 81)

Emerson equated the immeasurable mind of Deity with the Holy Spirit, the revealer of all truth, and his special relationship was clearly to this aspect of God. For him, in the condition of the time as he viewed it, the "unforgivable sin" must be untruth. "All that is clearly due today," he said, "is not to lie" ("The Transcendentalist," 99). Perhaps nowhere did he more humbly or more eloquently state his experience than in this passage from "The Over-Soul":

> The soul gives itself, alone, original and pure, to the Lonely, Original and Pure, who, on that condition, gladly inhabits, leads and speaks through it.... It is not wise,

but it sees through all things. It is not called religious, but it is innocent. It calls the light its own. . . . Behold, it saith, I am born into the great, the universal mind. (277)

Before the Crucifixion, Christ told his disciples: "I will pray the Father, and he shall give you another Comforter, that he may abide with you forever; even the Spirit of truth. . . . When he, the Spirit of truth, is come, he will guide you into all truth . . . he shall take of mine, and shall show it unto you." (John 16:13-7)

When not addressing the churchly congregation, Emerson chose to speak of the Over-Soul, by which he meant no less than the Holy Spirit, but purged of religious tradition and dogma. His joyous affirmation of this aspect of Deity was stated in a term of his own invention, based on his own experience, and accessible to others calling themselves Christian. It was characteristic of him to stick with what he himself truly knew.

Christ said to his disciples: "It is expedient for you that I go away; for if I go not away, the Comforter will not come unto you; but if I depart, I will send him unto you." (John 16:7) Would not Emerson have read into these words what we can imagine to have been his own understanding: "My outward authority must end, that it may come to life again within you. The I whom you see standing over against you in bodily separateness must pass from bodily sight, that my universal and unifying Spirit, the true I AM that I am, may in time come to rise as your own individuality within each one of you. I must die as separate man, that all human beings may at last rise into the godhead, the holy Manhood, that heals their separateness. You yourselves are also to become sons and daughters of God our Father. My apparent separation from you, and your apparent separateness from each other, are to be overcome—for those who will—by the unifying Spiritual Life that, as destined, I have made possible for you to receive in full measure."

SPIRITUAL EVOLUTION

The kind of Christianity Emerson could believe in would realize that Deity's sacrificial involution into humanity's slow historical becoming had an evolutionary purpose. The purpose was that we should not only have been made at potentially in the image and likeness of Divine Powers, but that we should come eventually to *wield* in freedom, and on ever higher levels, those same powers. In the fullness of time, the whole human condition should be raised up, finding within itself the divine powers of creative freedom. It was God's will that the human being should eventually cease from lapsing and start becoming. Son of God became Son of Man, in order that all people might in freedom find the possibility within themselves, similarly, to become Sons of God. It was the beloved disciple who testified that to them that believe on the divine name, the I AM, the Light of the world, He gave power to become the Sons of God.

Of this involutionary-evolutionary prospect Emerson meant to bear steadfast witness. Yet it was from experience and with feeling that he observed, "This one fact the world hates; that the soul becomes; for that forever ... shoves Jesus and Judas equally aside" ("Self-Reliance," 158).

The most perfected individual, of course, falls infinitely short of equality with the Creator, even as a single drop drawn from the ocean's vastness is by no means equivalent to the unsurveyable ocean as a whole. Yet is not the drop, however small, in essential respects qualitatively identical with the encompassing greatness from which it is drawn? Paul affirms that every human being must be recognized as true scion and heir of the Highest. To ready ourselves for the inheritance prepared for us from the beginning, we have only to *become* what we were always intended to be:

> For as many as are led by the Spirit of God, they are the sons of God. For ... ye have received the spirit of adoption, whereby we cry, Abba, Father. The Spirit himself beareth

witness with our spirit, that we are the children of God; and if children, then heirs; heirs of God, and joint heirs with Christ; if so be that we suffer with him. . . . (Romans 8:14-18)

One feels Emerson's assent. He would wholeheartedly agree that the testimony of the Apostle beautifully supported his own conviction. Yet he would still question whether "Christian" congregations themselves realize the implications of the soul's *becoming*. Have they understood that the evolving human soul finds its anchor only in the Absolute and that this Absolute is ultimately to be found only within, not outside, the soul itself?

Emerson found fault with the idea that Jesus *was* God, or the *only* begotten Son of God; with the idea that Jesus was the unique and indispensable Savior of all human souls; and with suppositions that his words, as recorded in Scripture, are the last to be spoken through man or woman by Divinity—"as if God were dead." He was repelled by any idea that churchly blessings, sanctions, confessions, absolutions, or other rites—however comforting and inspiring at times—are *essential* to the soul's salvation; and that to be baptized, whether merely with holy water or with the Holy Spirit unto speaking in tongues, makes the difference between salvation and damnation.

Emerson did not so much deny the actualized divinity of Christ Jesus as he was at pains to affirm the potential divinity dwelling also in all human beings, and in himself. For him, the words of the eighty-second Psalm spoke truth: "Ye are gods, and all of you are children of the Most High;" and he was no doubt fully aware, too, of Christ's challenge to the Pharisees: "Is it not written in your law, I said, Ye are gods?" (John 10:34)

Of course, all creatures in the whole of creation can rightly be called children of the Creator, but it is self-evident that only to human beings, and even to them only in the maturity of their soul's development, is it possible for the Father to impart the spark of his own self-existent, creative, and eternal essence. For only in the completely awakened aspect of his or her nature does the individual human being rise above *creature* status to become a freely *creative*, or actual, son or daughter of God.

> We do not yet possess ourselves, and we know at the same time that we are much more. ("The Over-Soul," 267)

> Within man is the soul of the whole ... the eternal ONE. This energy does not descend into individual life on any other condition than entire possession.... Ineffable is the union of man and God in every act of the soul. The simplest person who in his integrity worships God becomes God; yet for ever and ever the influx of this better and universal self is new and unsearchable. ("The Over-Soul," 262, 274-5)

Emerson's allegiance, first and last, was to truth. On the subject of Christianity, he was scrupulously honest. It was not in his nature to belittle, distrust, or disbelieve. Where at all possible, his judgments were affirmative. Yet he could not abide hypocrisy. Where religious forms were empty, where the so-called faith of the faithful was but a self-deluding, self-congratulatory convention, he could not but call a spade a spade. Obviously it was not to the formalities of religious worship in themselves that Emerson objected. "Forms are as essential as bodies; but to exalt particular forms, to adhere to one form a moment after it is outgrown, is unreasonable, and it is alien to the spirit of Christ" ("The Lord's Supper," 117)

> I am not engaged to Christianity by decent forms, or saving ordinances; it is not usage, it is not what I do not understand, that binds me to it—let these be the sandy

foundations of falsehoods. What I revere and obey in it is its reality, its boundless charity, its deep interior life, the rest it gives to mind, the echo it returns to my thoughts, the perfect accord it makes with my reason through all its representations of God and His Providence; and the persuasion and courage that come out thence to lead me upward and onward.... That for which Paul lived and died so gloriously; that for which Jesus gave himself to be crucified; the end that animated the thousand martyrs and heroes who have followed his steps, was to redeem us from a formal religion, and teach us to seek our well-being in the formation of the soul. ("The Lord's Supper," 117-8)

Emerson's advice to the Divinity School students was altogether positive. He rejected the idea of attempting to "project and establish a Cultus with new rites and forms." For in the end, and perhaps not long in coming, these themselves would become false to their originating spirit. "Rather," he said, and this admonition summed up all the conviction and striving of his own life,

> let the breath of new life be breathed by you through the forms already existing. For if once you are alive, you shall find they shall become plastic and new. The remedy to their deformity is first, soul, and second, soul, and evermore, soul. ("Divinity School Address," 83-4)

NOTES

1. Emerson, "The Last Supper," in *The Complete Essays and Other Writings of Ralph Waldo Emerson*, Brooks Atkinson, ed. (New York: Random House, 1950), 116. Page numbers for all further references to this book are given in the text by essay title.

2. Bliss Perry, *The Heart of Emerson's Journals*, entry of October 19, 1838, in *The Heart of Emerson's Journals* (Boston: Houghton Mifflin, 1926), 138.

3. This reference I can no longer find. For a contrasting, balancing statement, see "Self-Reliance," p. 152:

"In your metaphysics you have denied personality to the Deity, yet when the devout motions of the soul come, yield to them heart and life, though they should clothe God with shape and color. Leave your theory, as Joseph his coat in the hand of the harlot, and flee."

7

EMERSON'S GOAL: A SCIENCE OF THE SPIRIT

When a faithful thinker, resolute to detach every object from personal relations and see it in the light of thought, shall, at the same time, kindle science with the fire of the holiest affections, then will God go forth anew into the creation. —Emerson, *Nature*

If the auguries of the prophesying heart shall make themselves good in time, the man who shall be born, whose advent men and events prepare and foreshadow, is one who shall enjoy his connection with a higher life, with the man within man; shall destroy distrust by his trust, shall use his native but forgotten methods, shall not take counsel of flesh and blood, but shall rely on the Law alive and beautiful which works over our heads and under our feet.
—Emerson, "New England Reformers"

SHADOW, IMAGE, AND REALITY

EMERSON's mind, in equal measure with its piety, was of an inquiring nature. He sought the spirit not as one who could be comforted with traditional or churchly faith, but as one who demanded to know clearly for himself. He felt that his task was to champion the spirit in a new way. He did so by directing his attention to the same human intelligence that underlay the striking advances of scientific and practical enterprise in his own day. But in his hands, and as seen through his eyes, this intelligence was to be redirected. It should seek to lift itself to a higher level. As he essayed to follow the workings and trace the laws of intelligence, his genius led him to distinguish, even as his beloved Plato had done, between the thought-shadows cast upon the rear wall of the mental cave that is ordinary consciousness and the actual beings and events outside the mouth of the cave that cast those shadows. Only one whose attention has turned from the secondary play of shadows upon the cave wall to the primary realities of the world of light stretching away from the cave's entrance can speak, as Emerson does, of

> the influx of the all-knowing Spirit, which annihilates before its broad noon the little shades and gradations of intelligence . . . we call wiser and wisest.[1]

The ordinary use of the mind—that is, intellectuality as usually employed—is brain-based. As understood by Emerson and Plato, it is therefore an exercise carried out inside the human skull. Admittedly, this mentality can *infer* much from observation of the play of sensory shadows which the outside world of spirit-reality casts into this cave. But so long as the human intellect remains turned away from rather than toward the world of light, in which the *actuality* of what it would study lives, mental truths will remain merely shadows or images as seen in a mirror. When intelligence, however, turns from the derived image to the presence of the *original*, it has new things to say, and its tone becomes one of authority.

> We know truth when we see it, from opinion, as we know when we are awake that we are awake. . . . We are wiser than we know. If we will not interfere with our thought, but will act entirely, or see how the thing stands in God, we know the particular thing, and every thing, and every man. For the Maker of all things and all persons stands behind us and casts his dread omniscience through us over

things.... We distinguish the announcements of the soul, its manifestations of its own nature, by the term *Revelation*.... For this communication is an influx of the Divine mind into our mind. ("The Over-Soul," 268-9)

We are all discerners of spirits. ("The Over-Soul," 271)

Oriental wisdom has long held that "the mind is the slayer of the real." The justice of this maxim becomes evident when we recognize that in the "reflections" of ordinary thinking—even of what we know as highly trained scientific thinking—what takes place, as the word itself suggests, is a conversion of the movements of real life, of actual spirit being, into static mirror-images. In this sense, the merely reflective mind cannot help divesting the objects it perceives with its bodily senses of the creative, ideal power that first brought them into being and that continues to sustain them in their reality. This ordinary mind, therefore, "slays the real."

For Asian wisdom as for Transcendental insight, the thoughts of the "reflective" mind, despite their usefulness in practical ways, remain in and of themselves essentially unreal. However accurately they qualify and quantify the sensory facts in order to infer nature's "laws," their concepts remain but logical abstractions. At last, they are only negatives of real being. *Self-existent* life and being is something our ordinary thoughts do not have. Nor are they able to experience such life, or acknowledge its reality. And so, little by little, as we become honestly aware of the limitations of this particular kind of experience, it dawns upon us that in attempting to explain the ineffable immediacies of real life, our dry thoughts cannot help reducing them all to lifeless abstractions.

Thus the external world as usually conceived lacks both vitality and inwardness; it is merely an array or assemblage of things. These physical things, as interpreted by the physical sciences, evince nothing higher than the interplay of external forces. This interplay, in its turn, weaves a web of material necessities in which the human soul and spirit must inevitably feel trapped.

> I see not, if one be once caught in this trap of so-called sciences, any escape for the man from the links of the chain of physical necessity. Given such an embryo, such a history must follow. On this platform one lives in a sty of sensualism, and would soon come to suicide. But it is impossible that the creative power should exclude itself. Into every intelligence there is a door which is never closed, through which the creator passes. The intellect, seeker of absolute truth, or the heart, lover of absolute good, intervenes for our succor, and at one whisper of these high powers we awake from ineffectual struggles with this nightmare. We hurl it into its own hell, and cannot again contract ourselves to so base a state. ("Experience," 347)

If ordinary abstract thought inevitably conjures the *determinism* of a dead, mechanically operating world-process, can such thinking possibly be brought to life? Can it be strengthened so as to pass from the static reflection of life to participation in its meaningful, active reality? Emerson grappled with this question. The problem he chose to face was how to release the cave-bound form of thinking from the unreality of its shadow-existence. He expressed his confidence in an enhanced ability of human thought to share in the spiritual life of the real world, and he tried to set an example of how a transformed use of the mind lifts the unfreedom of passive reflection into the freedom of living experience.

> I could not be, but that *absolute life* circulated in me, and I could not *think* without *being* that absolute life.[2] [Emphasis added]

THE RESURRECTION OF THOUGHT

The resurrection of spiritual power in cognition begins not with mistrust of the ordinary kind of thinking, but rather with faith in its sleeping possibilities, which ask only to be awakened.

> In yourself is the law of all nature ... in yourself slumbers the whole of Reason; it is for you to know all; it is for you to dare all. ("The American Scholar," 62)

So bravely does Emerson encourage himself along with others. So confident is he of what to some extent he truly has, and yet has not, experienced himself. Despite his journal entry to this effect—"One step remains, but yet we cannot take it"[3]—he was intuitively positive, as well as prophetic, of what can be and must be, that is, of the eventual transformation of natural scientific method into a spiritual scientific mode of cognition.

> Man stands in strict connection with a higher fact never yet manifested. There is power over and behind us, and we are the channels of its communications.... This open channel to the highest life is the first and last reality, so subtle, so quiet, yet so tenacious, that although I have never expressed the truth, and although I have never heard the expression from any other, I know that the whole truth is here for me. ("New England Reformers," 466)

As Emerson viewed it, the advance of inquiry from the death-dealing to the life-giving mind involves a paradox. Two seemingly opposite requirements must be met. The first is precisely what the natural sciences of the West have for centuries been at pains to establish, namely, complete objectivity in the pursuit of knowledge. The discipline of objectivity requires the subordination—supposedly even the total exclusion—of all "subjective" or purely human reactions and feelings. Emerson himself is in no doubt that rigorous objectivity is required by the search for truth. And he found the intellect in its abstract form well able to satisfy this requirement.

> Intellect separates the fact considered, from you, from all local and personal reference, and discerns it as if it existed for its own sake.... Intellect is void of affection and sees an object as it stands in the light of science, cool and disengaged. The intellect goes out of the individual, floats over its own personality, and regards it as a fact, and not as *I* and *mine*. He who is immersed in what concerns person or place cannot see the problem of existence. This the intellect always ponders. ("Intellect," 292-3)

This first condition, then, demands of the would-be knower that for the sake of truth he or she be willing to abandon all self-reference. Knowledge of the thing under study being the goal, one must forsake one's own "standpoint" and "viewpoint," and in the moment of truth cease, as it were, to be a separate self.

The question raised by this first requirement is daunting. When as thinkers we cease to be ourselves, what condition ensues? As we "float" above our own personality, are we left hanging in the air of high abstraction, or do we take upon ourselves to go further in this adventure of the spirit? Can we go further, to invite, await, and experience in the world of light that living reality of which our hitherto abstract concepts have been but lifeless images?

> By the same fire, vital, consecrating, celestial, which burns until it shall dissolve all things into the waves and surges of an ocean of light, we see and know each other, and what spirit each is of. ("The Over-Soul," 271)

Emerson's view is that the prevailing methods of science as we know them, in their necessary and laudable commitment to objectivity, have stopped halfway. They have developed conceptual thinking to a high degree—an entirely positive achievement. But as a result science has found itself suspended in an in-between realm that, while it has gone beyond and risen above "created" nature in the merely factual aspect, still falls short of apprehending the creative reality underlying all physical manifestations. Conceptual thought does not experience the world of living Ideas as understood by Plato. To rise into this further experience of truth, Emerson admits, is easier said than done. It requires courage, patience, and love.

> What is the hardest task in the world? To think. I would put myself in the attitude to look in the eye of an abstract truth, and I cannot. I blench and withdraw on this side and on that. I seem to know what he meant who said, "No man can see God face to face and live." ("Intellect," 295)

> Thoughts let us into realities. Neither miracle nor magic nor any religious tradition, not the immortality of the private soul is incredible, after we have experienced an insight, a thought. I think it comes to some men but once in their life, sometimes a religious impulse, sometimes an intellectual insight.[4]

If reflective intellection is brain-based and done in the cave of the skull, it is no simple matter to turn from its shadowy abstractions to the world of light that casts these shadows. The thinker is asked to free his or her thinking from dependence on the physical brain—in other words, to leave the cave at least partly. As Emerson himself indicated, "the intellect," in pursuing truth, "goes out of the individual, floats over its own personality." As he said in another place, it is "almost a going out of the body, to think" ("Wealth," 711). Abstract, objective intelligence is well on the way to this accomplishment; yet it fears to complete what it has begun. Actually to *enter* the world of living Ideas, or creative spiritual being, is "to look in the eye of an abstract truth," "to see God face to face"; and this step imperils one's very selfhood, insofar as one's sense of self is body-based.

Emerson was intrepid in following his quest to its limit, but he was also honest with himself and with his readers. He knew it was seldom that he could, by grace, actually take the step that waited always to be taken, and then he could take it only in part. But he had no doubt of the necessity of making this advance. Humanity cannot go backward to earlier, perhaps more vital but less fully conscious states; yet when the soul's life, for nourishment, breathes only the thin air of abstraction, it inevitably becomes ever more anemic. The forward step must be taken. As a young man, in his very first book, *Nature*, Emerson indicated in epigrammatic form the first essential for this new beginning.

> *The problem of restoring to the world original and eternal beauty is solved by the redemption of the soul. The ... blank we see when we look at nature, is in our own eye. The axis of vision is not coincident with the axis of things, and so they appear not transparent but opaque. The reason why the world lacks unity ... is that man is disunited with himself. He cannot be a naturalist until he satisfies all the demands of the spirit. Love is as much its demand as perception. Indeed, neither can be perfect without the other.* [Emphasis added] (*Nature*, 41)

Let us attempt to sort out the main ingredients in this densely packed diagnosis and prescription, considering it point for point.

✦ ✦✦ Emerson first testifies that the world as we perceive it has lost its "original and eternal beauty." He realizes that this sacred aura of beauty, so deeply felt and joyfully celebrated by the cultures of times past, can return again only when human beings regain the sense for the higher, invisible glory that Whitman called "the Light of the light."

> For the world is not painted or adorned, but is from the beginning beautiful; and God has not made some beautiful things, but Beauty is the creator of the universe. ("The Poet," 321)

> But this beauty of Nature which is seen and felt as beauty, is the least part.... The presence of a higher, namely, of the spiritual element is essential to its perfection. (*Nature*, 11)

> A beauty not explicable is dearer than a beauty which we can see to the end of. It is nature the symbol, nature certifying the supernatural, body endowed with life.... ("The Poet," 326)

✦ ✦✦ To come into the presence of this Beauty requires "redemption of the soul," which is to say, a radical advance from the merely intellectual way of seeing things. Emerson finds, indeed, that when the scientifically educated but spiritually unawakened mind of modern times looks at nature, it sees a "blank." This blank is the briefest word to describe how the natural world looks when it is shorn not only of spiritual beauty but also of intrinsic meaning. To scrutinize minutely the face of a fellow human being, for example, yet lack any awareness of the vital thoughts and feelings in and behind the expressions of that face, would be to see it as a blank. The essential *meaning* of this face would have vanished. But it is quite in this way that so many today have come to see and conceive of the "facts"—that is, the face—of nature. Thus Emerson, too, even as Melville, has his own comment to make about the "whiteness of the whale"—the blankness in the face of nature shorn of God.

The blankness that meets our eye as observers, begins then with the quality of our own mind. When we ourselves are not fully present in our looking, when we have left behind, unused, major components of our own soul; then our zeal for objectivity has made even of *us* a bland, almost blank object. It should cause no surprise that, having given too little to the act of cognition, we get out of it far less than we ought.

✦ ✦✦ Emerson finds that the world as the modern mind views it is not only blank but "opaque"—that is, not really intelligible or see-throughable. We know much of physical detail, but a deeper sense of the "Whence? and Whither?" of the whole quite escapes us. As human beings conditioned to the critical, objective, abstract use of our minds, we work hard to make the most of lives lived in the context of a blank, enigmatic natural order wherein our human aspirations, loves, and values are total strangers. For nature as we conceive it *is* indifferent, and even inimical—to what is *humanly* most precious to us. As to what the whole of nature itself is about, we have no real idea.

Nature remains opaque to the mind that feels obliged to view things only from the outside, purely as onlooker. In this case, "the axis of vision is not coincident with the axis of things." Our vision will begin to coincide with what is being observed only when we try to see the beings of nature from within, as it were, as though by looking not at but through their own eyes, from their own center.

✦ ✦✦ The world "lacks unity" because we have lost feeling for the duty to bring our own indivisible wholeness to the contemplation of things in *their* indivisible wholeness.

> Empirical science is apt to cloud the sight, and by the very knowledge of functions and processes to bereave the student of the manly contemplation of the whole. (*Nature*, 36)

What we call objective scientific thinking is not what D.H. Lawrence, in Emerson's own spirit, felt it should be: "man in his wholeness, wholly attending." The more details of details the ceaselessly subdividing scientific disciplines bring to light, the farther away we find ourselves from a meaningful comprehension of things in their integrity. Our predilection for postmortem *analysis* is not balanced by an equal zeal to develop the power of *synthetic* vision. Such synthesis as we intellectually undertake but shuffles together again in dead form the living entity we have already dismembered.

> The naturalist is led from the road by the whole distance of his fancied advance.[5]

♦ ♦♦ This situation, Emerson says, will not change until "love" is added to "perception." By perception he means simply the attention usually given to the factual materiality of things as these are seen from the outside—and equally, as they are "known" when our thirst for "knowledge" has cut them apart and turned them analytically inside out. The opacity of blank facts thus perceived does not have the power to awaken love in the human heart. Love cannot be added to perception until the full inwardness of the observer's soul meets and joins with the inwardness—the living, creative Idea—hidden in what is being observed.

> Neither by detachment, neither by aggregation is the integrity of the intellect transmitted to its works, but by a vigilance which brings the intellect in its greatness and best state to operate every moment. *It must have the same wholeness which nature has.* [Emphasis added] ("Intellect," 300)

The question may well be asked: Can a proper scientific objectivity *permit* what Emerson is calling for—the imaginative and intuitive use of the soul's full power—as this is typified in love? The answer, he says, must be affirmative, because science is presently failing in the basic task it originally set for itself, namely, to come to the Truth of the universe that surrounds us and to which we belong.

> All science has one aim, namely, to find a theory of nature. We have theories of races and functions, but scarcely yet a remote approach to the idea of creation. *(Nature,* 3)

Emerson is sure of one thing: that a scientific method that really hopes to gain knowledge of what built the world and continues to be its life must find ways to open itself to the spirit.

> Through all its kingdoms, to the suburbs and outskirts of things, it [nature] is faithful to the cause whence it had its origin. It always speaks of Spirit. *(Nature,* 34)

> That which intellectually considered we call Reason, considered in relation to nature, we call Spirit. Spirit is the Creator. Spirit hath life in itself. *(Nature,* 15)

> A Fact is the end or last issue of spirit. *(Nature,* 19)

✦✦✦ The development of openness to spiritual reality has its own strict requirements. To be sure, such awareness must be objective and exact, as any true knowledge. But openness to the spirit will never be achieved without reverence, a trusting heart, and purity of motive. The end in view must be recognized as a sacred and holy one.

> 1. There is a probity of the Intellect, which demands, if possible, virtues more costly than any Bible has consecrated. It consists in an absolute devotion to truth, founded in a faith in truth.... I will speak the truth in my heart, or think the truth against what is called God.[6]

It is the office, I doubt not, of this age to annul that adulterous divorce which the superstition of many ages has effected between the intellect and holiness. The lovers of goodness have been one class, the students of wisdom another; as if either could exist in any purity without the other. Truth is always holy, holiness always wise.[7]

THE CHILD'S AWARENESS

Emerson saw in childhood the innocent wonder, selfless reverence, and heartfelt enthusiasm he felt must be recovered in maturity, after the individual has passed through the critical, self-conscious stage of rational analysis and intellectual abstraction. The child, just entering upon physical life, briefly foreshadows a mood of soul that has significant implications for adult cognition later on. The mature adult will have to retain or regain something entirely comparable to this mood, if his or her inquiry into truth is to proceed again from selfless wonder and is to prove capable of sustaining love between us and the universe we inhabit.

> To speak truly, few adult persons can see nature. Most persons do not see the sun. At least they have a very superficial seeing. The sun illumines only the eye of the man, but shines into the eye and the heart of the child. The lover of nature is he whose inward and outward senses are still truly adjusted to each other; who has retained the spirit of infancy, into the era of manhood. (*Nature*, 6)

Emerson observed, however, that among us the promise of spiritual communion with the wonderful world, as this is exhibited by early childhood, never properly "grows up." Instead of maturing and transforming their best childhood powers, most adults allow these to atrophy and be forgotten, while other, inferior, faculties of the mind press forward to establish exclusive dominion.

> Infancy is the perpetual Messiah, which comes into the arms of fallen men, and pleads with them to return to paradise. (*Nature*, 39)

> The history of mankind is the history of arrested growth. This premature stop, I know not how, befalls most of us in early youth; as if the growth of high powers, the access to rare truths, closed at two or three years in the child, while all pagan faculties went ripening on to sixty.[8]

What Emerson calls "pagan" faculties are, of course, those of earthbound seeing and thinking, which inquire boldly enough, to be sure, but have to confess that though they believe themselves to be open-minded toward all possibilities, they have never yet detected any trace of God's hand in what goes on in earthly experience. A certain arrogance characterizes the ordinary powers of intellect. From this unholiness of outlook, the sacred aspects of the world conceal themselves. What remains for cognition, Emerson calls "pagan," by which apparently he meant worldly, the opposite of sacred. "God-forsaken" might have been closer to his intention, for actually the so-called pagan's sense of the world seems always to have been touched in one way or another by a reverence for the spirit that is similar to the child's own sense—imaginative and intuitive rather than intellectual.

Emerson's evocation of childhood in order to illustrate his call for a higher form of cognition casts a special light on the problem of objectivity. On the one hand, children make no attempt to eliminate from their immediate observation of things the aesthetic and moral impressions they receive from them and that affect them deeply. Obviously, and fortunately, being unable to exclude these aspects from their naive, participatory kind of cognition, children respond fully—with their whole emotional and volitional being—to what they encounter. In this sense we could maintain that children are anything but objective, and are therefore certainly not a fitting model for scientists who are obliged to exclude subjective reactions from their inquiries. Yet, for Emerson, the natural child is in fact less self-bound, less brain-based, therefore less subjective, than most philosophers and scientists, despite all their scruples.

It is by our entry into, and close identification with, the cave of our particular heads that we adults come to our feeling of selfhood; and once this self-feeling has taken firm root in us, it is extremely hard to free ourselves from it. The child's consciousness, on the other hand, has not yet quite parted company with the universality out of which it has come. It has not yet entered fully into the confining limitations of bodily separateness, its personal cave. In this sense, early consciousness is actually so free of personal subjectivity that for some time it does not even identify itself as "I"; rather, it refers to itself in the third person, as though regarding itself from outside. This is the very trait that distinguishes what we call the objective way of seeing things. As Emerson remarked, the mind of the very young child is still "whole," because it feels itself still at one with the cosmic whole out of which it has emerged. And because this is so, he says, the child's observant eye remains "as yet unconquered"—meaning it is not yet corrupted or warped by the *self*-reference that so soon will set it as "subject" over against the rest of the world as "object."

The example of the child, then, is fruitful for the theory of knowledge. As Christ said, "Except ye turn, and become again as little children, ye shall not enter into the kingdom of heaven" (Matthew 18:3)—which seems to warn: You will not again experience the world as the child still does, in that integrity or wholeness wherein alone its spiritual reality is to be found.

In the matter of the child's awareness, Emerson finds a formidable challenge for those who would lift cognition to the height of spiritual Truth. For the child's example would require of them, as far as full objectivity goes, to *observe* of course with care, but then—their mind being empty of all save wonder—"having observed, observe again from the same unaffected, unbiased, unbribable, unaffrighted innocence" ("Self-Reliance," 147) as that of the child, who—as Thomas Traherne and William Wordsworth have testified—still sees the world in God. Not observe and then think, but observe and then observe again and again, patiently, with love, awaiting to gain the clues of wisdom not from one's own busy thinking-guessing, but as light instilled into the quietly receptive, participatory soul by the object itself.

In maturity, Emerson implies, our perception of the world should still be kindled by the trustful, childlike wonder that is the matrix from which love is born. Maturity should bring the child's diffuse, instinctive *feeling* of the spiritual background of physical existence to fully conscious awareness of that same spirit—but now in the realm of *thought*. Thinking itself should become, and should be felt to be, a spiritual event, an objective inspiration received from a living source. There should be an actual beholding of the self-sustaining, creative Ideas that are at work in the world with their intelligent, formative power. Such a further development can take place, however, only when "inward and outward senses are still truly adjusted to each other"; that is, when thought power, grounded in wonder and matured as love, has risen to become the gift of vision, before which the spirit of things, their actual being, reveals itself.

> Out of the human heart go as it were highways to the heart of every object in nature. ("History," 141)

> Whilst common sense looks at things or visible Nature as real and final facts, ... imagination ... is a second sight, looking through these.
> The vision of the intellect is not like the vision of the eye, but is union with the things known. ("Intellect," 292)

DEEP CALLS UNTO DEEP

Hidden depths in the human soul reach out toward hidden aspects of the great surrounding world. For the modern person, the quest for closer contact necessarily starts with thinking. But if our thoughtfulness is to make real contact with the life, the soul, the spirit—in other words, with the inward or "subjective" aspects of the objective world—cogitation must pass beyond the kind of objectivity that ends in abstractions. To apprehend the spiritual concretely, as being, the thinker must eventually become seer.

Having met the first requirement of modern consciousness, the seeker after truth must go further, to satisfy the paradoxical second demand. For if life is to be imparted to the thinking that is still dead, then certain of the so-called subjective responses of the soul, which quite legitimately had to be excluded at first, shall now be invited back. Reverence, devotion, love, aesthetic appreciation, and moral sense, as these live in the human heart and will, shall all be reaffirmed and used. They are themselves now to be purified by the same criterion of objectivity as the one that has been achieved in simple observation and intellection. Holistic knowing requires total engagement.

> In the uttermost meaning of the words, thought is devout, and devotion is thought. Deep calls unto deep. But in actual life, the marriage is not celebrated. (*Nature*, 41)

By being willing to exclude the soul's more intimate and profoundly felt responses—its power of wholehearted identification with that which confronts it—from scientific inquiry, humankind has indeed learned the discipline of objectivity and thereby gained a firm footing in the external world of "facts." The same discipline is needed in the further development of cognition if it is to advance, as it must, from the seen to the unseen. For Emerson believed that the disunion or divorce between nature and spirit, which has for some centuries been growing ever wider, can and must be bridged.

It is clear to Emerson that knowledge will not become wisdom, and we will not discover the inwardness that is also the loveliness and lovableness of world reality—for which our longing is intense, whether or not we allow ourselves to be aware of it—until we enlist our own intensified and purified inwardness. The necessity of this step, however, is not yet taken seriously by those who claim to speak with authority about the scientific method.

> There are innocent men who worship God after the tradition of their fathers, but their sense of duty has not yet extended to the use of all their faculties. And there are patient naturalists, but they freeze their subject under the wintry light of the understanding.... But when a faithful thinker, resolute to detach every object from personal relations and see it in the light of thought, shall, at the same time, kindle science with the fire of the holiest affections, then will God go forth anew into the creation. (*Nature*, 41)

On the one hand, the necessary limitations of the path of natural science in respect to things spiritual have long been acknowledged. They are not challenged by the religious. But on the other hand, the further supposition that religious piety itself has nothing in turn to give to scientific inquiry is taken equally for granted by the religious as well as by the scientists. Thus, even as the laboratories, in all their painstaking research, have not found God within the sensory world, the churches, for all their piety, have also ceased to look for him there. Both kinds of striving, the scientific and the religious, are failing to provide what cognition of full-fledged reality requires. When the quest is for truth, one may take either the more scientific path or the more religious, but the kinds of truth the two paths have thus far led to, manage to split the world into two realms that—this is rarely confessed—are in principle opposed to each other. Between them there is little communication, much less fructification. Emerson sought to reconcile and make fruitful both realms, each of which, due to its isolation from and immunity to the other, has been rendered essentially sterile.

> All the facts in natural history taken by themselves, have no value, but are barren, like a single sex. But marry it to human history [that is, to the human soul's deeper experience of the factual world], and it is full of life.
> (*Nature*, 16)

> All our science lacks a human side. . . . The motive of science was the extension of man, on all sides, into nature, till his hands should touch the stars, his eyes see through the earth, his ears understand the language of beast and bird, and the sense of the wind; and, through his sympathy heaven and earth should talk with him. But that is not our science. These geologies, chemistries, astronomies, seem to make wise, but they leave us where they found us.[10]

Emerson was not unaware that the scientifically discovered facts of natural history help to explain various bodily features of human existence, but he saw their relevance as limited to those aspects that are not essential. They leave out of account the soul and spirit that make human beings distinctively human. It is the religious orientation that *purports* to explore and develop the spiritual dimension of human nature, but the spirit, as theologically considered, remains for the most part a high abstraction—something "out of this world." And instead of casting a brilliant light into the actual Whence? and Whither? of earthly and cosmic natures, this spirit has little to do with the natural creation. Such an unworldly or other-worldly spirituality quite fails to lift, leaven, or fructify the sciences of this world in their preoccupation with matter.

Emerson's own aim was *one* world, a world in which material nature in all its aspects and in every process, reveals the creative spirit of which it is, after all, but the material manifestation.

> Once men thought Spirit divine, and Matter diabolic; one Ormuzd, the other Ahriman. Now science and philosophy [should] recognize ... how each reflects the other as face answers to face in a glass: nay, how the laws of both are one, or how one is the realization [or manifestation] of the other.[11]

> The noblest ministry of nature is to stand as the apparition of God. It is the organ through which the universal spirit speaks to the individual, and strives to lead back the individual to it. (*Nature*, 34)

POETRY AND TRUTH

It is the poet above all who typifies for Emerson the right approach to the kind of knowing that can raise material appearance into spiritual revelation, allowing "God" to shine articulately through into human consciousness. The poet deserves praise, therefore, because he or she stands for the function of creative art in general; and genuine art always issues from the union of matter and spirit that science and religion separately, fail to achieve. But in speaking of poetry as art, Emerson remains still the man of thought, the inquirer after *truth*. For him, "poetry" comes closer to vital truth than does "prose," for poetry attempts to render the spiritual aspects of reality in a living way. "*God himself does not speak prose.*"[12]

Emerson's idea of the higher form that science should take when enlivened by artistic feeling and deepened by moral intuition could be called a poetic, imaginative, or intuitive science—a "joyous science." He was entirely of Novalis' opinion": "*Je poetischer, je wahrer.*" The more poetic, the truer. As he himself said, "Poetry, if perfected, is the only verity, is the speech of man after the real, and not after the apparent."[13]

> Poetry is the perpetual endeavor to express the spirit of the thing, to pass the brute body and search the life and reason which causes it to exist.[14]

> Science is false by being unpoetical.[15]

What we confront in nature—in the cosmos as a whole and in each separate detail, so long as these remain but physical appearances—is a preliminary, static, revelation of divine creativeness. Within themselves, all things conceal the will to a further and living revelation of themselves; but the perceptions of our bodily senses and the interpretations of our ordinary intellect bring so-called objective facts to a halt for our consciousness, before what they have to say has been heard. The question is: How can we gain nature's confidence so as to transcend these limitations in our knowledge of her?

> Science does not know its debt to imagination.[16]

> [The] insight which expresses itself by what is called Imagination, is a very high sort of seeing, which does not come by study, but by the intellect being where and what it sees; by sharing the path or circuit of things through

forms, and so making them translucid to others. The path of things is silent. Will they suffer a speaker to go with them? A spy they will not suffer; a lover, a poet, is the transcendency of their own nature—him they will suffer. ("The Poet," 331-2)

The poet turns the world to glass.... For through that better perception he stands one step nearer to things, and perceives ... that *within the form of every creature is a force impelling it to ascend into a higher form*; and following with his eyes the life, uses the form which expresses that life. [Emphasis added] ("The Poet," 329)

The condition of true naming, on the poet's part, is his resigning himself to the divine *aura* which breathes through forms, and accompanying that. ("The Poet," 332)

By using the example of the poet, as representing all true artists, Emerson sets before us a thought that is basic to his whole concept of the function of the human knower in the realm of nature:

All the facts [of nature] are symbols of *the passage of the world into the soul of man, to suffer there a change and reappear a new and higher fact*. He uses forms according to the life, and not according to the form. This is true science. [Emphasis added] ("The Poet," 329)

The highest minds of the world have never ceased to explore the double meaning, or shall I say the quadruple or the centuple or much more manifold meaning of every sensuous fact. ("The Poet," 320)

What is implied here is much more than the usage lesser artists and poets often make of natural facts, employing them according to purely subjective fantasy rather than objective imagination. The issue concerns the actual life and meaning of these facts themselves. The concept is a difficult one, but it was formulated by Emerson already in *Nature*, his first book.

> But when, following the invisible steps of thoughts, we come to inquire, Whence is matter? and Whereto? many truths arise to us out of the recesses of consciousness. We learn that the highest is present to the soul of man; that the dread universal essence, which is not wisdom, or love, or beauty, or power, but all in one, and each entirely, is that for which all things exist, and that by which they are; that spirit creates; that behind nature, throughout nature, spirit is present; one and not compound it does not act upon us from without, that is, in space and time, but spiritually, or through ourselves: therefore, that *spirit, that is, the Supreme Being, does not build up nature around us, but puts it forth through us*, as the life of the tree puts forth new branches and leaves through the pores of the old. [Emphasis added] (*Nature*, 35)

> The soul of God is poured into the world through the thoughts of men.[17]

These statements are admittedly hard to follow. Yet they drive to the heart of what is at issue in the question of whether and how natural science can rise from its present legitimate form to the higher, equally legitimate, and even more necessary and fruitful form of the spiritualized science Emerson strove for. Making more explicit the analogy suggested by Emerson may be helpful.

The seed of a plant contains the "moral force," the Idea, that will eventuate in a beautiful flower or a mighty tree. But true as this is, the same seed being set in a place of honor on a velvet cushion, to be watched and studied over time, will never unfold what lies hidden within it. To bring forth the real possibility that remains unseen and unknown within the seed, it must be taken off the cushion and buried in the darkness of fertile soil. Only then can its germinal magic be released. The seedling that emerges will in turn have further need of an atmosphere of light and warmth for its continuing unfoldment. One phase will then follow another, until blossom, fruit, and the generation of new seed have made their appearance. But is that the whole story? Emerson says, No, there is more to come forth, and in some sense, the main part. This "more" is a series of still higher manifestations of the plant's mysterious nature and powers.

The *entire* physical plant, as represented in the totality of these successive stages of manifestation, can itself be regarded, so to speak, as still only a seed, one that, like all seeds, aspires to a further expression, ever more explicit, ever more intelligibly spiritual, of the secrets of its being. But such expression can issue only when these impalpable aspects of the plant nature have found their own proper ground wherein to germinate and bring forth something at the still higher level to which they aspire. That ground becomes available only when the plant as a whole has been lovingly welcomed into an appropriate form of human consciousness. Patient, trustful powers of will, heart, and mind, acting together in the soul seeking truth, are the new soil, as well as the atmosphere of warmth and light, required by the invisible, waiting, further potentialities of the God-force within the plant. Its aspiration, which had otherwise been balked, can now be realized. In this new environment it can emerge, stage by stage, even as the fostering human consciousness itself rises by advancing to subtler, spiritually ever more objective levels of cognition.

> The soul's advances are not made by gradation, such as can be represented by motion in a straight line, but rather by ascension of state, such as can be represented by metamorphosis—from the egg to the worm, from the worm to the fly. ("The Over-Soul," 265)

2. [True poetic] expression is organic, or the new type which things themselves take when liberated. As, in the sun, objects paint their images on the retina of the eye, so they, sharing the aspiration of the whole universe, tend to paint a far more delicate copy of their essence in his mind. Like the metamorphosis of things into higher forms is their change into melodies. ("The Poet," 331)

When even planets, stars, and constellations also transform themselves into such "melodies," we have come to the reality of what Pythagoras knew as the "harmony of the spheres." The whole world process in its evolving articulation becomes a divine music, and through this music higher meaning is revealed, a meaning that resounds only in the soul that has opened itself to inspiration.

CREATION AWAITS THE SONS OF GOD

Thus we approach the meaning of Emerson's at first baffling statement that "the Supreme Being does not build up nature around us but puts it forth through us." Nature's music cannot be heard as external sound by the physical ear. It can sound forth only in the human soul when thinking yields to inspiration.

In this connection, it may not be amiss to cite an equally baffling assertion made by St. Paul with respect to the essentials of our relation to nature. When set side by side, the two statements, St. Paul's and Emerson's, help to clarify each other.

> For the earnest expectation of the creation waiteth for the manifestation of the sons of God. . . . Because the creation itself also shall be delivered from the bondage of corruption into the glorious liberty of the children of God. For we know that the whole creation groaneth and travai-

leth in pain together until now. And not only they, but ourselves also who have the first fruits of the Spirit, even we ourselves groan within ourselves, waiting for the adoption, that is, the redemption of the body. (Romans 8:19-23)

This longing for "redemption" from the "bondage of corruption" which, according to Paul, all of nature shares with humankind insofar as human beings have not awakened to the essential in themselves, has traditional *religious* connotations that tend perhaps to obscure their value for an understanding of the role of spiritualized *cognition*. The bondage from which all the creatures of nature groan to be delivered is their mere appearance, as rendered static by our own supposition that they are only what they physically seem to be. For in fact they are more. Behind the story of limitation and transience they tell to the physical senses and to the physically oriented mind, all beings have more to say and show of their essential reality—of the sense in which they are "of God."

What Paul calls "the first fruits of the Spirit" are powers of imaginative and inspired consciousness in which human individuals first begin to awaken to their own reality. Human beings, who are favored by the potentiality of such consciousness, owe for this privilege—to all the beings of nature in whom conscious selfhood has not yet been attained—a sharing of their "glorious liberty." For it is only in and through this enhanced consciousness that they can find themselves clearly reflected in the truth of their being.

Thus nature waits for the appearance of human beings who have come to know themselves not as the cleverest of animals but as the "sons of God," and who therefore look with awakened and awakening eyes upon the rest of creation. For it is through the loving consciousness of those who have found spiritual freedom that all of earth's creatures are lifted as from an enchantment.

> But the natural man receiveth not the things of the Spirit of God; for they are foolishness unto him, neither can he know them, because they are spiritually discerned. (I Corinthians 2:14)

For St. Paul, as the result of his own awakening, realized that the human being is not just the entity physically perceived, and nature is not just nature in the same sense, both being equally mortal and as it were equally expendable. Human beings in their full potentiality are made by God, and the I AM which is God can awaken in them. Nature, too, is made by God, but limited to a lower stage of consciousness. Of itself, nature does not come to self-realization. As Emerson says,

> The world proceeds from the same spirit as the body of man. It is a remoter and inferior incarnation of God, a projection of God in the unconscious. (*Nature*, 56)

Our position calls upon us to realize what we owe to the rest of creation. Nature cannot come into its own self-experience until we have shown the way by taking the first step. The divine beauty, harmony, and love underlying all of nature become affirmed and further advanced here on earth only to the degree that we, in our awakened freedom, invite them into our purified, spiritualized consciousness.

Humanity's hope stems from our potentially direct relation to the spirit, which strives to become full awareness, heart of love, and power of thought within us. Nature's hope, however, lies in us, for so divine wisdom has ordained it. The question that arises is: How can it be that the kingdoms of nature have this intimate and fatal dependency upon the free will of humankind? To this question Emerson offers always the same clue:

> The Universe is the externization of the soul.... The earth and the heavenly bodies, physics and chemistry, we sensually treat, as if they were self-existent; but these are the retinue of that Being we have. ("The Poet," 325)

> From whatever side we look at Nature we seem to be exploring the figure of a disguised man. Nature is so pervaded with human life that there is something of humanity in all and in every particular.[18]

> In the bottom of the heart it is said: "I am, and by me, O child! this fair body and world of thine stands and grows. I am: all things are mine: and all mine are thine."[19]

> The thoughts [a man] delights to utter are the reason for his incarnation.... Did he not come into being because something must be done which he and no other is and does? Hereto was he born, to deliver the thought of his heart from the universe to the universe; to do an office which nature could not forego, nor he be discharged from rendering.[20]

THE MORAL ELEMENT

From what has already been said, the importance Emerson gave to the moral element in cognition is evident. For him, the necessity that moral purification precede the development of spiritual insight was an absolute. This was so not only because he finds moral values implicit in the natural creation itself, but also because without moral discipline the lens of human consciousness can be neither clarified nor focused. If heart and will are not clean, clear, quiet, and caring, they will be unable to perceive or to identify with the spectrum of moral values that nature exemplifies.

> The moral law lies at the centre of nature and radiates to the circumference. It is the pith and marrow of every substance, every relation, and every process. (*Nature*, 23)

> Therefore science always goes abreast with the just elevation of the man.... Since everything in nature answers to a moral power, if any phenomenon remains brute and dark it is because the corresponding faculty in the observer is not yet active. ("The Poet," 326)

INTELLECT AND INTUITION

But our review of Emerson's many-sided efforts to characterize what he envisioned as the spiritualization of natural science cannot leave unmentioned his philosophic distinction between what we might call intellect and intuition. Following Kant's distinction between *Verstand* and *Vernunft*, Emerson called these contrasting faculties of the human soul, respectively, "understanding," and "Reason."

> This relation between the mind and matter is not fancied by some poet, but stands in the will of God, and so is free to be known by all men. It appears to men, or it does not appear. Every property of matter is a school for the understanding—its solidity or resistance, its inertia, its extension, its figure, its divisibility. The understanding adds, divides, combines, measures, and finds nutriment and room for its activity in this worthy scene. Meantime, Reason transfers all these lessons into its own world of thought, by perceiving the analogy that marries Matter and Mind. (*Nature*, 19-20)

Reason, in Emerson's mind, stood not for a single stage or kind of cognition but for all the stages that rise above that of common understanding, whether these be called imagination, inspiration, or intuition. In one place or another, he sought to suggest distinctions between each of these cognitive levels, but he used Reason as an inclusive concept to cover the whole effort and journey of consciousness as, through strengthened love and faith, it mounts toward beholding creative spiritual reality. For him, this reality was the real world of "immortal necessary uncreated natures, that is Ideas" (*Nature*, 31). The discoveries to which Reason progressively gains access are the kind of revelation Emerson's religiously scientific and scientifically religious soul sought.

> At present, man applies to nature but half his force. He works in the world with his understanding alone. He lives in it and masters it by a penny-wisdom; and he that works most in it is but a half-man.... His relation to nature, his power over it, is through the understanding, as by manure; the economic use of fire, wind, water, and the mariner's needle; steam, coal, chemical agriculture; the repairs of the human body by the dentist and the surgeon.... Meantime, in the thick darkness, there are not wanting gleams of a better light—occasional examples of the action of man upon nature with his entire force—with Reason as well as understanding.... These are examples of Reason's momentary grasp of the sceptre; the exertions of a power which exists not in time or space, but an instantaneous in-streaming causing power. (*Nature*, 40)

Emerson never asked that intellect ("understanding") be abandoned. He sought only to discover how the reflective thinker, out of his or her own healthy intelligence, can go further and develop the intuitive certainty and spiritual power that are achieved by the genuine seer. The following passage from *Nature* attempts to characterize this transition as a progressive series of steps.

> To the senses and the unrenewed understanding, belongs a sort of instinctive belief in the absolute exist-

ence of nature. In their view man and nature are indissolubly joined. Things are ultimates, and they never look beyond their sphere. The presence of Reason mars this faith. The first effort of thought tends to relax this despotism of the senses which binds us to nature as if we were a part of it, and shows us nature aloof, and, as it were, afloat. Until this higher agency intervened, the animal eye sees, with wonderful accuracy, sharp outlines and colored surfaces. When the eye of Reason opens, to outline and surface are at once added grace and expression. These proceed from imagination and affection, and abate somewhat of the angular distinctness of objects. If the Reason be stimulated to more earnest vision, outlines and surfaces become transparent, and are no longer seen; causes and spirits are seen through them. The best moments of life are these delicious awakenings of the higher powers, and the reverential withdrawing of nature before its God. (*Nature*, 27-8)

What is indicated here as "the first effort of thought," or of Reason, brings about the first stage of spiritualized knowing, namely, "imagination." Emerson suggests that what to the physical eye had seemed an inert, solid tree becomes for imagination alive and "as it were, afloat." It floats because attention has shifted from the fixity of the mineralized object to its fluent, buoyant, and vital relationship with influences streaming in from cosmic space, from sun, moon, and stars. The tree is seen not in its motionless appearance, as something already achieved, but in its becoming, as a column of living sap that conjures and flows into characteristic forms.

Why should not ... we participate the invention of nature? This insight, which expresses itself by what is called Imagination, is a very high sort of seeing, which does not come by study, but by the intellect being where and what it sees. For if in any manner we can stimulate this instinct, new passages are opened for us into nature;

the mind flows into and through things hardest and highest, and [the perception and experience of] metamorphosis is possible. ("The Poet," 331-2)

For the human being whose "eye of Reason" is opening, the relatively frozen and uncommunicative *forms* of material reality begin, as it were, to melt and move. They become expressive *gesture*, such gesture as is made by a living, intelligent *presence*. "More earnest vision" seeks a still clearer sense of this presence, in order to understand the "moral" quality and significance of its expressive gesturing. It thus approaches the creative Ideas, the archetypes that shape and wield material existence. On this path, Imagination makes way for Inspiration, as mere life yields to soul presence. The beholding that has first been quickened to life evolves further and becomes a still more intimate and higher kind of experience: a spiritual hearing. The whole world becomes a construct and expression of musical tone. Earthly forms are no longer just alive; they have also ceased to be mute. Nature sounds and resounds intelligibly. Spiritual presence and meaning begin to make themselves known.

> Like the metamorphosis of things into higher organic forms is their change into melodies. Over everything stands its daemon or soul, and, as the form of the thing is reflected by the eye, so the soul of the thing is reflected by a melody. ("The Poet," 331)

The poet and the musician are inspired, even though perhaps but semiconsciously, when they attempt by physical means to render what they sense as the musicality of the universe. For Emerson, such artists foreshadow what he believed possible as a higher form of objective *cognition*.

As the beings of the world begin to reveal their nature through tones and sounding that are heard by the awakened spiritual ear, their utterance becomes increasingly coherent. They may be said to speak the names, primal spiritual "Words" or Ideas, which they essentially are. Thus only, are they at last fully known. And so, as the climax of Reason's unfoldment, intuitive wisdom dawns.

> We denote this primary wisdom as Intuition, whilst all later teachings are tuitions. In that deep force, the last fact behind which analysis cannot go, all things find their common origin. For the sense of *being* which in calm hours rises, we know not how, in the soul, is not diverse from things, from space, from light, from time, from man, but one with them and proceeds obviously from the same source whence their life and being also proceed. [Emphasis added] ("Self- Reliance," 155)

The important feature of Intuition, as Emerson conceived it, is that through it alone does the thinker who has become seer and hearer of divine Reality achieve for the first time full *certainty* in knowledge. For knowledge is sure only when it realizes complete *identification* of the knower with the spirit of what he knows. At the level of pure being—not matter, not life, not soul, but primordial spirit—this becomes possible.

IN CONCLUSION

Perhaps Emerson's own observation, though lifted from a different context in "The American Scholar," offers a fitting last word in this matter of comparing the merits and requirements of natural science as we presently know it with the spiritual science Emerson himself did so much to prepare:

> If there is any period one would desire to be born in, is it not the age of Revolution; when the old and the new stand side by side and admit of being compared; when the

energies of all men are searched by fear and hope; when the historic glories of the old can be compensated by the rich possibilities of the new era? This time, like all times, is a very good one, if we but know what to do with it. (60)

What Emerson, whose mind "in equal measure with its piety was of an inquiring nature," did with his own time, was to try to remove the chasm that existed between traditional religion and modern science. He wanted a science that was spiritual and a religious faith that was thoroughly grounded in science.

The religion which is to guide and fulfil the present and coming ages, whatever else it be, must be intellectual. The scientific mind must have a faith which is science.... Let us have nothing now which is not its own evidence.[21]

NOTES

Emerson felt sure that the goal to which he aspired so strongly would yet be achieved in Western culture. It would happen because it must: humanity's further development required it. This conviction on his part seems to justify mention of my own belief that an authentic realization of the thing Emerson prophesied has appeared in our time (see Appendix C).

1. Ralph Waldo Emerson, "Divinity School Address" in *The Complete Essays and Other Writings of Ralph Waldo Emerson*, Brooks Atkinson, ed. (New York: Random House, 1950), 82. Page numbers for further references to this book are given in the text with essay title.
2. William H. Giliam et al., eds., *The Journals and Miscellaneous Notebooks of Ralph Waldo Emerson*, 14 vols. (Cambridge: Harvard University Press, 1960), vol. 5, 391.
3. This thought is suggested often by Emerson, but I fail to find the particular reference.
4. Ralph Waldo Emerson, "Inspiration," *The Complete Writings of Ralph Waldo Emerson* (New York: Wise, 1929), 809.
5. Emerson,"Beauty," in *The Complete Writings*, 606.
6. Emerson,"Natural History of Intellect," in *The Complete Writings*, 1274.
7. Emerson,"The Method of Nature,"in *The Complete Writings*, 68.
8. Emerson, "Natural History of Intellect," in *The Complete Writings*, 1265.

9. Emerson, "Poetry and Imagination," in *The Complete Writings*, 732.
10. Emerson, "Beauty," in *The Complete Writings*, 606-7.
11. Emerson, "The Sovereignty of Ethics," in *The Complete Writings*, 1010.
12. Emerson, "Poetry and Imagination," in *The Complete Writings*, 730.
13. Ibid., 732.
14. Ibid., 731.
15. Ibid., 729.
16. Ibid.
17. "Perpetual Forces," in *The Complete Writings*, 973.
18. Emerson, "Natural History of the Intellect," in *The Complete Writings*, 1253; and *Nature*, in *Essays*, 35.
19. Emerson, "The Method of Nature," in *The Complete Writings*, 64.
20. Ibid., 60.
21. Emerson, "Worship," in *The Complete Writings*, 594.

8
RADICAL INDIVIDUALISM AND SOCIAL REFORM

> *I say of all this tremendous and dominant play of solely materialistic bearings upon current life in the United States, with the results already seen, accumulating, and reaching far into the future, that they must either be confronted and met by an at least equally subtle and tremendous force-infusion for purposes of spiritualization, for the pure conscience, for genuine aesthetics, and for absolute and primal manliness and womanliness—or else our modern civilization, with all its improvements, is in vain, and we are on the road to a destiny... equivalent in its real world, to that of the fabled damned.* —Whitman, Democratic Vistas

> *...all failed to see that the Reform of Reforms must be accomplished without means.* —Emerson, "Lecture on The Times"

NOW, AS THEN

DESPITE their very different personalities, Walt Whitman and Ralph Waldo Emerson agreed perfectly in their concept of individuality. Spiritualization of the individual's selfhood-consciousness was the goal they shared, and it was on this basis that they built their hopes for social reform. Perhaps each is better known today for his seemingly self-sufficient attitudes than for his concern about social improvements, but the message of both in the latter respect was vivid and urgent. It becomes especially relevant just now as we near the end of the twentieth century and the millennium, and when the feeling is strong—and rightly so—that our society must radically change many of its ways of doing things.

It seems that practically all would-be reformers, now as then, allow themselves to become preoccupied with what they imagine to be their main problem first and last, which is: By what techniques of pressure or persuasion can they manage to mobilize the numbers and the money that will be needed to bring their proposals to legal enactment? Yet though these techniques may in practice seem to work, they are actually foreign to the spirit of the reformers' original idea. This becomes evident when we note where many reformers think power actually lies, and in what they place their trust. "Where and how shall we find the *might* that can establish our right?" is the question of their little faith.

Rarely do we hear an Emersonian or Whitmanian voice raised in objection. We seem to have forgotten what these men and others of their time tried so hard to instill into the American consciousness, namely, that the place to begin is at the beginning. The beginning is always spirit. Not money, not numbers, not laws, can be trusted to do the job. The only power that really makes and really lasts is the power of the spirit. All reform that can be counted on to continue working as intended depends upon lasting changes taking place in the hearts and minds of people.

Let us remember the profound connection Emerson and Whitman saw between the economic and political ills of their time and the anemia of the spiritual climate, which they held to be still more basic. We look first to Whitman, then to his great friend.

WHITMAN

Walt Whitman spoke passionately rather than analytically about the debilitating effect of moral indifference and skepticism upon culture, politics, and economic life. He was profoundly distressed that what should be America's best contribution to human society was so little appreciated and so greatly endangered. His appeal was essentially religious, not of the church but of the individual soul's own experience.

It is unfortunate that the conceptions of Whitman's character and significance that prevail today, one hundred years after his death, have been unduly influenced by a narrow fascination with enigmatic aspects of his personal life. The deeper moral-religious quality of his spirit remains practically unknown to many readers, though it is abundantly plain throughout *Leaves of Grass* and becomes explicit in his *Democratic Vistas*. His function and rank as an American "herald of the spirit" in the religious sense cannot be missed in the latter work.

Published in 1871 when Whitman was fifty-two, *Democratic Vistas* is the voice of maturity, but the convictions to which it gives impassioned utterance had long been vital to the author. He felt that the problems facing humanity, and notably his own country, called urgently for a priestly level of vision and commitment. But he believed that this priestly function was much less likely to be exercised by those who preach from the pulpit than by the wielders of the literary pen. In his day, the individual writer or author—the "literatus"—accounted for what today issues more anonymously from the combined mass media.

> Viewed today, from a point of view sufficiently overarching, the problem of humanity, all over the civilized world is social and religious, and is to be finally met and treated by literature. The priest departs, the divine literatus comes.[1]

> In the civilization of today it is undeniable that over all the arts, literature dominates, serves beyond all—shapes

the character of church and school—or, at any rate, is capable of doing so. Including the literature of science, its scope is indeed unparalleled. (396)

Certainly those best remembered for providing spiritual nourishment and guidance to the Americans of Whitman's time were the outstanding literary figures. The situation in our own day, though rendered more impersonal and amorphous by new techniques of communication, remains essentially the same.

But Whitman had hope for literature only to the extent that it actually provides the *spiritual* content modern humanity needs. Such abstract ideals as "democracy" and "freedom" will never gain vital, creative power for citizens who are merely literate, no matter how great the flood of worldly news—information, opinion, and propaganda—they receive.

> For know you not, dear, earnest reader, that the people of our land may all read and write, and may all possess the right to vote—and yet the main things may be entirely lacking? (393)

The fundamental need and lack in the United States, said Whitman, is of

> native authors, literatures, far different, far higher in grade, than any yet known, sacerdotal, modern ... permeating the whole mass of American mentality, taste, belief, breathing into it a new breath of life, giving it decision, affecting politics far more than the popular superficial suffrage ... accomplishing (what neither the schools nor the churches and their clergy have hitherto accomplished, and without which this nation will no more stand, permanently, soundly, than a house will stand without a substratum), a religious and moral character beneath the political and productive and intellectual bases of the States. (393)

RADICAL INDIVIDUALISM AND SOCIAL REFORM

To strengthen this character was a responsibility Whitman felt to be peculiarly his own. Such was the thrust and signature of his whole life's effort. He dedicated himself to the task of digging, as it were, the spiritual "substratum" for the economic and political "house" the New World was attempting to build. Recognition of the necessity for this foundation to be firmly laid, he believed, could

> give more compaction and moral identity ... to these States, than all its Constitutions, legislative and judicial ties, and all its hitherto political, warlike, or materialistic experiences.... For, I say, the true nationality of the States, the genuine union, when we come to a mortal crisis, is, and is to be, after all, neither the written law, nor (as is generally supposed) either self-interest, or common pecuniary or material objects—but the fervid and tremendous Idea, melting everything else with resistless heat, and solving all lesser and definite distinctions in vast, indefinite, spiritual, emotional power. (397-8)

What is the "tremendous Idea"? It is the realization of our spiritual origin and destiny. When the nation lacks this experience and understanding, "It is as if we were somehow endowed with a vast and more and more thoroughly appointed body, and then left with little or no soul." (400)

> I hail with joy the oceanic, variegated, intense practical energy, the demand for facts, even the business materialism of the current age, our States. But woe to the age and land in which these things, movements, stopping at themselves, do not tend to ideas. As fuel to flame, and flame to the heavens, so must wealth, science, materialism—even this democracy of which we make so much—unerringly feed the highest mind, the soul. (460)

Democracy speaks for the honored equality of human beings in respect of their social rights and duties. Genuine economic welfare is built upon the friendly collaboration of men and women who work to satisfy material needs. Both are essential. But still more basic is the realm of spiritual self-development, whence the vision of worthwhile purpose and the vitality to pursue such a purpose flow into all spheres of human activity. As Whitman said:

> For my part, I would alarm and caution even the political and business reader, and to the utmost extent, against the prevailing delusion that the establishment of free political institutions and plentiful intellectual smartness, with general good order, physical plenty, industry, etc. (desirable and precious advantages they all are), do, of themselves, determine and yield to our experiment of democracy the fruitage of success. (398-9)

> For I say at the core of democracy, finally, is the religious element. (414)

As to the health of the religious element in America, Whitman's observations left no room for complacency.

> Never was there, perhaps, more hollowness of heart than at present, and here in the United States. Genuine belief seems to have left us. The underlying principles of the States are not honestly believed in ... nor is humanity itself believed in.... We live in an atmosphere of hypocrisy throughout.... A lot of churches, sects, etc., the most dismal phantasms I know, usurp the name of religion.... From deceit in the spirit, the mother of false deeds, the offspring is already incalculable. (399)

It was part of Whitman's genius that he always conceived of his nation's destiny in evolutionary terms. First, of course, there had to be the physical discovery of the Western world that would show such an aptitude for focusing upon and mastering material realities. Whitman had this special gift in mind when he called America "the most positive of lands," for he realized that materialism has its own destined role to play; it has its own kind of germinal/spiritual as well as practical justification. But unless the truths of materialism lead *beyond* themselves in the right way at the right moment, they are death-dealing, and death follows from them into every sphere of social life.

When and how, Whitman asked himself, shall the advance from physical to spiritual discovery of the "New World" be made?

> We stand, live, move, in the huge flow of our age's materialism—in its spirituality. We have founded the most positive of lands. The founders have passed to other spheres—but what are these terrible duties they have left us? (447)

America is the "daughter of a physical revolution" that started with the breakthrough to the West by Columbus and was confirmed by the revolutionary disengagement of the Colonies from Europe; but she was always destined, Whitman hoped and believed, to be the "mother of the true revolutions, which are of the interior life." (449)

What then is to be done? Somehow the concepts, the basic ideas that presently determine the nation's course, must undergo a transformation. Our eyes and expectations must be raised. Science and technology, and the education based upon them, must be spiritualized. Both political and economic life will have to be re-envisioned and reshaped correspondingly. Such inspiration for change will have to come from inspired writers, "stars of the first magnitude": souls, indeed, who have penetrated the mystery of death, to find in it the secret of the Life of life.

> In the future of these States must arise poets immenser far, and make great poems of death. The poems of life are great, but there must be poems of the purport of life, not

only in itself, but beyond itself.... Faith, very old, now scared away by science, must be restored, brought back by the same power that caused her departure—restored with new sway, deeper, wider, higher than ever. (463)

The same cognitive *wonder* and *will to understand* that prompted scientific investigation in its materialistic phase (and felt compelled in the process to eliminate all attempts to inquire into unseen higher worlds) should by now have arrived at the stage where it is not only possible but desirable, to shift its emphasis and transform its method. If humanity is not to be driven into still deeper darkness, science itself must find the way to supplement its physical empiricism with a spiritual empiricism, and religion must make ready to supplant blind faith with seeing faith, the kind of faith St. Paul developed as "the *evidence* of things *not* seen."

The elevating and etherealizing ideas of the unknown and of unreality must be brought forward with authority, as they are the legitimate heirs of the known, and of reality, and at least as great as their parents.... Let us take our stand, our ground, and never desert it, to confront the growing excess and arrogance of realism. (459)

Then that which was long wanted will be supplied, and *the ship that had it not before in all her voyages will have an anchor*. [Emphasis added] (463)

Whitman was convinced that spiritual sight must supplement physical sight, that spiritual knowledge must rise up from material knowledge, and that this normal evolutionary advance was an absolute requirement of the time and the times to come. As he brings his *Democratic Vistas* to conclusion, he confesses that everything depends henceforth upon the introduction into our American culture of an altogether higher, truer language and manifestation of the spirit than natural science as such has hitherto supplied or, indeed, is inherently capable of supplying.

> It really seems to me the condition, not only of our future national and democratic development, but of our perpetuation.... I say of all this tremendous play of solely materialistic bearings upon current life in the United States, with the results already seen, accumulating, and reaching far into the future, that they must either be confronted and met by at least an equally subtle and tremendous force-infusion for purposes of spiritualization ... or else our modern civilization, with all its improvements, is in vain, and we are on the road to a destiny, a status, equivalent, in its real world, to that of the fabled damned. (466-7)

Whitman, the supposedly everlasting optimist, confessed to a certain dread regarding "the America of our hopes." This dread concerned what he saw as a lack of the will to strive for *genuine* individuality. Failing this effort, society, in his view, had no purpose. Yet precisely through this endeavor, calling as it does for courage, faith, and initiative of soul, society stood to realize its rightful hopes in every practical sphere.

Individualism was basic to all of Whitman's thought and effort toward social reform, and his zeal in this cause was no less radical than Emerson's. In the "simplicity of unsophisticated Conscience," he found the essential of true "I am" consciousness; and in the spiritually awakened individual, he beheld both the root and the flowering of true religion.

> The ripeness of Religion is doubtless to be looked for in this field of individuality, and is a result that no organization or church can ever achieve.... Religion, although casually arrested, and, after a fashion, preserved in the

churches and creeds, does not depend at all upon them, but is a part of the identified [or truly "individualized"] soul, which, when greatest, knows not bibles in the old way, but in new ways—the identified soul, which can really confront Religion when it extricates itself entirely from the churches, and not before. . . .

I should say, indeed, that only in the perfect uncontamination and solitariness of individuality may the spirituality of religion positively come forth at all. Only here, and on such terms, the meditation, the devout ecstasy, the soaring flight. Only here, communion with the mysteries, the eternal problems, whence? whither? Alone, and identity, and the mood—and the soul emerges, and all statements, churches, sermons, melt away like vapors. . . . Bibles may convey, and priests expound, but it is exclusively for the noiseless operation of one's isolated Self, to enter the pure ether of veneration, reach the divine levels, and commune with the unutterable. (433-4)

EMERSON

Both Whitman and Emerson could have agreed upon a formula sure to arouse in conventional minds a misunderstanding: "The more individual, the more social." For is not individualism, presumably, just that which insists upon going its own way, at whatever cost to social bonds?

Presently we shall be trying to understand what it is that justifies the words on social solidarity I have put into the mouths of both Whitman and Emerson. Before going further, however, and to balance Whitman's critique of the social conditions in which he found himself, let us turn to Emerson's views on aspects of that same society. To him, the economic effects of egotism pretending to be individualism and the political effect of "public opinion" pretending to be the voice of democracy were especially unfortunate.

On the Economy

Emerson observed that his fellow Americans were attuned primarily to the economic side of life. While he found no fault with this predilection as such and could readily acknowledge, as did Whitman, its benefits even to the human soul, he obviously had to consider it a fatal error when a nation allowed itself to hope more from the power of money than from that of moral ideas and ideals.

> The Americans have many virtues, but they have not Faith and Hope. I know no two words whose meaning is more lost sight of. We use these words as if they were as obsolete as Selah and Amen.... The Americans have little faith. They rely on the power of a dollar; they are deaf to a sentiment. They think you may talk the north wind down as easily as raise society.[2]

It was the appropriate moral sentiments that Emerson found wanting in the mainstream of the nation's economy—the feelings of genuine human solidarity and concern. Sheer selfish gain (the illusory aspect of economic endeavor) he saw too often as the primary motive; service and communal effort (the really essential and fruitful aspects) came second. Naturally, he wanted the order reversed.

> The general system of our trade ... is a system of selfishness; is not dictated by the high sentiments of human nature; is not measured by the exact law of reciprocity, much less by the sentiments of love and heroism, but is a system of distrust, of concealment, of superior keenness, not of giving but of taking advantage. (71)

Selfishness calls upon the mind to be shrewd and clever rather than truthful. Unless this underlying purpose has been actually replaced by a nobler sentiment—one more favorable both to truth and to the long-term interest of the economy itself—the ugly motive inevitably goes on to corrupt much besides the negotiations of "trade"; indeed, it affects every undertaking in which money becomes the goal.

> But by coming out of trade you have not cleared yourself. The trail of the serpent reaches into all the lucrative professions and practices of man. Each has its own wrongs. Each finds a tender and very intelligent conscience a disqualification for success. Each requires of the practitioner a certain shutting of the eyes, a certain dapperness and complaisance, an acceptance of customs, a sequestration from the sentiments of generosity and love, a compromise of ... integrity. (72)

Emerson followed the destructive play of egoism into all that concerned the ownership and use of *property*. The insistence upon what is mine, what belongs to me and is therefore not yours and need not be shared with you, no matter what your condition of want, is a denial of solidarity with the rest of the human race. No person should imagine that he has either an original or an ultimate claim upon what earth existence offers to be shared by all its guests. The reality is that natural resources of every kind, whether the air and waters and produce of the earth itself, or the light and warmth of the sun above, are beauties not earned but freely given. Such are not to be "possessed" in any absolute sense. All are meant for the common welfare and development of humanity as a whole.

To Emerson, an excessive concern with acquiring and protecting private property must be traced back to a want of true self-reliance.

> Men have looked away from themselves and at things so long that they have come to esteem the religious, learned and civil institutions as guards of property, and they deprecate assaults on these, because they feel them to be

assaults on property. They measure their esteem of each other by what each has, and not by what each is. But a cultivated man becomes ashamed of his property, out of new respect for his nature. Especially he hates what he has if he sees that it is accidental—came to him by inheritance, or gift, or crime; then he feels that it is not having; it does not belong to him, has no root in him and merely lies there because no revolution or no robber takes it away. But that which a man is, does always by necessity acquire; and what the man acquires, is living property, which does not wait the beck of rulers, or mobs, or revolutions, or fire, or storm, or bankruptcies, but perpetually renews itself wherever the man breathes.[3]

The injustice of prevailing laws that are at pains to protect the absolute ownership of properties but say little about social obligations in the use of them, is painfully felt by those who from the beginning lack both property and the means to acquire it. But Emerson, in his usual cool way, observed that if egoism should dominate in the craving of the poor, and still be what persuades the well-to-do to lighten their lot by conferring upon them from time to time minor benefits, right action will obviously not replace wrong.

> Let the amelioration in our laws of property proceed from the concession of the rich, not from the grasping of the poor. Let us begin by habitual imparting.... Let me feel that I am a lover. I am to find my reward in the act. (78)

Neither grasping demands on the part of the poor, nor patronizing concessions by the wealthy will establish justice in the matter of property. Only a radically different spirit will ever achieve more than the temporary appearance of equity. That different spirit, to speak plainly, is love; and, of course, love works its wonders only when freely offered from the hearts of individuals. It lies beyond the power of cleverness to contrive, or law to command, the opening of the individual human heart.

> The criticism and attack on institutions which we have witnessed has made one thing plain, that society gains nothing whilst a man, not himself renovated, attempts to renovate things around him.... No one gives the impression of superiority to the institution, which he must give who will reform it. It makes no difference what you say, you must make me feel that you are aloof from it; by your natural and supernatural advantage do easily see to the end of it—do see how man can do without it. Now all men are on one side. No man deserves to be heard against property. Only Love, only an Idea, is against property as we hold it. ("New England Reformers," 455)

It may come as a surprise to those who have tended to think of Emerson as cold, that he speaks so simply and warmly of the power of love.

> Let our affection flow out to our fellows: it would operate in a day the greatest of all revolutions.... Love would put a new face on this weary old world in which we dwell as pagans and enemies too long, and it would warm the heart to see how fast the vain diplomacy of statesmen, the impotence of armies and navies, and lines of defence, would be superseded by this unarmed child. Love will creep where it cannot go, will accomplish that by imperceptible methods—being its own lever, fulcrum, and power—which force could never achieve. (78)

The conscious concept of *property*, or "mineness," begins obviously with the "I am" consciousness, and can evolve for the better only as that evolves. It will always mirror our idea of our own nature and proper relationship with the rest of humanity. The problem of property ownership is clearly of great social concern, but its origin and its solution derive primarily from one's concept of selfhood. What is the authentic and ultimate purpose of life, and what therefore may be considered real requirements and real security, within this earth existence whose benefits should accrue to all?

Much in the field of criminality is related to the property question. Here, too, Emerson's opinion was consistent. He observed that only essential goodness can cast out evil, for in the end no threat of social force, in the form of law and punishment, will eliminate or even control criminality.

Only the trust of loving hearts that see deeply enough into their own and other hearts to find *reason* for trust, can tame and heal the wildness of hearts that have succumbed to hate.

> Our age and history, for these thousand years, has not been the history of kindness, but of selfishness. Our distrust is very expensive. The money we spend for courts and prisons is very ill laid out. We make, by distrust, the thief, the burglar, and incendiary, and by our court and jail we keep him so. An acceptance of the sentiment of love throughout Christendom for a season would bring the felon and the outcast to our side in tears, with the devotion of his faculties to our service. (78)

On Politics

Emerson's comment on the political life of his day foreshadows a phenomenon that we may imagine is peculiar to our own time, when opinion-polling on political issues has become a veritable industry. But the idea behind it must already have been fully operative in the last century. In his study of American democracy, Alexis de Tocqueville observed that in America "public opinion" exercised a coercive influence on public policy that went well beyond what any European monarch or tyrant would have dared to try imposing.

And in his "Self-Reliance," Emerson feelingly acknowledged this power.

> For nonconformity the world whips you with its displeasure.... The sour faces of the multitude... have no deep cause, but are put on and off as the wind blows and a newspaper directs. Yet is the discontent of the multitude more formidable than that of the senate and the college.... When the ignorant and the poor are aroused, and when the unintelligent brute force that lies at the bottom of society is made to growl and mow, it needs the habit of magnanimity and religion to treat it godlike as a trifle and of no concernment. ("Self-Reliance," 151)

Politicians are now accustomed to pay an attention that amounts to subservience to every sign of a shift in public opinion, as this is reported daily by one poll or another. Because it lacked our electronic devices, society a hundred and fifty years ago was less developed in this respect, but essentially not different. And the theory that sanctifies this behavior was doubtless called then, as it still is now, "democratic." It is what passes for the sacred rule "of the *people*, by the *people*, for the *people*."

But if such be the idea of popular sovereignty, what will ultimately prevent an incessant opinion-polling from entirely displacing the formalities of occasional vote-casting as the central engine of democratic government? And what is to prevent democracy itself from turning, as Plato long ago predicted it eventually would do, into a mobocracy?

We can at least surmise Emerson's view of how a rightly conceived popular government need not become mob rule, and need not therefore call eventually for a dictator, a single domineering ego, to bring order out of the chaos created by the clamoring multitude of discordant small egos. For Emerson pictured the situation when pharaohs and kings were in their right time and place. In that period, many such rulers received an education that taught and disciplined them to feel most intimately that their earthly power was always to be understood as subject to a higher authority—that of the spirit itself. The "divine right of kings," upon which they were being trained to enter, implied strictest responsibility, and the duty of unquestioning obedience to this higher authority. The obedience of genuine pharaohs and kings was to the spirit of their land and people, conceived according to inspirations they habitually sought and received. This kind of inclusive and objective concern, painfully acquired and heeded, was the reason the best of ancient priest-kings felt it only right to speak, each of himself, in the plural as "we" rather than "I."

Then came the stage in human development, as required by the further evolution of the "I am" consciousness, when democracy inevitably began to set monarchy aside. This step could go well or ill. It would go well only to the extent that "the people," as individuals, would choose *not* to pull kings down out of ignorant scorn for the very idea of divine right, but would instead feel inspired and obliged to raise themselves up in accord with the example royalty had once set before them. Such an elevation of each commoner's consciousness to noble standing would, of course, be presumptuously false, unless it presupposed the royal kind of self-discipline, which is to say, the strict obedience to what the citizens recognized in their souls as higher, broader, and more far-seeing than mere self-interest. To be king-like, citizens would have habitually, of their own free choice, to subordinate their personal preferences to concern for the welfare of the social organism as a whole.

I know of no place where Emerson spelled out his view in just this manner, but it is altogether consistent with his conception of true individuality. The high calling of human selfhood is not to be taken for granted, nor confused with self-concern and self-preference. It is a moral elevation achieved precisely through subordination of the lesser, private self to a higher and more inclusive Self.

> When private men shall act with original views, the lustre will be transferred from the actions of kings to those of gentlemen. The world has been instructed by its kings.... It has been taught by this colossal symbol the mutual reverence that is due from man to man. The joyful loyalty with which men have everywhere suffered the king, the noble ... to walk among them by a law of his own ... and represent the law in his person, was the hieroglyphic by which they obscurely signified their consciousness of their own right and comeliness, the right of every man. ("Self-Reliance," 155)

In the question that immediately followed the above in "Self-Reliance," together with its suggestion of an answer, Emerson indicated what he meant by "original" as contrasted with personal or idiosyncratic views:

> What is *the aboriginal Self*, on which a universal reliance may be grounded?... Here is the *fountain* of action and thought. Here are the *lungs* of that inspiration which giveth man wisdom and which cannot be denied without impiety and atheism. [Emphasis added] ("Self-Reliance," 155-6)

Emerson's reliance on the "aboriginal" universal Self is a far cry from our present reliance on public opinion as the basis for democracy. To the question of whether mere numerical majorities, as tabulated by either poll or vote, shall be taken as dependably expressing the true "will of the people," Emerson would answer in the negative. For private citizens can so readily fail to remember their duty to consult and obey the higher Self, who holds in view the welfare of *all* the people. They then speak from their selfish interest, and the addition of their testimony to that of no matter how many other such selves will not serve the more deeply buried, actual public will. When such a superficially majoritarian judgment becomes mandatory as law, it will likely result in a policy that pleases no one for long and that may even come to serve purposes quite the opposite of what had been hoped for.

Emerson's warning against the numerical idea of democracy and his concept of the requirements for truly democratic government find expression in words such as these:

> Is it not the chief disgrace in the world, not to be an unit; not to be reckoned one character; not to yield that peculiar fruit which each man was created to bear, but to be reckoned in the gross, in the hundred, or the thousand, of the party, the section, to which we belong; and our opinion predicted geographically, as the north, or the south? Not so, brothers and friends—please God, ours shall not be so.... We will walk on our own feet; we will work with our own hands; we will speak our own minds.... The dread of man and the love of man shall be a wall of defence and a wreath of joy around all. *A nation of men will for the first time exist, because each believes himself inspired by the Divine Soul which also inspires all men.* [Emphasis added] ("The American Scholar," 63)

> Leave this hypocritical prating about the masses.... Masses! The calamity is the masses. I do not wish any mass at all, but honest men only, lovely, sweet, accomplished women only.... Away with this hurrah of masses, and let us have the considerate vote of single men spoken on their honor and their conscience.[4]

"But now we are a mob," Emerson said. He did not go on to say that if we are a mob, and too proud, besides, to change our ways of political thinking and doing, we shall yet be forced one day to realize that the process we are allowing to establish itself is indeed tending to become a fractious and intemperate mobocracy, rather than a democracy graced by high wisdom and deep harmony. For the true form of the latter society to take shape, he maintained, it is paradoxical but necessary that we citizens realize individually that we must, indeed, "go alone."

> The reformers summon conventions and vote and resolve in multitudes. Not so, O friends! will the God deign to enter and inhabit you, but by a method precisely the reverse. It is only as a man puts off all foreign support and stands alone that I see him to be strong and to prevail. He is weaker by every recruit to his banner. ("Self- Reliance," 169)

The Essence of Reform

Emerson expressed "respect and joy" in contemplation of the social reforms that were springing up on all sides in the last century. But he felt all the more compelled to insist upon "the paramount duties of self-reliance."[5] He found the impulse towards reform "sacred" in its original motivation—but "in its management and details, timid and profane."

> For the origin of all reform is in that mysterious fountain of the moral sentiment in man, which, amidst the natural, ever contains the supernatural for men. *That* is new and creative. *That* is alive. *That* alone can make a man other than he is. Here or nowhere resides unbounded energy, unbounded power.[6] [Emphasis added]

> By new infusions alone of the spirit by which he is made and directed, can he be re-made and reinforced. ("Lecture on The Times," 87)

Clearly, the essence of Emerson's contention was that it is *right* that makes might, not the other way around. He foresaw eventual failure for associations that hope to gain power by the *might* of numbers, when many of those presumed to be marching together are still, in fact, less than truly at one with the "right" for which they are asking to be counted.

But let there be one man, let there be truth in two men, in ten men, then is concert for the first time possible: because the force which moves the world is a new *quality*, and can never be furnished by adding whatever *quantities* of a different kind. [Emphasis added] ("New England Reformers," 457)

It is no wonder, however, that projects for reform do attract widespread interest, causing associations of all kinds to gather, originally with good intentions.

The world is awaking to the idea of union, and these projects show what the world is thinking of. It is and will be magic. Men will live and communicate, and plough, and reap, and govern, as by added ethereal power, when once they are united.... But this union must be inward, and not one of covenants, and is to be reached by a reverse of the methods they use. The union is only perfect when all the uniters are isolated.... The union must be ideal in actual individualism. ("New England Reformers," 457-8)

Words pass the eye so easily, so swiftly, these days, because, being so seldom coined from original thought, they rarely challenge real thinking. We are usually right in assuming that they are saying what we have already heard and know. Then, if a sentence calls special attention to itself because it is a little out of the ordinary and therefore seems a trifle awkward, we readily forgive the author and press on, depending upon something later to relieve the momentary embarrassment. But with Emerson as with Whitman, one needs to pause for reflection at such moments, letting novelty and paradox ring in their own way, until their surprising and doubtful message at last justifies itself. What, for example, is the meaning of sentences such as those just cited?

— The union is perfect only when all the uniters are isolated.
— The union must be ideal in actual individualism.
— The dread of man and the love of man shall be a wall of defence and a wreath of joy around all.

The "dread of man" and the "fear of God" mean essentially the same thing. They are but the shortest way of saying: Here we stand in the presence of something momentous and incalculable. If we can realize that in the human being who stands before us we confront a living, breathing, incarnate spirit (fully unconscious of the fact though he or she may be), we will want, as it were, in this presence to take the shoes off our feet! We shall beware of ignoring or trying to circumvent or dismiss this spiritual being, for it must have the last word, and from that word, when spoken from its freedom to choose, there is no appeal. Be aware! Then, just as one's so-called "fear" or "dread"—actually awesome respect—before God finds balance in a keener love for His holiness and infinite goodness, so the holy respect due to every man and woman as an Individual in whom divinity lives and is even now at work, will turn into a "wreath of joy." This joy is awakened by our new sense of the beautiful possibilities waiting to emerge from the Individuality of such a person.

And "the union is perfect only when the uniters are isolated" implies, of course, that any union or consensus of citizens will be genuine, fruitful, and lasting only when it has been arrived at without persuasion or coercion, but according to the conscience of each individual standing alone, uninfluenced in the moment of choice and decision. Such union has magical strength because, being based in the free conviction of souls who are obedient to higher guidance, it makes way for the action of the universal spirit.

INDIVIDUALISM AND SOCIAL REFORM

In the paradox of the "I am" consciousness, as this awakens in individual souls, lies the secret of effective rather than ineffective social reform. What is this mystery? It concerns the actual presence and effective working, the "new infusion," of immortal power into the mortal world. It concerns the realization that the spirit is not merely a theoretical ideal, an abstraction remote from life, something that operates in a higher but other world. The spirit is what lights up and works powerfully in the present world, wherever the human "I" becomes conscious of its own immortal reality.

In the *individual* who can properly be so called, the *universal* comes to the fore. Characteristic of this universal is the fact that its working is not limited by either space or time. And while it has initially aroused the reformer by silently sounding as the voice of his or her own conscience, that is also the way in which it will make itself heard within the inwardness of all souls who are free to listen.

The social reformer, when confronted by practical necessities, may at first be put off by talk of individualism. But following Emerson's argument, his activist zeal will take a radically new form. His main effort will be to conform personally to the Idea he wishes to serve. To realize the necessity of this effort requires strengthened faith in the power inherent in the Idea as such. The battle of the reformer with himself is the most productive of all, and the one most worth fighting. By such strategy, Truth, Love, and Justice themselves manifest with magic effect, without diversion or distortion. Their formative, reformative spirit is free to work, beyond calculation or even knowledge. No emotional propaganda suffices to activate this magic power. Obedience in self-reform comes first; knowledge of its mysterious effectuality, later.

Emerson said, "That which we admire, we become." And "What we love, that we have; but by desire we rob ourselves of the love." Social activism is energized by love for an Idea. But when love passes over to desire, the activist will begin to confuse the urgency of his or her personal hopes and ambition with the will of the higher world.

While one commonly imagines that it is only natural to *desire* what one loves, this notion must be uprooted. In physical life, when we wish to work upon objects according to our ideas, it is indispensable that we exert our will to reach for them, draw them to ourselves, and take hold. But in spiritual life, the reverse dynamic prevails; what is willfully reached for, actually recedes. It is the will that has subdued its personal desire, to grow through admiration, praise, thanksgiving, and trust, that the objectively spiritual, the beloved Idea, approaches, and by which it is enabled immediately and effectively to manifest its *own* power—in the reformer and in those he would reach.

Visualizing this process, we can see how it is that the more quietly and confidently centered in acceptance the would-be activist becomes—"Not by my will, but Thine be it done"—the more correspondingly free his Idea is to work without restraint or confinement in fields far as well as near, which, being of universal nature and potency, it will not fail to do. It will move people, or leave them unmoved, according to its wisdom. In thoroughly practical ways, the Idea itself will work in and through the reformer, as he abandons the illusion that he is the one who should be trying, by his cleverness and pressure, to establish it in the world. For in the really real world the efforts of self-will are, in fact, counterproductive.

Such paradoxical truths announce and affirm themselves only in the peace and stillness of the trusting individual's heart. The stiller it becomes, the more miraculous is their working. One feels that Whitman had this fact in mind when he spoke of "the perfect uncontamination and solitariness of individuality." It was Emerson's experience when he said that *"the Reform of Reforms must be accomplished without means."*

INDIVIDUALISM IN
THE REFORM OF EDUCATION

Whitman and Emerson found in Individuality the best assurance for social harmony and progress. From the deepened inner life of individuals, from the aptitudes, powers, conscience, and guidance that genuine individuals carry within themselves, flows everything a society needs to support its life and know the blessings of security and fulfillment. The question, then, becomes extraordinarily important: *What can a society do to insure that this primary source of creativeness is protected and enhanced?* To answer this question in practical terms for our own time, we must go a little, but only a little, beyond the situation as it appeared to those of the last century. We must ask: What exerts the most intensive influence during the most formative years upon the evolution of "I am" consciousness in the young? Society's answer to this question is evident in its ever-renewed hopes for education. There is need, therefore, to examine the relationships between education and individuality, as these favor or harm the development of the latter.

The observed fact, in this century as in the last, is that American education, whether seemingly independent or supported and controlled by the State, habitually avoids the spiritual dimension. But it is just and only in this dimension that individuality is born and lives.

Already in his own culture, Emerson was distressed by the ignorance, skepticism, and fear of the spirit that caused such evasion. In our time the seeking for the spirit has perhaps become even more urgent and widespread than it was in the days of Transcendentalism; yet the blockade against mention of it in the nation's schools is no longer a mere evasion. It has become an established custom, and for the state school system, a legal requirement.

Education today is the prime matrix of all phases of both cultural and spiritual development. Yet to serve society as society needs to be served, which means, to be leading rather than misleading, and inspiring rather than dispiriting, education should always be seeking and celebrating the essential spirit of things—of life and very existence. It should certainly be appealing under all circumstances to "the divine sentiments" of youth. Such a more fundamental, more spiritual because more spirited, education is what teachers, parents, and students all profoundly need and want. But matters of conscience, conviction, and deepest commitment, all of which have to do with the spirit, belong in the individualistic sphere, where liberty to choose and freedom to differ should be the absolute rule. These matters should stand beyond the influence of *ad hoc* economic motives, as well as beyond "the web of government" (including democratic government). The proper concern of the latter is never individualistic pluralism but always "same and equal treatment for all."

The result of attempting to subordinate the liberty principle to the equality dynamic, as has been done for a hundred and fifty years or so—placing under conformist, leveling state control what should be a thoroughly indi-vidualistic undertaking, variously initiated and freely chosen—has been perhaps the most basic reason for the progressive materialization of American society. The Constitution's First Amendment, could its foresight have extended a little further toward our time, would undoubtedly have recognized that the same wall of separation it set so firmly between institutional religion and the state should, for the same reasons and in equal measure, have been set up between science and the state, art and the state, culture a...nd morality in general and the state. To secure these freedoms for the full development of Individuality and to bring the First Amendment up to date, *the wall that now requires to be raised is that between the state and all forms of education.*

This requirement was not yet apparent to Emerson though it was certainly implicit in his whole outlook and conviction. He still shared at least some of the early hopes for what was emerging as the "public" or state school system. His attention, however, was aways directed primarily to the thoughts people think: the ideas they allow to shape their lives. These thoughts, he felt, could and *would* take a spiritual and a socially fruitful direction (by no matter how great a variety of ways) if the schools and churches stood on their own feet—as was *not* the case—and if they insisted in all their undertakings upon freedom to follow their conscience, which they were not doing.

> If the truth must be told, thought is as rare in colleges as in cities.... The College should hold the profound thought, and the Church the great heart to which the nation should turn, and these two should be counterbalancing to the bad politics and selfish trade. But there is but one institution, and not three. The Church and the College now take their tone from the City, and do not dictate their own.[7]

Evidently Emerson saw the greater danger, threatening the freedom of both school and church, coming from the interference of financial interests rather than from political manipulation. But whether the one or the other was the more guilty of intruding where it did not belong, behind the whole zeal for so-called popular education he detected a still more fundamental danger. He saw fear, and behind the fear, lack of faith in the power of spiritualized intelligence. At bottom was a hidden fear of the spiritual dimension as such. Such fear manifested itself in the strenuous efforts made by all educational means (except the spiritual), to subdue the passionate, unpredictable, perhaps radical "spirit" of the young by introducing "diversions and opiates" of various kinds. Once the school began to supplant the Church's control of social behavior through its religious sanctions, how otherwise than by such educational stratagems were the gross appetites and selfish impulses of human beings to be held in check?

In alluding ... to our system of education, I spoke of the deadness of its details. But it is open to graver criticism than the palsy of its members: it is a system of despair. The disease with which the human mind now labors is want of faith. Men do not believe in the power of education [despite their zeal for it]. We do not think we can speak to the divine sentiments in man, and we do not try. We renounce all high aims. We believe that the defects of so many perverse and so many frivolous people who make up society are organic, and society is a hospital of incurables. I notice too that the ground on which eminent public servants urge the claims of popular education is fear; "This country is filling up with thousands and millions of voters, and you must educate them to keep them from our throats." We do not believe that any education, any system of philosophy, any impulse of genius, will ever give depth of insight to a superficial mind. Having settled ourselves into this infidelity, our skill is expended to procure alleviations, diversions, opiates. We adorn the victim with manual skill, his tongue with languages, his body with inoffensive and comely manners. So have we cunningly hid the tragedy of limitation and inner death we cannot avert. Is it strange that society should be devoured by a secret melancholy which breaks through all its smiles and all its gaiety and games? ("New England Reformers," 458-9)

One thing, at least, society had felt it could do educationally. By appealing strictly to the intellectual mind, so-called public education hoped to avoid the battling dogmatisms of the religious confessions. Doubtless, a well-developed rationality would suffice also to control animal passions and enable students to steer a steady course. However, Whitman's warning was ignored: namely, that if this rational mind should lack grounding in firsthand spiritual experience and conviction, it would prove incapable—"when we come to a mortal crisis"—of holding its own against either major temptations or dire threats.

Emerson wondered, indeed, whether we have actually experienced, and should really believe, that intellectual training alone can *ever* find or hold to the noble path in life. Apparently not, for

> even one step farther our infidelity has gone. It appears that some doubt is felt by good and wise men whether really the happiness and probity of men is increased by the culture of the mind in those disciplines to which we give the name of education. Unhappily too the doubt comes from scholars, from persons who have tried these methods. In their experience the scholar was not raised by the sacred thoughts amongst which he dwelt, but used them to selfish ends. He was a profane person, and became a showman, turning his gifts to a marketable use.... It was found that the intellect could be independently developed, that is, in separation from the man [that is, the individual in his balanced wholeness], as any single organ can be invigorated; and the result was monstrous. A canine appetite for knowledge was generated, which must still be fed but was never satisfied, and this knowledge ... never took the character of substantial, humane truth, blessing those whom it entered. ("New England Reformers," 459)

Emerson realized that the knowledge demanded by the "canine appetite"—which characterizes both intellectual curiosity and worldly ambition, in the materialistic preoccupations and power goals of both—could never satisfy the human soul. No amount of eating to serve this appetite would ever add up to nourishment for the human soul.

The lesson here is that when *spirituality* is banned from an educational system, the thing that remains to dominate the whole is *intellectuality*. When heart and soul are placed out of bounds, "brain-power" is left to do its own thing. Sheer brain-power lacks conscience. It is clever and shrewd rather than good, and at least as ready to be devious as straight. As such, it is easily enlisted by the instinctive drives and desires of the untransformed self. "Pure intellect," said Emerson, "is the pure devil when you have got off all the masks of Mephistopheles." [8]

The deepest stirrings and aspirations in human nature have, as far as most education is concerned, been effectively excommunicated. They could have been used to permeate and lift the whole enterprise of human knowledge, and in so doing could have made acquaintance with the reality of their own higher calling. Instead, schools hold these inspiring, creative forces away from either recognition or exercise. Confined within a conspiracy of silence, students in their spiritual ignorance nowadays turn to the only outlet that remains open to them. But that opening invites and entices to lower levels of experience. On such levels, these urgent powers become destructive rather than constructive.

Emerson realized that this disappointment, this blockage of the light and warmth and the liberating high zest every soul instinctively demands, accounts for (to use our current terms, which differ but slightly from his) drug and sex abuse, alcoholism and gluttony, gambling fever and consumerism, violence, and the appetite for war. Such were and are the spawn of an educational enterprise that presumes to teach all things—without the spirit.

Man's health and greatness consist in his being the channel through which heaven flows to earth, in short, in the fullness in which an ecstatical state takes place in him .... in the fact that enthusiasm is organized therein.[9]

The reason of idleness and of crime is the deferring of our hopes. Whilst we are waiting we beguile the time with jokes, with sleep, with eating and with crimes. ("Nominalist and Realist," 441)

Not through the unleavened intellectual mind but through its enhancement as imagination, inspiration, and intuition, did Emerson expect the human soul to find what it sought as release from the confinement of its separate personality, and from the dullness of existence when viewed only from the outside. Preparation for these higher states should be the basic task of education, for only through them will the soul find the life it seeks, by coming, as Emerson says, "nearer to the fact."

All men avail themselves of such means as they can, to add this extraordinary power to their normal powers, and to this end they prize ... music, dancing, theatre ... war, mobs, fires, gambling, politics, or "love"... which are several coarser or finer *quasi*-mechanical substitutes for *the true nectar, which is the ravishment of the intellect by coming nearer to the fact.* These are auxiliaries to the centrifugal tendency of a man, to his passage out into free space, and they help him to escape the custody of that body in which he is pent up, and of the jail-yard of individual relations in which he is enclosed. [Emphasis added] ("The Poet," 332-3)

The one thing which we seek with insatiable desire is to forget ourselves, to be surprised out of our propriety [our "selfness"].... Nothing great was ever achieved without enthusiasm. The way of life is wonderful; it is by abandonment.... Dreams and drunkenness, the use of opium and alcohol, are the semblance and counterfeit of this [enthusiasm], and hence their dangerous attraction for men. For the like reason they ask the aid of wild passions, as in gaming and war, to ape in some manner these flames and generosities of the heart. ("Circles," 290-1)

But never can any advantage be taken of nature by a trick. The spirit of the world, the great calm presence of the Creator, comes not forth to the sorceries of opium or of wine. The sublime vision comes to the pure and simple soul in a clean and chaste body. That is not an inspiration [or imagination, or intuition] which we owe to narcotics, but some counterfeit excitement and fury.... For poetry is not "Devil's wine," but "God's wine." ("The Poet," 333)

What can raise academic intellectuality above itself, to higher forms of consciousness that free the true Self from its bodily fetters, can be called enthusiasm or passionate faith, or persistent prayerful effort. But the briefest and most comprehensive word for it is love.

What is love, and why is it the chief good, but because it is an overpowering enthusiasm? Never self-possessed or prudent, it is all abandonment. Is it not a certain admirable wisdom, preferable to all other advantages, and whereof all others are only secondaries and indemnities, because this is that in which the individual is no longer his own foolish master, but inhales an odorous and celestial air, is wrapped round with awe of the object, blending for the time that object with the real and only good, and consults every omen in nature with tremulous interest? When we speak truly—is not he only unhappy who is not in love? his fancied freedom and self-rule—is it not so much death? He who is in love is wise and is becoming wiser.... And the reason why all men honor love is because it looks up and not down; aspires and not despairs.[10]

The ultimate task of education, then, is to cultivate love. Love is the very substance of Individuality, both its motive and its fulfillment. Ultimately, love alone nourishes, heals, empowers, and exalts. Love is "the one remedy for all ills, the panacea of nature," said Emerson. But whence comes love? It comes from sensing the presence of the lovely and lovable. What opens the heart to be aware and what makes either nature or humanity lovable? It is, on all counts, the presence of God—as the spirit of truth, of beauty, and of goodness. Where the Spirit is felt or discerned, however dimly, love is awakened. It is love that reconciles the hitherto irreconcilable and solves the apparently unsolvable. "We must be lovers, and at once the impossible becomes possible" ("Man the Reformer," 78).

Such reflections about the role of education, as its great possibilities struggle to free themselves from external controls, as well as from fear of the spirit, bring us to the heart of Emerson's as well as Whitman's conception of the relation between social reform and radical individualism. For the only impulses for social reform that can be depended upon to issue constantly and with lasting effect are those flowing from a free spiritual life, such as can be expected from schools of individual initiative and individual choice. *All* forms of education, too, must "go alone," if they are to prove themselves capable of serving *all* the people, in all their diversity of conscience and conviction—and thereby contribute what is necessary for society's basic well-being.

NOTES

1. Walt Whitman, "Democratic Vistas," in *The Portable Walt Whitman*, Mark Van Doren, ed. (New York: Viking Press, 1945), 393. Page numbers for further references to this book are given in the text by poem title.

2. Ralph Waldo Emerson, "Man the Reformer," *The Complete Writings of Ralph Waldo Emerson* (New York: Wise, 1929), 77. Page numbers for further references to this essay are given in the text.

3. Ralph Waldo Emerson, "Self-Reliance," in *The Complete Essays and Other Writings of Ralph Waldo Emerson*, Brooks Atkinson, ed. (New York: Random House, 1950), 168. Page numbers for further references to this book are given in the text by essay title.

4. Emerson, quoted by John Jay Chapman in *The Shock of Recognition*, Edmund Wilson, ed. (New York: Grosset and Dunlap, 1955), vol. 1, 600.

5. Emerson, "The Times," in *TheComplete Writings*, 86.

6. Ibid., 84.

7. Emerson, "The Celebration of Intellect," in *The Complete Writings*, 1287-8.

8. B. Perry, ed., *The Heart of Emerson's Journals* (New York: Houghton Mifflin, 1926), 207.

9. Emerson, "Method of Nature," in *The Complete Writings*, 65.

10. Ibid., 67.

EPILOGUE:

The Paradox of the "I am" Experience

While attempting in various ways to characterize what these prophetic individuals had in common, I felt the need to clarify in my own mind the issue they faced and that we still face. What is this riddle modern souls are trying to solve? What is the battle, underlying all others, that is being fought in this historical epoch? How and why does it happen that humanity seems to be parting ways with itself: one impulse driving us ever deeper into materialism, and the other trying to draw us up toward spiritual experience?

Trying to make plain talk about these questions, I wrote a short chapter in addition to the foregoing. But since it referred primarily to events of our own time, ignoring the circumstances of the nineteenth century and citing its authors hardly at all, I had to agree with friends that this chapter did not belong with the others. Yet because in principle and according to my feeling, the statement, such as it is, does belong with the book, it follows herewith. May it serve as hail and farewell to readers who have cared to stay with the discussion this far.

* * *

They were nearly all Islanders in the Pequod, *Isolatoes* too, I call such, not acknowledging the common continent of men, but each Isolato living on a separate continent of his own. (Melville, *Moby Dick*)

Let it be granted... that some sources of human instruction are almost unnamed and unknown among us; that the community in which we live will hardly bear to be told that every man should be open to ecstacy or a divine illumination, and his daily walk elevated by intercourse with the spiritual world. Grant all this, as we must, yet I suppose none of my auditors will deny that we *ought* to seek to establish ourselves in such disciplines and courses as will deserve that guidance and clearer communication with the spiritual nature. [Emphasis added] (Emerson, "Man the Reformer")

It is a matter of daily experience that the shock we feel upon collision with an external object helps to increase our awareness of our own existence. It is reasonable, therefore, to believe that the very origin of the human being's consciousness of himself or herself as "I"—not the origin of the essential spirit, the "I Am" as such, but that of the individual's *consciousness of selfhood*—is to be looked for in the contact, confrontation, or interaction of the immortal spirit with the mortal physical body. This contact is made anew every morning, when the soul that has "passed out" during sleep returns to awareness in the body, and one awakens to self-possession and self-consciousness. Historically, for the human race as a whole, it is this ever closer bonding of human souls with their physical bodies—with the bodily senses and the bodily mind serving them—that accounts for the progressive awakening of humanity to an ever more distinct sense of subjective personality, on the one hand, and to objective, material reality on the other. This stimulating impingement or contact of the spirit with its bodily vehicle is a matter of incarnation. The human spirit, which is of a universal nature, self-existent and immaterial, unites ever more closely with its local, bodily manifestation, and progressively stronger "I am" consciousness results. The more firmly bonded to its particular body is the incarnating spirit of a human being, the less well does it remember its origin in universal spirituality. It simply takes for granted the situation as it appears to be, namely, that it actually belongs to this body which was only meant to serve it for a time, and that since it apparently came into existence as a function of this body, it is reasonable to imagine (and fear) that it will cease to exist when, as is unavoidable, this body is destroyed by death.

Yet, paradoxically, our sense of self—despite our belief that we are born of, are dependent upon, and may reasonably be supposed to perish with this transient body—develops a powerful self-importance and a formidable self-will. Despite the narrowly limiting aspects of its presumed physical origin and quite possible decease, it lays claim to *intrinsic* dignity, high respect, and unquestionable rights. Despite the fact that it looks out at the world from its body-based standpoint, which naturally restricts its view, it undertakes to judge all things. It seeks to know the nature of every kind of being everywhere—and to proclaim universal principles of morality for the guidance of humanity for all time.

So long as the incarnation process is still but tentative and exploratory, whether as in the childhood of an individual of today or in humanity's historical childhood, the "I" consciousness comes only partly to birth. Awareness of selfhood remains indistinct and tentative. But the incarnating spirit's deeper penetration of the material body brings to the soul ever sharper self-definition, for it is the separateness of the body as an object among objects that first gives the soul its sense of being a distinct identity. Because of its close union with its particular body, the soul comes to feel set apart and self-enclosed, yet at the same time wide-awake to all *bodily* aspects of the world surrounding it.

A price, however, is paid for the soul's brightened but outward-turned consciousness. It loses contact with the spiritual aspects of its own nature. Though increasingly self-conscious, it remains *Self*-ignorant. Because its attention is quite taken up with the external world around it, the soul loses contact with its own inwardness. In consequence, it also loses touch with the inward life of the rest of the world. The higher, impalpable aspects of sun, moon, and stars, of river, forest, and mountain, of flower and animal become problematic, something only to be guessed at. If there is thought, or feeling, or intention at work somehow in or behind the natural creation, they certainly do not appear to the bodily senses. Nor are they known by the intellectual mind, which interprets for the senses. All such hypothetical inward realities have been overlaid by the brightened veil of external appearance.

For the soul that is asleep to its own essential being, the rest of the world becomes an enigma. It has nothing *essential* to reveal concerning itself. It resembles a still-life, and remains as mute and superficial. In the language of fairy tales, the world with all its creatures has fallen asleep, as it did at a certain point for Sleeping Beauty. In the shock of pricking her finger with the spindle, the princess whom we may think of as the historically evolving human soul in its descent into distinct, separative "I am" consciousness, actually *awoke*, in an external way, to herself and to the world. But inwardly—and this is the paradox that the fairy tale is concerned to portray—both she and the world around her fell fast asleep, almost as though turned to stone, each stone ignorant of its neighbor.

When the world becomes "objective" in the sense of being but an assembly of "objects," it becomes, by the same token, essentially unknown. As to its hypothetical inward or subjective realities, it becomes unknowable. And the soul that has been awakened only by and to its own physicality, then is as a stranger to itself as well as to the life, soul, and spirit of the world into which it has awakened. The objects it encounters through the agency of its material senses are all unmistakably material. The only aspects of their nature that remain available to the observer's body-based consciousness are but assorted objective processes: mechanical, chemical, electrical. . . .

What alienates the self-conscious soul from even its own reality, as well as from that of the rest of nature, comes also between it and its fellow human beings. People too become unknowns, about whom only surmises are possible. Human beings whose awakeness is still primarily physical, tend to walk among their fellow human beings almost indifferently, merely as bodies passing among bodies. The minor "shock" transmitted by the external encounter of one with another does heighten to some extent the awareness in each party of its own separate selfhood, but it could also have served to stimulate an intuitive, loving interest in each concerning the subjective reality of the other. As a rule, this does not happen.

The spiritual being that existed before it took on a body, and that will continue to be after this particular body has been laid aside, remains quite undiscovered. As has been suggested, for the consciousness of many so-called practical persons, this alleged but physically imperceptible being is, at most, only a theoretical construct.

The wall that separates the *physically* awakened soul from its own reality, from that of its fellows, and from the kingdoms of nature, separates it also from God. For God, as Love, and as very Essence of Self-existent Being, does not appear in bodily form. The senses of the body never knowingly collide with Him. His reality, therefore is not only unknown but moot. To the bright but outward-turned consciousness, God becomes hardly so much as a problem—

rather, a doubtful supposition left over from bygone times whose consciousness never advanced beyond the mythical and which can therefore be more or less safely ignored.

* * *

Turning now to the special relationship our own country appears to have with the historical development of "I" consciousness in humanity, we realize that the discovery of America coincided quite closely with the beginning of what may be called "modern" times. Its story is one that illustrates, and has been conspicuously motivated from the first by the development of the kind of ego-consciousness that is praised and prized today—politically and economically—as individualism. Among the nations of the world, the distinguishing feature of America has always been its pursuit of "life, liberty, and happiness" along both individualistic *and* materialistic lines. Americans are justly proud, for example, of what they have developed as the "rugged individualism" of "free enterprise." Such enterprise gives scope for the unfettered exercise of personal abilities, and it has proved effective in mastering many material aspects of human life on earth.

As time goes on, however, unfolding events of the present century are beginning to force recognition that sheer "enterprise" has a shadow side, one that tends to be typical of the American scene, for it tends to mean enterprise not only *by* the individual, in his or her freedom to act on the basis of ability and experience, but also *for* the individual, in his or her pursuit of personal gain.

On their shadow side, capitalism, the absolute ownership of land, the profit motive, and competition in the market place, with all of which America still identifies herself uncritically (despite certain marginal feelings of guilt and concern), can be seen as merely names for the will of each ego to assert itself in contest with other egos—and tough luck take the hindmost! Yet most Americans assume that this contest is creative—indeed, the essence of dynamic creativity — and they experience in it the heightening of their sense of individual worth. That the battle has so often led, and still leads, to the exploitation of the peace, harmony, health, and beauty of the natural environment is less impressive to the enterprising individualist even today than the material gains momentarily accruing to himself or herself.

What is true of America in these respects is, of course, more or less equally characteristic of all Western nations since the time of the discovery of America. But America likes to think of herself as leading the way in respect to both the free initiative of individual persons and material development of the body social. Its national pride, like the nationalisms of other countries in the modern age, may be regarded as but an expanded form of "I" or "ego" consciousness. As such, it witnesses further to the fact that the time in which we have long been living, and toward which we have yet to look ahead, is one that favors the still further development of an attitude that by nature is not only competitively acquisitive, but unbelieving and lonely as well.

It is comparatively easy of course, to underscore in this way the negative by-products of materialistic individualism. It is certainly possible to forecast in such terms the devolution of rugged individualism into an ever uglier materialism, with ever colder human relationships—initial indifference turning into suspicion and fear, followed by competitive scheming that ends in brutal strife—with natural disasters accompanying. Such can be seen ahead, if materialistically inclined egocentrism does not begin to recognize the paradoxically opposite, more demanding but also far more rewarding possibilities that lie buried within it—and that patiently, or not so patiently, wait their turn to be realized.

What, then, can be said on the opposite, positive side of the situation as it now stands? The development of distinct

"I am" consciousness, even in its present half-way state, has had obvious benefits. On the personal side, surely one must reckon the general acknowledgment of human dignity, the legal establishment of human rights, the stimulation of individual initiative, and the sharpening of critical judgment. On the objective, physical side, practical energies have brought about tremendous changes in the conditions of life on earth, many of them beneficial.

As a direct result of an awakened mentality and a clear, factual perception of the outer world, the triumphant exploits of modern science have been achieved. The application of scientific discoveries and technical inventions to the practical problems of earthly life have been made possible. From these factors, whole civilizations have arisen and are still arising. And in contrast to whatever may be deplored about our being cut off from intimate connection with our fellow beings, shall we not praise developments that seem to point in quite the opposite direction, for example, the wonders of instant verbal and visual communication, by which the limitations of space and time, as well as many of the drudgeries of human labor, are being overcome? Is it not an extraordinarily hopeful thing that the whole of our hitherto divided humanity is apparently being drawn together in closer acquaintanceship, for the organization of improvements in human welfare? (At the present moment, indeed, many claim that the future clearly belongs to the technical tools and skills of "communication.")

It must be admitted, however, that fascination with the marvels of electronic communication has succeeded in diverting notice from the fact that as the flood of information grows in volume, intensity, speed of delivery, and ability to be stored, personal memory is being eroded at the same time and personal comprehension is being swamped. What is so urgently being heaped upon the physical senses fails to enlighten as it was originally expected to do. Individual comprehension has no time to gather itself, to judge patiently with alertness of soul, and to act from ripe conviction. It is overridden, shouted down. Group-suggestion takes its place. Self-initiated activity gives way to passive reception and managed response. As far as individual integrity, intelligence, and initiative are concerned, the admittedly magnificent boon of communications technology is on the way to proving a threat of the first order. Its social implications must therefore be considered fully as appalling as they are encouraging. They open the way, on a scale never before conceived, for the collective manipulation, bemusement, and coarsening of humanity by unsurveyably powerful forces.

At every turn, we are confronted by paradox, in the great headway being made by scientific materialism, derived as it is from the still exclusively physical orientation of the "I-it" consciousness. One such paradox may be seen in the fact that, because modern humanity's technical understanding and control of nature have made such astounding advances on all fronts, ours is imagined to be a scientific age. It would seem to follow that vital interest, insight, and a wholesome love for knowledge now characterize most of the world's advanced and affluent peoples. Were this truly the case, it should be taken as positive indeed. Yet feelings that long ago were common, namely, those of being at home in the cosmos and intimately observant of both earthly creatures and the starry heavens, are more recently replaced—for the majority of people who enjoy the benefits of modern education—by a comparative ignorance and indifference of soul. The scientific concepts that are so fit for technical use have nothing in themselves to warm or exalt human hearts that long to love. While they fascinate some, they leave most in apathy and in poverty of soul and spirit.

The passionate, creative forces in humanity are being forced to seek outlets that have nothing to do with knowledge, or even with lucid consciousness. The life-quickening thrill, the love-enkindling warmth, and the soul-satisfying communion that could and should be engendered by contact with the visible/invisible world are for large numbers of human beings giving way to self-centered depression, to an irritable restlessness, and to perverse cravings. Only the eagerness felt by the comparatively few who stand to win status, money, or power through the clever use of physically oriented intelligence momentarily prevents them from realizing that they, too, are burdened by these same feelings of disappointment and alienation.

Despite praiseworthy advances in biology, psychology, and sociology, the individual soul knows not why it is so often lonely, confused, fearful, depressed, resentful, and angry. It feels itself a stranger to its own destiny, and it is moved to take the truly paradoxical way out. It tries to find "release" through the very means most certain to render it more completely captive and helpless. Gambling, gluttony, alcoholism, drug addiction, lust, greed, and violence are phenomena made more attractive through the subversive stimulation provided by the urgent mass media.

Perhaps a word may be ventured about the relationship among nations that has come into being in the era of speedy and incessant communication. Much has been achieved in the form of multinational pacts and alliances. Provincial horizons have been greatly widened and a myriad of new ways of mutual intelligence and cooperation developed. Surely all this is to be included on the positive side, justifying confidence and hope? Yet in the midst of the closely woven network that has been established among the nations, fear still flourishes. Misunderstanding and distrust, hesitation and delay, plotting and scheming, are still basic to the policies of the leading powers. Technical progress has made warfare more violent, devastating, and inhuman than ever before. In spite of the remarkable transformations now being witnessed in many countries, which certainly support new hopes for freedom, prosperity, and peace, the accumulating worldwide dangers of warfare technology remain in ready reserve. They have not lost their threatening power—and they have a will of their own.

The sudden and dramatic changes in many East European nations are being hailed as triumphs of spiritual and cultural freedom, of political democracy, and of entrepreneurial capitalism. They do, indeed, very dramatically open a new era in international relations, but it is one whose emerging character remains painfully uncertain, because it is subject to all the paradoxes we have been considering. Unless there is a genuine, conscious turning toward the spirit—and real freedom in that turning, especially in the field of education—one cannot trust the substitution of so-called democratic techniques and procedures, or the alleged all-purpose magic of the market economy, to accomplish what needs to be done. These social techniques have long been well established in America, but of themselves they have not protected our country from the degenerative consequences of egoistic materialism. These inevitable consequences have gathered and compounded here in the United States to the point where they can no longer be ignored. Yet their reality, and their fundamental cause, are still far from being generally recognized. Indeed, immense effort is in fact being expended—whether consciously or not—to prevent this recognition.

In the case of the newly emerging nations, should the freedom they have longed for and seemingly won not lead to genuine *freedom for all forms of cultural and spiritual activity, especially education*, but instead to an illusory "freedom" that but permits and encourages resurgence of the prideful egoisms known as ethnicism, racism, sectarianism, and nationalism—we can foresee only a replication and further complication of the very issues that account for strife and suffering in the established Western democracies, yet whose *root* cause still waits to be named or dealt with.

* * *

The problematic aspects of the historical epoch whose beginning coincides more or less with the discovery of America are painfully enough felt by all, even when not consciously acknowledged. My purpose in alluding to them here in what may seem pessimistic terms has been to suggest that the *minuses* following upon the materialistic orientation of the sense of self, as it has emerged and evolved thus far, are threatening to outweigh and foreclose the *pluses* that require to be realized in the future that is already upon us.

The writers whom we have called heralds of the spirit here in America had a common purpose. They sought to remind their fellow citizens that the true goal of the adventure upon which their beloved nation was embarking was spiritual, not material. The fruits of an individualism, an "I" consciousness that properly understands itself, are certainly independence, freedom of thought, unfettered initiative, and enterprise. But they are not egoism and selfishness. They are not a mortal competition of all against all. They are not the substitution of material comforts and prizes for spiritual insight, compassion, and creativeness. Rather than condoning heedlessness in the exploitation of the natural environment, a spiritually conscious individualism would be supporting a vivid sense of responsibility for the protection and enhancement of our beautiful earth. Beauty, not ugliness; health, not disease; and joy, not pain—all these should follow from humanity's intervention in the natural order.

In all these respects a beginning is being made, and much has been achieved. But the motives behind most of the new concern have been *fears* of various kinds—to which, of course, the mortal self is always vulnerable—rather than what flows from the invulnerable nature of the spiritual Self, which is love.

If a further development of "I" consciousness, through further preoccupation of the soul with its bodily instrument, is to become a victory rather than a defeat for humanity, it must be balanced by a much closer identification with the spirit that should be living consciously within that body. Recognition of this spirit was instinctive in earlier, dreamier times. The culture of the native Americans bears eloquent witness of this fact. But in our day, what was once instinctive cannot be regained in the fully conscious way that the modern soul demands, unless there is courage to admit and build upon what we unconsciously still know to be true. Unless through a new awakening to the spirit, wholeness and depth are restored to humanity's experience of life, the same materialism that has led the human soul into an initial but illusory aspect of selfhood will inevitably go on to lead it altogether out of acquaintance with the reality of its own being—the spiritual reality that waits, still hidden, within it.

For the profoundly and prophetically concerned writers whose work we have reviewed in at least a few aspects, it was clear that the Self, the "I" in its essence, has not been created by the instrumentality of matter. Its reality existed before, and will continue to exist after, the bonding with matter. This same spiritual reality lies behind the creation and continuing evolution of all things, and the time has come to be clearly conscious of the fact, as a matter not of traditional faith alone, but of modern objective, fully conscious experience. Only through an intuitive realization of this direct kind can today's individual soul find genuine understanding and love for neighbor, for nature, for God—for Selfhood itself. Failing such an intuitive awakening, the modern soul feels itself defenselessly dazzled by the brilliance, and helplessly captured by the forces, of an external order of things with which it feels no relationship of either security or communion.

To hold the balance between outwardness and inwardness, matter and spirit, spiritual Self-recollection must be greatly strengthened. It is as harbingers of this new strength that one best appreciates the mission shared by the American authors of our study, as they sought to bring light into their century—for its own sake, and for the sake of times still to come.

All three authors were heralds of the spirit in a culture apparently destined to be great in its adventure with both individualism and materialism—but one that was obviously fated also to suffer, and cause others to suffer, because of the naiveté with which it embarked in so great haste upon this hazardous adventure. They came to face and name the nemesis of modern times: the superficial consciousness of self, in conjunction with its equally superficial and illusory outlook upon the world. It is reassuring to observe that in their view, the battle was not to be won by minimizing either the one aspect or the other of the paradoxical situation. No one glorified the reality of true selfhood more than they. And none had greater appreciation for the wonders of the natural world, or gave greater honor to American material achievements. But equally radical and uncompromising was the insistence of all three upon Spirit—immortal spirit as the only *real* content of the awakening human soul; and spirit, indeed, as the ultimate reality of matter itself.

In comparing these three, I would say again, as I have suggested before, that Emerson's affinity with pure thought led him to that aspect of the spirit from which all things came in the beginning. Whitman's affinity with the mystery of the will led him to the spiritual fulfillment toward which all things strive in the end. Melville's unique gift derived from his awareness of the painfully bewildering predicament in which present-day human beings find themselves: would-be individual souls, striving to maintain equilibrium in a world where light struggles with darkness, life with death, love with hate, and hope with despair.

EPILOGUE

In the search for the truth of the troubled relationship between self and world, Emerson found ultimate reconciliation through his certainty of the spiritual origin of things. This he saw as intuitive thought and it led him toward the divine past out of which he envisioned the material world gradually being precipitated. Whitman found ultimate reconciliation in his certainty that time and cosmic purpose will in future perfect all things, as they gradually ascend toward higher states, through the divine impulse that ever gains in strength despite all hindrances. Melville, however, found reconciliation no easy task. His was the confusing experience, in heightened degree, of the self that in its depths knows itself spiritual, but that is born in a time ignorant and heedless of the spirit. In what happened to the Pequod and its crew—the American ship of state—Melville testified, if indirectly, to the disaster to be expected should America not awaken from its simplistic, self-centered dreams of fulfillment through material affluence and military power.

My own sense is that all who now look steadfastly to the light have every reason for confidence; for full assurance of security, and the certainty of being able to share in wonderful developments of beauty, goodness, and truth—despite the rending, but apparently necessary, turmoil occasioned by the breakup of old life-habits and understandings that even now is making way for the new.

CHRISTMAS, 1990

APPENDIX A

The discussion of "styles of being" in Chapter One reminds one of archetypal forms that are now typified in the animal kingdom, but which the ancients visualized as originally joining to compose the human form itself. These same styles or forms appear even in the way early Christianity portrayed the distinctive characters of its four great evangelists. As we know, traditional sculpture and painting have for centuries represented as an eagle the lofty tone and meaning of St. John; as cow or bull, the loving compassion of St. Luke; and as lion, the spiritual power conveyed by St. Mark. The fourth evangelist, St. Matthew, has been portrayed in specifically human or angelic form, as a composite of the other three.

Long before the advent of Christianity, ancient Egypt embodied its sense of the human mystery in a tripartite image, the Sphinx—the majestic, fearsome presence whose question to all who sought to approach it concerned precisely the meaning of human nature.

Ancient peoples saw the human head as essentially birdlike. They pictured the thoughts that wing into and out of our consciousness as birds that come to rest for a moment in a tree and then fly off again. In this sense, they imagined that thoughts perch on the head, even as the head itself perches on the rest of the body. Thus, the Egyptians portrayed the inspiring force of thought as a falcon with wings extended behind the head of the Pharaoh. The American Indians, too, in the ceremonial headdress of eagle feathers worn by their chiefs, indicated the same relationship of feathered bird to inspired or consecrated thought. In this case, the feathers outlined the top and back of the head, extending, understandably, also downward along the spine.

The mythic consciousness of times past saw the noble head as an eagle come to rest upon the shoulders, but for the middle and lower body they had to visualize other archetypes. Obviously the eagle had nothing to do with the human being's highly developed limb nature, since in all birds the legs are scarcely present, and the wings, though they can master the air, are incapable of taking hold of anything else. Also, in the bird, abdominal features are much reduced, since their process of digestion is comparatively simplistic and rapid.

Just what birds of the air do not have is the distinguishing feature of earthbound ruminants. People in past ages must have been deeply impressed by the contrast between the eagle, who spurns the earth, and the cow, which stands four-square on heavy legs and whose lowered head crops the earth's surface with such devotional appetite—the cow who, to facilitate her digestion, gladly lies down upon the earth after eating and who employs, besides, four stomachs and a complex, highly developed intestinal tract in the slow and ponderous work of assimilation. One ancient people in the East found in the cow the very prototype of warmth, of compassion, and of contemplative wisdom. As Emerson himself observed, "The cattle that lie on the ground seem to have great and tranquil thoughts."[1] While we cannot fathom all that those of India once saw and perhaps still see in the cow that remains sacred for them even today, we can be sure that this beast has always represented lofty, inspiring, spiritual forces of a kind that also constitute and work through the whole human being, especially the metabolic aspect. The cow is obviously attuned to the earth, but one felt that her metabolism is moved by the heavens, too.

Between the archetypal bird and the archetypal ruminant stands the third heraldic creature: the lion. This "king of beasts" represents the third basic aspect of human nature.

Between our upper being whose primary function is consciousness, and the lower being whose function is life, lies the middle body, whose task is in all ways mediatory—whose characteristic rhythms, indeed, are to be understood as *caused* by the alternating way in which the contrasting influences from above and below play into one another. In the chest, the contracted, static form and posture of the head, and the expansive mobility of abdomen and limbs, alternate rhythmically. They appear as the alternately open and closed structure of the bony rib-cage itself, as the diastole and systole of the heart muscle, as the inhalation and exhalation of the lungs, and even as the rhythmic peristalsis of the alimentary tract. In this middle region of the human body we may picture what D. H. Lawrence called the white or day consciousness of the "man" of nerves meeting the dark or night consciousness of the "man" of blood. Here death plays into life, and life into death.

This intermediating arena, where the cool antipathy of intellectual consciousness meets and mingles with the warm sympathy that is basic to the instinctive, unconscious forces of growth and reproduction, has from time immemorial been known as the bodily seat of feeling. Its central organ is the heart, and one can understand why tradition's symbol among animals for this middle world has been the lion, whose magnificent muzzle, chest, mane, and roar bespeak the powerful mingling of blood and breath.

As I have indicated, it seems helpful to suggest that these same functional forms, celebrated in myth and art, may be seen respectively and notably represented in Emerson, Whitman, and Melville.

1. Ralph Waldo Emerson, "Nature," Brooks Atkinson, ed., *The Complete Essays and Other Writings of Ralph Waldo Emerson* (New York: Random House, 1950), 406.

APPENDIX B

Passage to India!
Lo, soul, seest thou not God's purpose from the first?
The earth to be spann'd, connected by network,
The races, neighbors, to marry and be given in
    marriage,
The oceans to be cross'd, the distant brought near,
The lands welded together.

A worship new I sing,
You captains, voyagers, explorers, yours,
You engineers, you architects, machinists, yours,
You, not for trade or transportation only,
But in God's name, and for thy sake O soul.

* * *

O vast Rondure, swimming in space,
Cover'd all over with visible power and beauty,
Alternate light and day and teeming spiritual darkness,
Unspeakable high processions of sun and moon and
    countless stars above,
Below, the manifold grass and waters, animals
  mountains, trees,
With inscrutable purpose, some hidden prophetic
  intention,
Now first it seems my thought begins to span thee.

Down from the gardens of Asia descending radiating,
Adam and Eve appear, then their myriad progeny
    after them,
Wandering, yearning, curious, with restless
    explorations,
With questionings, baffled, formless, feverish,
    with never-happy hearts,
With that sad incessant refrain, *Wherefore
    unsatisfied soul? and Whither O mocking life?*

Ah who shall soothe these feverish children?
Who justify these restless explorations?
Who speak the secret of impassive earth?
Who bind it to us? what is this separate Nature
    so unnatural?
What is this earth to our affections? (unloving earth,
    without a throb to answer ours,
Cold earth, the place of graves.)

Yet soul be sure the first intent remains, and shall be
    carried out,
Perhaps even now the time has arrived.

After the seas are all cross'd, (as they seem already
    cross'd,)
After the great captains and engineers have
    accomplish'd their work,
. . . .
Finally shall come the poet worthy of that name,
 The true son of God shall come singing his songs.

Then not your deeds only O voyagers, O scientists and
    inventors, shall be justified,
All these hearts as of fretted children shall be
    sooth'd,
All affection shall be fully responded to, the secret
    shall be told,

All these separations and gaps shall be taken up and
    hook'd and link'd together,
The whole earth, this cold, impassive, voiceless
    earth, shall be completely justified,
. . . .
Nature and Man shall be disjoin'd and diffused no
    more,
The true son of God shall absolutely fuse them.

* * *

The medieval navigators rise before me,
The world of 1492, with its awaken'd enterprise,
Something swelling in humanity now like the sap of
    the earth in spring,
The sunset splendor of chivalry declining.

And who art thou sad shade?
Gigantic, visionary, thyself a visionary,
With majestic limbs and pious beaming eyes,
Spreading around with every look of thine a golden
    world,
Enhuing it with gorgeous hues.

As the chief histrion,
Down to the footlights walks in some great scena,
Dominating the rest I see the Admiral himself,

(History's type of courage, action, faith,)
Behold him sail from Palos leading his little fleet,
His voyage behold, his return, his great fame,
His misfortunes, calumniators, behold him a prisoner,
    chain'd,
Behold his dejection, poverty, death.
(Curious in time I stand, noting the efforts of heroes,
Is the deferment long? bitter the slander, poverty,
    death?

Lies the seed unreck'd for centuries in the ground?
    lo, to God's due occasion,
Uprising in the night, it sprouts, blooms,
And fills the earth with use and beauty.)

* * *

Passage indeed O soul to primal thought,
Not lands and seas alone, thy own clear freshness,
. . . .
O soul, repressless, I with thee and thou with me,
Thy circumnavigation of the world begin,
Of man, the voyage of his mind's return
To reason's early paradise,
Back, back to wisdom's birth, to innocent intuitions,
Again with fair creation.

* * *

O we can wait no longer,
We too take ship O soul,
Joyous we too launch out on trackless seas,
Fearless for unknown shores. . .
. . . .
Caroling free, singing our song of God,
Chanting our chant of pleasant exploration.
. . . .

Ah more than any priest O soul we too believe in God,
But with the mystery of God we dare not dally.

O soul thou pleasest me, I thee,
Sailing these seas or on the hills, or waking in the night,
Thoughts, silent thoughts, of Time and Space and
    Death, like waters flowing,
Bear me indeed as through the regions infinite,
Whose air I breathe, whose ripples hear, lave me all over,

Bathe me O God in thee, mounting to thee, I and my
    soul to range in range of thee.

O Thou transcendent,
Nameless, the fibre and the breath,
Light of the light, shedding forth universes, thou
    centre of them,
Thou mightier centre of the true, the good, the loving,
Thou moral, spiritual fountain—affection's source—
. . . .
Thou pulse—thou motive of the stars, suns, systems,
That, circling, move in order, safe, harmonious,
Athwart the shapeless vastnesses of space,
How should I think, how breathe a single breath, how
    speak, if, out of myself,
I could not launch, to those, superior universes?

Swiftly I shrivel at the thought of God,
At Nature and its wonders, Time and Space and Death,
But that I, turning, call to thee O soul, thou actual Me,
And lo, thou gently masterest the orbs,
Thou matest Time, smilest content at Death,
And fillest, swellest full the vastnesses of Space.

Greater than stars or suns,
Bounding O soul thou journeyest forth;
What love than thine and ours could wider amplify?
What aspirations, wishes, outvie thine and ours O soul?
What dreams of the ideal? what plans of purity,
    perfection, strength?
What cheerful willingness for others' sakes to give up all?
For others' sakes to suffer all?

                    * * *

Passage to more than India!
. . . .

Passage to you, your shores, ye aged fierce enigmas!
Passage to you, to mastership of you, ye strangling
  problems!
You, strew'd with the wrecks of skeletons, that,
    living, never reach'd you.

Passage to more than India!
O secret of the earth and sky!
Of you O waters of the sea! O winding creeks and rivers!
Of you O woods and fields! of you strong mountains of
  my land!
Of you O prairies! of you gray rocks!
O morning red! O clouds! O rain and snows!
O day and night, passage to you!

O sun and moon and all you stars! Sirius and Jupiter!
Passage to you!
. . . .
Have we not stood here like trees in the ground long
  enough?
Have we not grovel'd here long enough, eating and
  drinking like brutes?
Have we not darken'd and dazed ourselves with books
  long enough?

Sail forth—steer for the deep waters only,
Reckless O soul, exploring, I with thee, and thou with me,
For we are bound where mariner has not yet dared to go,
And we will risk the ship, ourselves and all.

O my brave soul!
O farther farther sail!
O daring joy, but safe! are they not all the seas of
  God?
O farther, farther, farther sail![1]

1. Walt Whitman, "Passage to India," *Leaves of Grass* (New York: Aventine Press, 1931), 416-20.

APPENDIX C

The reference here is to Rudolf Steiner's extensive and immensely fruitful research—using the development of objective Imagination, Inspiration, and Intuition. Though Emerson's characterization of the successive forms taken by cognitive unfoldment is at times rhetorical and less decisive, the coincidence between his descriptions and those given by Steiner in *Stages of Higher Knowledge* is striking.[1] The latter confirms Emerson's prophetic affirmations, lending them the clarity of something fully experienced and actually practiced in the modern day.

One has the impression that had the New Englander (1803-82) known the Austrian (1861-1925) as a contemporary, he would have found in him a thoroughly congenial spirit, one who had in fact gone far to realize the cognitive advance so long awaited.

> I look for the hour when that supreme Beauty which ravished the souls of those Eastern men ... shall speak in the West also. The Hebrew and Greek Scriptures ... have been bread of life to millions. But they are ... fragmentary; are not shown in their order to the intellect. I look for the new Teacher that shall follow so far those shining laws that he shall see them come full circle ... shall see the world to be the mirror of the soul.[2]

Rudolf Steiner himself, in looking back, spoke of his predecessor as "one of the greatest spirits of the nineteenth century," and he called the book *English Traits and Representative Men* "one of the greatest achievements of the spiritual striving of mankind." He spoke of "noble spirits like Emerson," who "when during sleeping life they are in the spiritual world ... come into contact with truths, and future psychic knowledge" that have now matured to what is known now as anthroposophy (from lectures on the *Kalevala*, held in Dornach, Switzerland, in 1914).

I have been struck by the similarity between Emersonian Transcendentalism and what Rudolf Steiner, in its philosophical beginnings, called his own *empirical* (as contrasted with speculative or theoretical) Idealism. For him, Ideas were always more than mere mental constructs or generalizations. This they only seem to be, as mirrored by the reflective physical brain. For when encountered directly in higher states of consciousness, thoughts and ideas appear as living, causative identities. Higher cognition knows them in objective, immediate experience of their spiritual reality.

Speaking in this latter sense, Rudolf Steiner came to call the results of his own research into the ideal world "spiritual science" or anthroposophy. While Emerson apparently found the Kantian concept of "transcendental" idealism quite acceptable, Steiner, insisting upon the demands of an empirical approach—whose possibility Kant denied—thought the latter's doctrine a block to further progress in real knowledge of the spirit. Yet with Emerson's own use of the term to indicate "the tendency to respect the intuitions," Steiner would certainly have concurred.

Emerson was compelled to observe that the genius of Transcendental *experience* was "not yet incarnated in any powerful individual." My belief is that in the early part of the present century, Steiner himself clearly "incarnated" or represented the intuitive spirituality that was striving for release in these New England heralds. What in them had been still anticipatory, came to maturity in him. With it, he fought the battle for the spirit in the scientific way required by the formidable issues and obstacles of the present time.

Rudolf Steiner was only one among the many today who valiantly support and seek to advance the "perennial wisdom." Therefore, the making of so particular a reference to the Austrian seer can be misunderstood. Let not my calling attention to the scientific value of his seership, and the human value of his example, be confused with any kind of partisan zeal; for no doctrine, dogma, or sectarian impulse is being espoused. Modern individuals, among whom I count myself, resist being labeled "believers" or "followers"; but perhaps they feel all the more obliged to testify to the importance and usefulness of new truth wherever found. So, while gladly expressing my fundamental agreement and deeply felt sympathy with this particular pathbreaker's outlook, method, and achievements, I confess also a certain pleasure in taking this opportunity to quote, with reference to followership in general, Emerson's partly humorous yet entirely serious observation concerning the fate that disciples ever tend to inflict upon their beloved masters.

> Every new mind is a new classification. If it prove a mind of uncommon activity and power ... it imposes its classification on other men, and lo! a new system. In proportion to the depth of the thought, and so to the number of objects it touches and brings within reach of the pupil, is his complacency.... The pupil takes the same delight in subordinating everything to the new terminology as a girl who has just learned botany in seeing a new earth and new seasons thereby. It will happen for a time that the pupil will find his intellectual power has grown by the study of his master's mind. But in all unbalanced minds, the classification is idolized, passes for the end and not for a ... means, so that the walls of the system blend to their eyes in the remote horizon with the walls of the universe; the luminaries of heaven seem to them hung on the arch their master

built. They cannot imagine how you aliens have any right to see—how you can see; "it must be somehow that you stole the light from us." They do not yet perceive that light, unsystematic, indomitable, will break into any cabin, even into theirs.³

Any lover of Emerson knows what Walt Whitman meant when in *Specimen Days* he wrote this of the man whom he had first, from a distance, called "Master," but who came to be his beloved friend:

> The best part of Emersonianism is, it breeds the giant that destroys itself. "Who wants to be any man's mere follower?" lurks behind every page. No teacher ever taught, that has so provided for his pupil's setting up independently—no truer evolutionist.⁴

Whitman's call to all pupils to "set up independently," Emerson's championing of "self-reliance," and Steiner's powerful defense of the same thing (as "ethical individualism") encourage the present writer, even as he emphasizes the role of this one individual, to follow that master's example by remaining all the more open to greet "the immortal Light," wherever, whenever, and through whomsoever else it chooses also to shine.

1. Rudolf Steiner, *Stages of Higher Knowledge* (New York: Anthroposophic Press,1981).
2 Ralph Waldo Emerson, "Divinity School Address," in *The Complete Essays and Other Writings of Ralph Waldo Emerson*, Brooks Atkinson, ed. (New York: Random House, 1950), 84.
3. Emerson, "Self-Reliance," in Essays, 164.
4. Edmund Wilson, ed., *The Shock of Recognition* (New York: Grosset and Dunlap,1955), vol.1, 288-9.

www.ingramcontent.com/pod-product-compliance
Lightning Source LLC
Chambersburg PA
CBHW021959220426
43663CB00007B/882